THE CONSUMER IN PUBLIC SERVICES

Choice, values and difference

Edited by Richard Simmons, Martin Powell and Ian Greener

This edition published in Great Britain in 2009 by

The Policy Press
University of Bristol
Fourth Floor
Beacon House
Queen's Road
Bristol BS8 1QU
UK

Tel +44 (0)117 331 4054
Fax +44 (0)117 331 4093
e-mail tpp-info@bristol.ac.uk
www.policypress.org.uk

North American office:
The Policy Press
c/o International Specialized Books Services (ISBS)
920 NE 58th Avenue, Suite 300
Portland, OR 97213-3786, USA
Tel +1 503 287 3093
Fax +1 503 280 8832
e-mail info@isbs.com

© The Policy Press 2009

British Library Cataloguing in Publication Data
A catalogue record for this book is available from the British Library.

Library of Congress Cataloging-in-Publication Data
A catalog record for this book has been requested.

ISBN 978 1 84742 180 7 paperback
ISBN 978 1 84742 181 4 hardcover

Cover design by Qube Design Associates, Bristol
Front cover: image kindly supplied by www.alamy.com
Printed and bound in Great Britain by TJ International, Padstow

Contents

List of figures and tables

Figures

Tables

Acknowledgements

This book is the product of a lively seminar we convened in December 2006, entitled 'The differentiated consumer in public services'. A key focus for the contributors, drawn from a range of disciplines (political science, management, social policy, social work), was to think about difference and what it meant from their perspective in relation to public services and consumption. Papers presented at the seminar showed that people are working with a wide range of understandings in this regard. We hope to have captured some of this diversity in this book. We would like to acknowledge the support of the ESRC and the AHRC under the umbrella of their 'Cultures of Consumption' programme (www.consume.bbk.ac.uk) for enabling this gathering of people to come together, and also for supporting the research that led to the writing of several of the chapters contained within the book. The book would not have been possible without this.

Many thanks go to Emily Watt, Leila Ebrahimi and Jessica Hughes at The Policy Press for their kind attention and encouragement, and to the anonymous referee who provided helpful comments on the draft manuscript. Finally, huge thanks also to our contributors, who have responded quickly and good-humouredly to all the deadlines and requests we have strewn in their path.

Richard Simmons
Martin Powell
Ian Greener

Notes on contributors

Marian Barnes is Professor of Social Policy and Director of the Health and Social Policy Research Centre at the University of Brighton. She has previously worked at the Universities of Birmingham, Leeds and Sheffield. Much of her research has focused on user involvement and user self-organisation in health and social care, and on public participation and new forms of democratic practice.

Peter Beresford OBE is Professor of Social Policy and Director of the Centre for Citizen Participation at Brunel University. He is Chair of Shaping Our Lives, the independent national service user-controlled organisation and network and is himself a long-term user of mental health services. He is a Trustee of the Social Care Institute for Excellence, member of the advisory boards of Involve and the National Institute for Health Research. He is also a member of the Shadow Board of the Social Care Skills Academy. He has a long-standing interest in issues of participation and empowerment as a writer, educationalist, researcher and campaigner.

Johnston Birchall is a Professor of Social Policy at Stirling University. He specialises in the study of membership-based organisations, focusing on public service delivery agencies, mutuals and co-operatives; with Richard Simmons he has undertaken a series of ESRC-funded projects on the subject. He has written several books, including *The International co-operative movement* (Manchester University Press, 1997); *Decentralising public service management* (with C. Pollitt) (Macmillan, 1998); *The new mutualism in public policy* (ed) (Routledge, 2001), and *Co-operatives and the Millennium Development Goals* (International Labour Organisation, 2004). He is currently working on a book called *Member-owned businesses: Co-operatives and mutuals in an age of globalisation* for publication by Macmillan in 2010.

John Clarke is Professor of Social Policy at the Open University, where he has worked for more than 25 years on the political struggles involved in remaking welfare states. He has a particular interest in the ways in which managerialism and consumerism have reshaped the relations between welfare, states and nations. He is currently working with an international group on a project called Disputing Citizenship. His books include *Changing welfare, changing states* (Sage, 2004); *Creating citizen-consumers* (with Janet Newman and others) (Sage, 2007); and the forthcoming *Publics, politics and power* (with Janet Newman) (Sage, 2009).

Shane Doheny is Research Officer at Swansea University where he is currently working on a project which looks at contractual governance in the NHS. Shane completed his PhD on the concept of responsibility in welfare at the University of Bedfordshire. Since then, he has worked on a variety of research projects at the Universities of Bristol, Bath and Stirling, each of which focused on aspects of citizenship, governance and management.

Catherine M. Farrell is Professor of Public Policy and Management at the University of Glamorgan. Her research interests are in the areas of citizen participation in governance, citizens and consumers in public services and also improvement and effectiveness in public services. The vast majority of her work is focused on education services. She is currently working with a colleague on comparative education policy in Wales and Scotland. Catherine has published papers in a wide range of the quality UK public management and organisation journals.

Caroline Glendinning is Professor of Social Policy and Research Director (Adults, Older People and Carers) in the Social Policy Research Unit, University of York. From 2005 to 2008 she was involved in the National Evaluation of the Individual Budgets Pilot Projects. From 2008 to 2011 she is also Chair of the UK Social Policy Association.

Ian Greener is Reader in Social Policy at Durham University, where he teaches postgraduate students about research methods and runs taught postgraduate programmes. He is the author of *Healthcare in the UK: Continuity and change* (The Policy Press, 2008) and *Public management: A critical text* (Palgrave, 2009), as well as numerous peer-reviewed journal articles on consumerism and choice in healthcare and other public services.

Gill Hogg is Professor and Head of the School of Management and Languages at Heriot-Watt University in Edinburgh. After graduating from the University of Dundee she joined the NHS Scotland 'fast-track' graduate training scheme for managers and worked for six years at Lothian Health Board. Her PhD focused on the management of professional services and her recent research with Professor Angus

Laing and Dr Terry Newholm considers the impact of the internet on professional services.

Debbie Keeling is Research Associate within the Marketing Group at Manchester Business School, University of Manchester. Her expertise is based in Applied Psychology, and she has worked on a range of national and European projects with interests that span service innovation, social support and networks, virtual communities, motivation, technology acceptance, learning and innovation. She is a founder member of the MBS Second Life project and is particularly interested in consumer experiences and service provision in virtual worlds. She is a member of the Centre for Service Research and the Consumer, Retail and Services Group within MBS.

Angus Laing is Professor of Management at the University of Glasgow. He previously held the Beneficial Bank Chair of Marketing at the Open University Business School. His research interests centre on the consumption and delivery of professional services in contemporary societies. He has just completed a project examining the impact of the information revolution on service consumption as part of the ESRC 'Cultures of Consumption' programme and is presently working on a Department of Health project on patient use of e-health resources, as well as an ESRC project on the consumption of legal services. He has published extensively on issues of service consumption and management across the public and private sectors in a range of academic and professional journals as well as contributing to texts on marketing, consumption and public policy.

Ed Mayo is Chief Executive of Consumer Focus, the new statutory organisation campaiging for a fair deal for UK consumers. He has been described by *The Independent* as 'the most authorative voice in the country speaking up for consumers'. A passionate campaigner on consumer issues, Ed has helped to start a range of public interest initiatives, including the Fairtrade mark, the London Rebuilding Society and the cultural charity MERRY, which links Deptford in South London to Mozambique. Formerly the Director of the New Economics Foundation, he joined the National Consumer Council as Chief Executive in 2003. In the same year, *The Guardian* nominated him as one of the 100 most influential figures in British social policy. Ed is Vice Chairman of the social innovation charity the Young Foundation, and is on the Board of the Fairtrade Foundation.

Nick Mills is a researcher with a strong interest in citizenship and participation, particularly in areas around housing. He has worked on a number of projects aimed at increasing participation in public services and has conducted research on areas such as tenant participation, housing policy and homelessness. Nick has also worked on ESRC-funded research considering citizenship and consumerism in the areas of health, education and housing.

Catherine Needham is Lecturer in Politics at Queen Mary, University of London. Her research focuses on the reform of public services, with particular emphasis on the relative role of quasi-markets and consumer-centred models of decision-making compared with those based on notions of citizenship and publicness. Her publications include *The reform of public services under New Labour: Narratives of consumerism* (Palgrave, 2007) and *Citizen-consumers: New Labour's marketplace democracy* (Catalyst, 2003).

Terry Newholm is Lecturer in Marketing at Manchester Business School, University of Manchester. Previous academic positions include two years as a researcher with the Manchester Retail Research Forum at UMIST focusing on young consumers' lives, and a research fellowship looking at the evolving relationship between professionals and consumers. His research interests cover consumer theory, including multiple-selves and fragmentation, ethical consumption and voluntary simplicity, the representation of Corporate Social Responsibility to consumers, consumption and online consumer communities, and evolution in the consumption of professional services.

Martin Powell is Professor of Health and Social Policy at the Health Services Management Centre at the University of Birmingham. His research interests include health policy, New Labour's social policy, and citizenship and consumerism. With Ian Greener, he won an ESRC grant in the 'Cultures of Consumption' programme on 'Modes of Consumerism and Citizenship in the UK Welfare State'. They have published papers from this project in journals such as the *Journal of Social Policy* and *Human Relations*.

Eric Shaw is Senior Lecturer in the Politics Department, University of Stirling. He has written extensively on the Labour Party, including four books and numerous articles and book chapters. His most recent book is *Losing Labour's soul? New Labour and the Blair government 1997–2007* (Routledge, 2007).

Richard Simmons is Lecturer in Social Policy and Co-Director of the Mutuality Research Programme at the University of Stirling. He is interested in the ways in which tensions between different value bases are exposed in public action. Over the last ten years, his research has examined the governance and delivery of public services, user perspectives and involvement, and the role of co-operatives and social enterprises in a range of contexts. This includes projects under the ESRC's 'Democracy and Participation', 'Cultures of Consumption' and 'Non-Governmental Public Action' programmes.

Foreword

Ed Mayo

Our relationship with the state has filled the pages of novels and tracts for the last two centuries, but there has been far less attention to the everyday experience of this relationship and how we should understand and improve it.

Are we consumers, citizens, clients, users, passengers, patients or prisoners of public services? Well, people make sense of this relationship in different ways. As one of the people interviewed in research in this book states, "they just call me John". We should not be surprised that words are slippery if we are dealing with such a myriad of different public services. But it is no help if the thinking behind these services is slippery, because different ways of thinking about the 'public' in 'public services' can lead to very different outcomes.

To begin with, the post-war European consensus was that certain basic needs for health, education, shelter and security should be underwritten by the state. Tackling poverty, in particular, was where the market had failed, and it was the role of the welfare state to take the lead. But this is quite different from the social contract advanced in the USA, in which poverty was seen as an issue of discrimination, limiting the access of citizens to market opportunities and livelihoods.

What we have seen is that the benefits of the European model have come at a price, which is that the agency of individual service users was degraded over time. Service users were designed to be passive, conceptualised in a deficit model in which what they lacked was what public services provided. They were not partners. They were beneficiaries. Their obligation, as well as voting for the taxes required to sustain the work, was to be grateful. And, for a long time, they were. But the weaknesses of the bureaucratic state have led to the outcome that people tend to get the services that others – public service professionals – think that they ought to have.

One thing that people tend to value is the quality of how they experience services. Many public services, from health to welfare, achieve what professionals intend, but in the process generate a degree of stigma, denying people's dignity. As one woman said in a piece of research I was involved in: "she said to me 'are you on benefits?' and this man was sitting there, this young lad, and my face went bright red. I felt like smacking her."

Bright red and a smack or not, in future, this approach cannot work. People are perhaps used to better standards of service elsewhere in their lives. But also, the contribution that they make, from tackling crime and promoting health to saving for old age, can no longer be taken for granted.

It seems to me that the best and most sustainable way to improve the responsiveness of public services is to improve the expectations and entitlements of service users. If customers have a right to certain services, they will get treated with respect. But we also have work to do to sustain and expand the very mandate for public services, which is why the flavour of membership and citizenship is an important one to nourish alongside the model of users and consumers.

We need more sophisticated ways of understanding the relationship we have with public services, given their importance in our lives, but they are dependent on us too for their success. This book stands out in its attempt to do this, not short-circuiting issues of political theory but, equally, not limited to its abstractions. It should inspire better analysis, more humility and, we should hope, services that work and are sustained over time for John, you and me.

Ed Mayo
Chief Executive of Consumer Focus

ONE

Introduction: managing the 'unmanageable consumer'

Martin Powell, Shane Doheny, Ian Greener and Nick Mills

Introduction

The figure of the consumer has been central to New Labour's approach to modernising and reforming public services (Clarke, 2004; Clarke et al, 2007; Needham, 2007). However, both consumers and public services are problematic. First, it is possible to claim that government documents tend to see the 'consumer' in a narrow sense: the individual 'consumer as chooser' to use the term of Gabriel and Lang (2006). Choice is becoming the watchword of the 'new' public services (Le Grand, 2005, p 200). At the risk of some oversimplification (see later), commentators tend to associate choice or exit with economic consumers and voice with political citizens. The recent choice versus voice debate (eg Audit Commission, 2004; NCC, 2004; Office of Public Services Reform, 2005; PASC, 2005) clearly sees a role for both mechanisms. However, according to the Joint Memorandum from Ministers, *The case for user choice in public services* (2005, p 3):

> Both theoretical and empirical evidence points to choice serving as an important incentive for promoting quality, efficiency and equity in public services – and in many cases more effectively than relying solely or largely upon alternative mechanisms such as 'voice'.

However, Gabriel and Lang (2006, p 2) argue that the word 'consumer' is now so overused that it is in danger of collapsing into meaningless cliché, and that the consumer can mean all things to all people. They point to 'the theoretical softness of the concept of the consumer', and are 'impatient with one-dimensional views', claiming that it is time that different traditions of defining the consumer started to take notice of each other (pp 2, 3). In particular, they point out that one type – the 'consumer as chooser' – has monopolised the attention of writers (p 42), but many other 'faces' exist: the consumer as communicator, explorer, identity seeker, hedonist or artist, victim, rebel, activist and citizen.

Second, consumption of public services is more complex than consumption of private goods and services, because of the possible tension between efficiency and equity criteria, and individual and collective dimensions. Few would raise the problem of equity if some consumers did better than others in snapping up a bargain in a sale or negotiating a good discount in buying a new car. However, government should be concerned if some welfare consumers appear to be getting a better deal from state healthcare or education as compared to others. The debate is more complex than is often stated. Inequalities exist between citizens in services allocated under state bureaucratic mechanisms (Le Grand, 1982; but see Powell, 1995). It is not, then, a case of 'four legs good; two legs bad', comparing perfect equity in state bureaucratic systems with inequity in choice mechanisms, but an empirical examination of the type, level and distribution of inequity in both mechanisms. Supporters of public sector consumerism claim that choice mechanisms can *reduce* inequalities (see Le Grand, 2005, 2007; Clarke et al, 2007; Needham, 2007). Governments need to focus on consumers (plural) rather than *the* consumer, and what works for individual consumers may not be best for all consumers.

This text aims to widen the focus on the consumer of public services, beyond 'the consumer as chooser'. If New Labour's citizens can be 'activated, empowered, responsibilised or abandoned' (Clarke, 2005), then New Labour's consumers can be equally diverse. After briefly examining the broader context of citizens, consumers and clients in the welfare state, this chapter focuses on consumerism of public services and discovers that much recent writing tends to ignore a rich and diverse history of consumerism and choice in public services. It then examines the different faces of the consumer, before turning to focus on the different mechanisms of choice. It concludes that focusing on one face of consumerism and a few mechanisms of choice oversimplifies the great diversity associated with the terms and raises the question of whether consumerism in public services may be contextual: different faces and mechanisms may work for different people in different contexts.

Citizens, consumers and clients in the welfare state

Despite some early references to the consumer (eg Webb, 1928), most discussions of users in the welfare state have – at least until recently – focused on citizens and clients rather than on consumers. However, these terms are often undefined, thinly defined or differently defined.

Barnes and Prior (1995, p 58) write that describing someone as a user of services is a description of a complex and shifting relationship. Alford (2002, p 337) points to the lack of agreement on terms. Labels such as 'customer', 'consumer', 'client', 'user', 'stakeholder', 'citizen', 'taxpayer' or 'the public' are used in almost as many ways as there are writers about them. Clarke (2004) states that there are many words to describe our relationship with public services: citizens, clients, consumers, customers, members of the public, parents, patients, pupils, punters, service users, service survivors, victims and villains.

Many commentators use terms as if they are interchangeable (Gyford, 1991, p 167). Vigoda (2000) appears to use interchangeably the terms citizens, citizens/clients, citizens/consumers, citizens as clients and stakeholders/citizens, while Hudson (1998, p 456) writes of 'the client–citizen as consumer'. Alford (2002) presents a typology of citizens and clients, with the latter divided into 'paying customers' (eg mass transit – but clients or customers?), 'beneficiaries' (no economic exchange – ie free at the point of use) and 'obligates' (clients against their will, eg prisoners; consumer 'bads' rather than 'goods' – reluctant clients). However, there is no clear rationale for his typology, and it is not clear how 'paying customers' are a class of 'clients'. Moreover, he does not draw on the professionalism literature (see later), and while he discusses reciprocity in terms of restricted versus generalised exchange, he does not cite Titmuss (1970), Pinker (1971) or Janoski (1998). Gyford (1991, ch 7) differentiates between consumer, citizen and local shareholder. Deakin and Wright (1990, p 11) argue that it should not be forgotten (although it frequently is) that 'the difference between citizens and consumers is all important', pointing to Klein's (1984, p 20) focus on non-users or contingent users, or taxpayers or ratepayers.

A number of writers have attempted to introduce an analytical dimension to this confusion. Hirschman (1970) differentiated between exit, loyalty and voice. Commentators have largely equated exit with economic mechanisms and voice with political mechanisms, while tending to ignore loyalty (clients?) (see, eg Crouch, 2003; Needham, 2003; Audit Commission, 2004; NCC, 2004; Office of Public Services Reform, 2005; PASC, 2005; Gabriel and Lang, 2006).

Client

Many accounts situate the client in the context of professionalism (see, eg Powell and Greener, this volume, Chapter Six for healthcare). Sullivan (1994, p 118) sums up that it is 'widely acknowledged that the relationship between post-war welfare services and their users, was one characterised by clientism'. Perkin (1989) argues that the welfare state was a key part of a 'professional society', while Foster and Wilding (2000) write that the 1950s and 1960s were the 'golden age' for welfare professionalism. In short, the Webbs' expert administrators, H.G. Wells' 'New Samurai' or Douglas Jay's 'gentleman in Whitehall' all knew better than the user in the welfare state.

Gower Davies (1972, p 220), in his study of planning in Newcastle, argues that 'the customer is always right: he can choose, criticize and reject. The client, on the other hand, gives up those privileges and accepts the superior judgement of the professional. It is one of the aims of the would-be profession to convert its customers into clients.' Similarly, the Barclay Report on *Social workers: Their role and tasks* (1982, p xii) commented that the term 'client' was likely to provoke 'negative reactions ... as implying an undesirable degree of dependence and perhaps of stigma'. Gyford (1991) gives a number of examples of the public being regarded as objects and passive in the local government world. Saunders (1986, p 345) claims that:

> customers can exert power (albeit limited) within a market through their purses, pockets and pouches, but this is denied to a client within a system of state provision. Clients can complain, can vote, can demand, but in the end they have nowhere else to go, and no choice but to accept what they are offered. They are, in short, dependent in a way that is never true of customers in a competitive market.

Citizen

There is a vast literature on citizens in the welfare state, but citizens are often poorly defined and undifferentiated (but see, eg Janoski, 1998; Lister, 2003). Crouch (2003, p 53) claims that if a service is an attribute of citizenship, it is managed through concepts of rights, participation and democratic authority, although he realises that 'in practice the system did not always work like that'.

However, much of this assumes a particular type of citizen, and there are many different types (Isin and Turner, 2002). The essentially political nature of citizenship is at the heart of the republican rather than the Marshallian citizen. While republican (or Athenian citizens) are 'active', Marshallian citizens are passive. In this sense, the welfare state is based more on the citizenship of entitlement rather than on the citizenship of contribution. Indeed, 'citizens' are more like passive clients or subjects than active agents.

Claims such as Alford's (2002), that trends towards being 'customers' devalue citizens reducing them to 'passive' recipients of services rather than active agents, and Gabriel and Lang's (2006, p 173), that citizens are active members of communities, assume the dominance of republican rather than Marshallian citizenship in the welfare state. However, as Marquand (1992) points out, the institutions of social citizenship were not effectively subject to popular control. Exit won the argument because the culture provided too little space for voice.

Consumer

According to Newman and Vidler (2006, p 169), the consumer embodies the private (rather than the public), the market (rather than the state) and the individual (rather than the collective). Although there is a large recent literature on consumerism in public services, much of it has an unclear definition of the consumer, tends to see the consumer as monolithic or undifferentiated and tends not to refer to earlier literature on the subject (eg Lees, 1965; Titmuss, 1968; Williams, 1977; Clode et al, 1987; Potter, 1988; Deakin and Wright, 1990; Cahill, 1994).

Trentmann (2006, p 19) writes that consumers have been elusive characters, pointing to the problem of the 'under-historicized view of the consumer', before asking 'will the real consumer please stand up?' (p 26). 'Consumers' of welfare services or 'citizen-consumers' are not new terms (see, eg Strasser et al, 1998; Daunton and Hilton, 2001; Cohen, 2003; Hilton, 2003; Trentmann, 2005, 2006). Even before the consumer was 'discovered' (Webb, 1928), the cooperative theorist Percy Redfern had called on consumers to unite to 'build a new social order' and to 'live and act as citizens in the commonwealth of man' (1920, pp 42, 57).

Williams (1977, p 1) points to the notion of 'consumer detriment' coined by Caplovitz (1963) and taken up by the National Consumer Council. Consumer detriment is defined as poor people getting less or worse-quality goods and services, pound for pound spent, than richer ones. The book examines consumer detriment across a wide range of 'consumer services, both private and public, from buying a tin of peas to using the National Health Service'. She later concludes that there is a 'massive consumer detriment for poor consumers' (p 235).

Clode et al (1987, p 1) claim that consumerism has never needed much stimulus to flourish within what is less and less being described as the welfare state. The high-water mark of the dominance of public services by their producers was reached in the infamously recorded 'winter of discontent' in 1978–79. The text examines different types of consumerism – individual (eg vouchers), participative democracy (voice?), advocacy services, 'fiscal consumerism' (eg vouchers) and 'organisational consumerism' (eg school governing body), and schemes included the Kent Community Care Scheme, the Camden Consortium (mental health planning), the Nottingham Self-Help Team, the Advocacy Alliance, the Little Women Cooperative and the Liverpool Parent Governor Support Project. Deakin and Wright (1990, p 10) note that 'consumers' are not a monolithic category with clearly defined common interests, but may well have sharp disagreements of interest, which they will articulate with varying degrees of effectiveness.

Cahill (1994, p 177) claims that consumerism is an ideology, an 'ism', which has a power as great as that of the other ideologies such as socialism or liberalism. No 'Consumer Party', but both Labour and Conservative parties accept the primacy of consumption. He discusses the 'Citizen's Charter' and points out that an extension of citizenship would require a very different kind of Citizen's Charter (eg the right to travel). He claims that less emphasis is placed on the responsibilities, duties or obligations which stem from citizenship. If citizenship is to have meaning, then it has to include duties which the citizen owes to the wider society, to his or her family and friends, most notably in environmental issues. The ethic is difficult to put into practice because it is in direct contrast to the consumerist ethic of modern society. It is much easier to persuade people to spend their money and take home their packaging rather than to persuade them to bring their used bottles and cans to the supermarket's recycling centre on their next visit (pp 184–5). He concludes that private choices, especially in housing and transport, lead to restricted choices for the poor and give rise to new inequalities (p 192).

Multiple identities or hybrid citizens?

While some commentators have argued that there have been moves from citizens to consumers, others have pointed to multiple identities or hybrid citizens (Gyford, 1991, pp 19–20). Gyford (pp 27–8) points out that a 1988 Labour Party document, *Consumers and the community*, stated that 'We are consumers and citizens, citizens and electors, electors and tax-payers, tax-payers and contributors, contributors and producers', before claiming that it was 'essential' that the public sector orient itself more towards the consumer.

Stewart and Clarke, in a series of articles (eg 1987), have pointed to the public service orientation. This moves, in the words of Gyford (1991, p 169), from an instrumental focus on the consumer to a more developmental focus on the citizen. They claim that the customer is also a citizen and that there are citizens other than customers. 'Concern for the citizen as well as the customer distinguishes the public service orientation from the concern for the customer that should mark any service organisation.... Thus the public service orientation is not merely consumerism' (Stewart and Clarke, 1987, p 190; see Gyford, 1991, pp 169–70).

Writers such as Pollitt (1988), Needham (2003) and Clarke (2004) have pointed to 'citizen-consumers'. However, Harris (2004, pp 534–5) points out that the conventional story of shift from welfare statism to consumerism – from social development (the welfare state) to an era of social delimitation (consumerism) – is more complex, as welfare statism was an era of social delimitation as well as social development, and consumerism may not simply be an era of social delimitation, but has potential for social development. In terms of welfare statism as social delimitation, the service user was a client of the state, with implications for citizen passivity. He cites Marshall (1981, pp 141–2), that citizens were engaged in passive consumption of services, and social rights – unlike civil rights – 'are not designed for the exercise of power at all'. Service users surrendered power to professionals and entered a 'benign form of state clienthood'. Conversely, consumerism, conceptualised as rational agency, has an increasing emphasis on procedural rights. In other words, users in the classic welfare state were not 'citizens' but 'citizen-clients'.

Clarke et al (2005, p 175) point out that other expectations and identities might be in play alongside those of the consumer, including the deferential supplicant, the assertive rights claimant, the willing-to-be-patient member of the public, the anxious or distressed vulnerable person, the reluctant recipient and the outraged citizen-curmudgeon. There is no reason why people should remain tied to one identity. On the contrary, moving between different sorts of identifications and their implied relationships may well be a feature of the public's relationship with public services.

Consumer typologies

Keat et al (1994) point out that there are different kinds of consumer, but that they tend to be concealed by the concepts of neoclassical economic theory, with its blanket attribution of 'sovereignty' to consumers and their 'preferences'. However, these are clearly 'ideal types', and 'Economics 1.01 courses' do not uncritically subscribe to this. According to Wonnacott and Wonnacott (1979, pp 61–4), while the market has impressive strengths, it is also the target of substantial criticisms. They cite Galbraith that 'it involves an exercise of imagination to suppose that the taste so expressed originates with the consumer'. In this case, the producer (not the consumer) is sovereign. According to Galbraith, 'the consumer is a puppet, manipulated by producers with the aid of Madison Avenue's bag of advertising tricks'. They conclude that, although the market is a vital mechanism, it has sufficient weaknesses to provide the government with a major economic role. However, they do concede that economists generally favour broadly market solutions, citing Assar Lindbeck that: 'next to bombing, rent control seems in many cases to be the most efficient technique so far known for destroying cities'.

Contributors point to different types of consumer. Hugman (1994, pp 209, 219) differentiates between market consumerism and 'democratic consumerism' (see Beresford, 1988: market research versus democracy) and between collective and individual consumerism. Winward (2004, p 76) points out that the premise of the disorganised consumer has often been used to contrast consumers unfavourably with workers as a potential political force, 'Yet active consumer organisations – often of quite considerable size – exist throughout the world'.

In their seminal study of consumerism, Gabriel and Lang (2006) developed a typology to classify different motivations for consumer behaviour. This typology has proved to be influential on subsequent work, with both Edwards (2000) and Aldridge (2003) considering Gabriel and Lang's 'faces' of consumerism, before attempting to modify the classification. An explanation of their typology, together with subsequent developments, is shown in Table 1.1.

Edwards (2000, pp 11–13) differentiates between five types of consumer. 'All of these perceptions of the consumer are, to some extent at least, stereotypes, yet contain a grain of truth.' For our purposes, the most important types are the consumer as king, the view of the New Right, and the consumer as helpless fool or hapless victim, the view of social policy (Cahill, 1994).

Table 1.1: Different consumer 'faces'

Gabriel and Lang (2006)	Edwards (2000)	Aldridge (2003)
CHOOSER: rational consumer, requiring genuine options, finance, information	KING: 'an unconstrained rational actor seeking to maximise positive personal outcomes' (p 12)	RATIONAL ACTOR: 'calculative and selfish' (p 18)
COMMUNICATOR: using goods to communicate, leading to conceptions of the consumer as VICTIM, ARTIST or EXPLORER	See VOYEUR	COMMUNICATOR: maintains that these faces are the same
REBEL: using products in new ways as a conscious rebellion. Also refers to active rebellion (joyriding, looting, etc)	CRIMINAL: the professional shoplifter, causing costs to be passed on to other consumers	
IDENTITY SEEKER: as in social identity, gained from a group.	See VOYEUR	
HEDONIST OR ARTIST? Consumption as pleasure, noting that pleasure may be socially constructed	See VOYEUR	
VICTIM: referring to both created wants and consumer protection, although focusing on the latter, as in Aldridge	VICTIM: either seduced into buying unnecessarily or buying the wrong product	VICTIM: the rational actor making a mistake, or being incorrectly informed/advised
ACTIVIST: generally a potted history of consumer activism, from the Co-op to modern ethical/environmental groups	ANTI-CONSUMER: participating in boycotts, demonstrations, etc, consuming specific products	See COMMUNICATOR
CONSUMER OR CITIZEN? Tracing the tension between two concepts	N/A	Maintains that this is not a face of the consumer
EXPLORER: consumers buying without a clear idea, bargain hunting	VOYEUR: window-shopper; strongly tied to the role of consumption in identity formation. Could also apply to ARTIST, COMMUNICATOR or IDENTITY SEEKER	DUPE: characterisation of the critique of rationality. Could also apply to several other categories in certain contexts

There are several notable features about these typologies. First, all three note that each consumer 'face' is an incomplete representation of individual action: one consumer may assume any number of the 'faces' at different times and in different contexts. Second, each subsequent attempt to develop Gabriel and Lang's typology has resulted in a reduction in the number of consumer 'types'. Aldridge justifies this cut on the grounds that the original categories overlap to some extent, and certainly there does appear to be a degree of commonality between categories such as identity seeker and communicator. His alternative suggestion (Figure 1.1) comprises a simple matrix charting the twin themes of power and expression. Aldridge's matrix is chosen to represent the two major issues that he sees in consumption: power and consumer motivation. The construction of the matrix means that motivation and power are measured on a continuum, which in turn helps to break down some of the dualities that result from attempting to divide consumers up into stereotypes. This does not mean that these stereotypes are unrepresented, but rather that the model allows some variance between strong and weak versions of consumer 'faces'.

Baldock and Ungerson's (1994) overview of community care produces one of the few consumer typologies specifically developed with users of public services in mind. Like Aldridge's (2003), this is a

Figure 1.1: Consumerism matrix

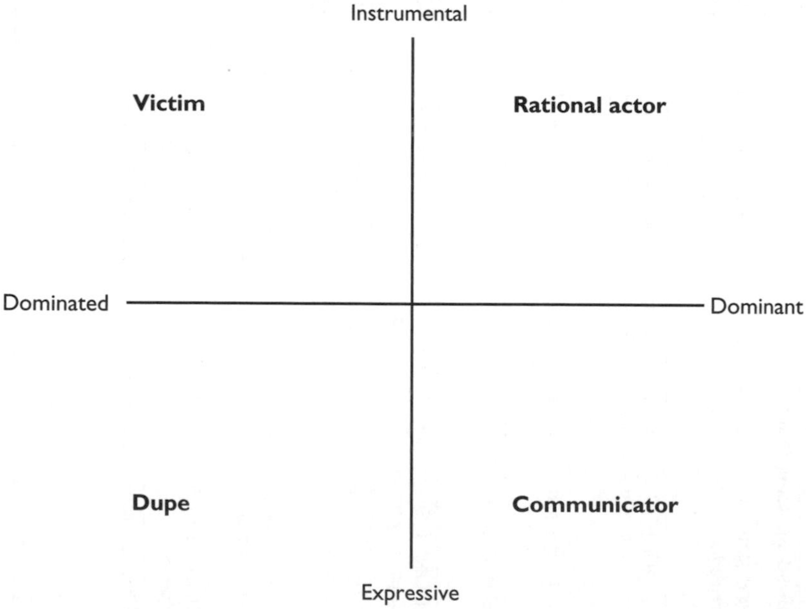

Source: Aldridge (2003)

2 × 2 matrix. There are differences in axes and types, but Baldock and Ungerson's 'consumer' is Aldridge's rational actor, a figure who can traverse private markets in order to receive the goods and services that are suitable for their needs (Figure 1.2).

Figure 1.2: Modes of participation in the care market

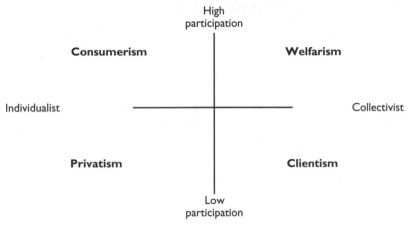

Source: Baldock and Ungerson (1994)

There are marked similarities between Symon and Walker's (1995) typology of tenants and Baldock and Ungerson's (1994) model. It is a fourfold typology, with the consumer again positioned as a rational, self-interested agent. This is contrasted with citizenship, with the latter representing political activism against the economic activism of the former. Symon and Walker are a little hazy on the different methods of participation, maintaining that consumers express themselves through 'exit', while also noting that consumers' views on a service may be actively sought by a housing provider in order to ensure their loyalty. The figure of the client is also used, although Symon and Walker note that this is increasingly rare in housing.

While these typologies are useful, they have not been generally applied to public services. Consumption occurs in shopping malls, supermarkets and coffee shops rather than in schools and hospitals. Gabriel and Lang (2006) tend to say little about social policy in their chapter on citizens and consumers. Edwards (2000), in his chapter on 'Never-never land – social policy, social divisions and consumer society', says little about social policy. Aldridge (2003) has no chapter on social policy. Cahill (1994) examines issues of home and sustainability rather than consumerism in public services. The Baldock and Ungerson (1994) typology was developed for community care, but its wider relevance is not clear and is not cited in Baldock's (2003) discussion of 'being a welfare consumer in a consumer society'. As Baldock (2003, p 65) puts it, the academic discipline of social policy finds consumerism difficult (but see *Social Policy and Society*, 2003).

Consumer mechanisms

Greener (2003) sums up the issues in his phrase 'Who choosing what?'. Perri 6 (2003, p 241) states that a consumer might be given a choice over the content of a service, its level, the identity of a gatekeeper or a provider, or the manner of access. Le Grand (2005, p 201) writes that the concept of user choice comes in many forms: choice of provider (where?), of professional (who?), of service (what?), of appointment time (when?) and of access channel (eg telephone, web or face-to-face – how?).

Leadbeater (2004, pp 20–5) states that there are different meanings of personalisation (see also Cutler et al, 2007). He produces a linear or hierarchical scale: a more customer-friendly interface with existing services (eg 24/7 call centres); giving users more say; giving users a more direct say over how money is spent; users not just as consumers but as co-designers and co-producers of a service; and self-organisation. He argues that, as we move from the first to the fifth option, the implications become more radical and disruptive, and that once you start personalising public services people will get an appetite for this and will want more. He argues that choice cannot provide a sole organising principle for a reform strategy. Users of public services want to be treated well, as customers, but that does not necessarily mean that they want to become consumers, shopping around for the best deal or even threatening to do so. We need to find a way to make public services responsive without turning the public sector into a shopping mall (p 52). However, no amount of talk about citizenship will empower consumers in their day-to-day engagement with public services. Voice for users – the more direct, informal and immediate, the better – is a vital component in public service reform. But citizenship – formal democratic representation – cannot be the sole organising principle for public service reform (pp 55–6).

Conclusions

We have seen that many different faces and mechanisms of consumerism exist. It follows that arguments favouring greater choice and consumerism could lead down very different routes. It is also likely that – to use a favoured phrase of New Labour – one size does not fit all. Consumerism and choice may be contextual: what works for some people in some settings may not be universal. Do the different conditions of public service choice (Barnes and Prior, 1995) mean that reforms are differentially empowering or disempowering in different areas? Are consumers choosers in education but victims in healthcare? Does government assume that consumers are choosers; and what follows if this assumption is not correct? Have consumers changed over time; were they victims but now rational actors? Potter (1988) asks whether the coat of consumerism in the public sector fits: it is possible that very different coats may be suitable in different contexts, including some where the garment resembles the 'Emperor's new clothes'.

This text explores beyond the consumer as chooser. It will analyse the faces and mechanisms of public sector consumerism in different public services. Chapters Two and Three give the context for New Labour's public sector consumerism, while Chapters Four and Five provide wider conceptual contexts. Chapters Six to Ten explore the faces and mechanisms of public sector consumerism in the services of healthcare, education, housing, criminal justice and social care. Chapters Eleven to Thirteen discuss wider perspectives of user groups and membership. Chapter Fourteen aims to draw together the material of the previous chapters and move towards a conclusion. The subtitle of the book is 'Choice, values and difference', and this is revisited in the concluding chapter. While the first term of the subtitle pervades the literature, the other terms are often implicit or hidden. We suggest that the varying faces and mechanisms of consumerism are linked to values, and that contexts are linked to difference. It is ironic that a government that stresses that 'one size does not fit all' appears to wish one size of consumerism to fit all. However, moving beyond the consumer as chooser suggests a wide range of faces, mechanisms, values and difference.

References

6, P. (2003) 'Giving consumers of British public services more choice', *Journal of Social Policy*, vol 32, no 2, pp 239–70.

Aldridge, A. (2003) *Consumption*, Cambridge: Polity.

Alford, J. (2002) 'Defining the client in the public sector: a social-exchange perspective', *Public Administration Review*, vol 62, no 3, pp 337–46.

Audit Commission (2004) *Choice in public services*, London: Audit Commission.

Baldock, J. (2003) 'On being a welfare consumer in a consumer society', *Social Policy and Society*, vol 21, no 3, pp 65–71.

Baldock, J. and Ungerson, C. (1994) *Becoming consumers of community care: Households within the mixed economy*, York: Joseph Rowntree Foundation.

Barclay, P. (1982) *Social workers: Their role and tasks*, London: Bedford Square Press.

Barnes, M. and Prior, D. (1995) 'Spoilt for choice? How consumerism can disempower public service users', *Public Money and Management*, vol 15, no 3, pp 53–8.

Beresford, P. (1988) 'Consumer views: data collection or democracy?', in I. Allen (ed) *Hearing the voice of the consumer*, London: PSI, pp 37–51.

Cahill, M. (1994) *The new social policy*, Oxford: Blackwell.

Caplovitz, D. (1963) *The poor pay more*, New York, NY: Free Press of Glencoe.

Clarke, J. (2004) 'A consuming public?', Lecture in ESRC/AHRB Cultures of Consumption series, Royal Society, London, 22 April.

Clarke, J. (2005) 'New Labour's citizens: activated, empowered, responsibilised or abandoned?', *Critical Social Policy*, vol 25, no 4, pp 447–63.

Clarke, J., Smith, N. and Vidler, E. (2005) 'Consumerism and the reform of public services', in M. Powell, L. Bauld and K. Clarke (eds) *Social Policy Review 17*, Bristol: The Policy Press, pp 167–82.

Clarke, J, Newman, J., Smith, N., Vidler, E. and Westmarland, L. (2007) *Creating citizen-consumers*, London: Sage.

Clode, D., Parker, C. and Etherington, S. (1987) *Towards the sensitive bureaucracy: Consumers, welfare and the new pluralism*, Aldershot: Gower.

Cohen, L. (2003) *A consumers' republic: The politics of mass consumption in postwar America*, New York, NY: Knopf.

Crouch, C. (2003) *Commercialisation or citizenship*, London: Fabian Society.

Cutler, T., Waine, B. and Brehony, K. (2007) 'A new epoch of individualisation? Problems with the "personalisation" of public sector services', *Public Administration*, vol 85, no 3, pp 847–55.

Daunton, M. and Hilton, M. (eds) (2001) *The politics of consumption: Material culture and citizenship in Europe and America*, Oxford: Berg.

Deakin, N. and Wright, A. (1990) *Consuming public services*, London: Routledge.

Edwards, T. (2000) *Contradictions of consumption: Concepts, practices and politics in consumer society*, Milton Keynes: Open University Press.

Foster, P. and Wilding, P. (2000) 'Whither welfare professionalism?', *Social Policy and Administration*, vol 34, no 2, pp 143–59.

Gabriel, Y. and Lang, T. (2006) *The unmanageable consumer* (2nd edn), London: Sage (first published 1995).

Gower Davies, J. (1972) *The evangelistic bureaucrat: Study of a planning exercise in Newcastle-upon-Tyne*, London: Tavistock.

Greener, I. (2003) 'Who choosing what?', in C. Bochel, N. Ellison and M. Powell (eds) *Social Policy Review 15*, Bristol: The Policy Press, pp 49–68.

Gyford, J. (1991) *Citizens, consumers and councils*, Basingstoke: Macmillan.

Harris, J. (2004) 'Consumerism: social development or social delimitation?', *International Social Work*, vol 47, no 4, pp 533–42.

Hilton, M. (2003) *Consumerism in twentieth century Britain*, Cambridge: Cambridge University Press.

Hirschman, A. (1970) *Exit, voice and loyalty*, Cambridge, MA: Harvard University Press.

Hudson, P. (1998) 'The voluntary sector, the state and citizenship in the United Kingdom', *Social Science Review*, vol 73, no 4, pp 452–65.

Hugman, R. (1994) 'Consuming health and welfare', in R. Keat, N. Whitley and N. Abercrombie (eds) *The authority of the consumer*, London: Routledge, pp 207–39.

Isin, R. and Turner, B. (eds) (2002) *Handbook of citizenship studies*, London: Sage.

Janoski, T. (1998) *Citizenship and civil society*, Cambridge: Cambridge University Press.

Joint Memorandum from Minister of State for Development of Health; Minister of State for Local and Regional Government; and Minister of State for School Standards (2005) *The case for user choice in public services*, London: Cabinet Office (http://archive.cabinetoffice.gov. uk/opsr/documents/pdf/the_case_for_extending_choice_in_public_ services.pdf).

Keat, R., Whitley, N. and Abercrombie, N. (eds) (1994) *The authority of the consumer*, London: Routledge.

Klein, R. (1984) 'The politics of participation', in R. Maxwell and N. Weaver (eds) *Public participation in health*, London: King's Fund, pp 49–65.

Le Grand, J. (1982) *The strategy of equality*, London: Allen and Unwin.

Le Grand, J. (2005) 'Inequality, choice and public services', in A. Giddens and P. Diamond (eds) *The new egalitarianism*, Cambridge: Polity, pp 200–10.

Le Grand, J. (2007) *The other invisible hand*, Princeton, NJ: Princeton University Press.

Leadbeater, C. (2004) *Personalisation through participation*, London: Demos.

Lees, D.S. (1965) 'Health through choice', in R. Harris (ed) *Freedom or free-for-all?*, London: IEA, pp 21–85.

Lister, R. (2003) *Citizenship: Feminist perspectives*, (2nd edn) Basingstoke: Palgrave.

Marshall, T.H. (1981) *The right to welfare and other essays*, London: Heinemann.

Marquand, D. (1992) *The progressive dilemma*, London: Heinemann.

NCC (National Consumer Council) (2004) *Making public services personal: A new compact for public services* (The Report of the Policy Commission on Public Services), London: NCC.

Needham, C. (2003) *Citizen-consumers: New Labour's marketplace democracy*, London: Catalyst.

Needham, C. (2007) *The reform of public services under New Labour: Narratives of consumerism*, Basingstoke: Palgrave Macmillan.

Newman, J. and Vidler, E. (2006) 'More than a matter of choice? Consumerism and the modernisation of health care', in L. Bauld, K. Clarke and T. Maltby (eds) *Social Policy Review 18*, Bristol: The Policy Press, pp 101–19.

Office of Public Services Reform (2005) *Choice and voice in the reform of public services*, Government Response to the PASC Report – Choice, Voice and Public Services, Cm 6630, London: The Stationery Office.

PASC (Public Administration Select Committee) (2005) *Choice, voice and public services*, Fourth Report of Session 2004–05, Volume 1, HC 49–1, London: The Stationery Office.

Perkin, H. (1989) *The rise of professional society*, London: Routledge.

Pinker, R. (1971) *Social theory and social policy*, London: Heinemann.

Pollitt, C. (1988) 'Bringing consumers into performance measurement', *Policy & Politics*, vol 16, no 2, pp 77–87.

Potter, J. (1988) 'Consumerism and the public sector: how well does the coat fit', *Public Administration*, vol 66, no 2, pp 149–64.

Powell, M. (1995) 'The strategy of equality revisited', *Journal of Social Policy*, vol 24, no 1, pp 163–85.

Redfern, P. (1920) *The consumers' place in society*, Manchester: Co-operative Union Limited.

Saunders, P. (1986) *Social theory and the urban question* (2nd edn), London: Hutchinson.

Social Policy and Society (2003) 'Themed section on consumerism and social policy', vol 2, no 1, Guest Editors: I. Shaw and A. Aldridge.

Stewart, J. and Clarke, M. (1987) 'The public service orientation', *Public Administration*, vol 65, no 2, pp 161–77.

Strasser, S., McGovern, C. and Judt, M. (eds) (1998) *Getting and spending: European and American consumer societies in the twentieth century*, Cambridge: Cambridge University Press.

Sullivan, M. (1994) *Modern social policy*, Hemel Hempstead: Harvester Wheatsheaf.

Symon, P. and Walker, R. (1995) 'A consumer perspective on performance indicators', *Environment and Planning C: Government and Policy*, vol 13, no 2, pp 195–213.

Titmuss, R. (1968) *Commitment to welfare*, London: George Allen and Unwin.

Titmuss, R. (1970) *The gift relationship*, London: George Allen and Unwin.

Trentmann, F. (ed) (2005) *The making of the consumer*, Oxford: Berg.

Trentmann, F. (2006) 'The modern genealogy of the consumer', in J. Brewer and F. Trentmann (eds) *Consuming cultures, global perspectives*, Oxford: Berg, pp 19–69.

Vigoda, E. (2000) 'Are you being served? The responsiveness of public administration to citizens' demands: an empirical examination in Israel', *Public Administration*, vol 78, no 1, pp 165–91.

Webb, B. (1928) *The discovery of the consumer*, London: Ernest Benn Limited.

Williams, F. (ed) (1977) *Why the poor pay more*, London: Macmillan.

Winward, J. (1994) 'The organized consumer and consumer information co-operatives', in R. Keat, N. Whitley and N. Abercrombie (eds) *The authority of the consumer*, London: Routledge, pp 75–90.

Wonnacott, P. and Wonnacott, R. (1979) *Economics*, London: McGraw Hill.

TWO

The consumer and New Labour: the consumer as king?

Eric Shaw

Traditionally the left turned its back on choice as the preserve of the right. In a consumer society where the consumer is king, vacating this political terrain is not a feasible strategy for progressive politics. (Alan Milburn, 2004 quoted in Joint Memorandum from Ministers, 2005, p 1)

Introduction: New Labour and framing

'The figure of the consumer', Vidler and Clarke have written, 'stands at the heart of New Labour's approach to the reform and modernisation of public services.' Consumerism, that is, 'the commitment to organising services around a public understood as consumers of services', emerged after 2000 as the central motif in the Blair government's narrative, 'a generic organizing principle for public service reform' (Vidler and Clarke, 2005, pp 19, 20; see also Clarke et al, 2007). What were the main elements of New Labour's consumer narrative? Why was it adopted and so vigorously propounded? To what extent did it amount to a major break with past Labour (and traditional social democratic) thinking?

A key objective of this chapter is to elucidate New Labour's understanding of 'consumerism'. In so doing it shall draw heavily on Schon and Rein's concept of the frame. Frames can be understood as analytical devices which supply order and intelligibility to a complex, ever-shifting and confusing world (Schon and Rein, 1994). The first part of the chapter, after a brief sketch of the concept of 'framing', consists of a discussion of what will be called New Labour's 'diagnostic frame'; that is, the way it defined the problem of 'modernising' the public services (for reasons of both space and political saliency, we focus on education and healthcare). The next section considers New Labour's 'prescriptive frames'; that is to say, its major policy prescriptions which emerged from this diagnosis, The final section explores ambiguities and problems within New Labour's consumerist narrative.

In this chapter I draw upon documentary research (government papers of various types and ministerial policy speeches) and a series of interviews conducted mainly between 2004 and 2007. The people interviewed include former government ministers, former government advisers and MPs, and clinicians. Some were on the record but most were off (for a list, see Shaw, 2007).

A central organising principle of the New Labour approach to public policy is its repudiation of 'ideological thinking'. It believed in approaching issues 'without ideological preconceptions' and searching for practical solutions 'through honest well constructed and pragmatic policies' (Blair and Schroder, 1999). It made decisions (it claimed) on the grounds of the merits of the case and the feasibility of all policy options, grounded in a scrupulous investigation of their likely consequences. As the mantra had it, 'what matters is what works', whatever a policy's ideological provenance.

It is true that New Labour displayed a willingness to experiment, to look at issues with fresh eyes, to challenge received willingness and to sweep aside the barnacles of past belief. To this extent it was, indeed, 'non-ideological'. But is it possible to adopt an approach that is wholly practical and solely evidence based? I would suggest not. For example, how does one know 'what works'? Given uncertainty, imperfect information, constraints of time and analytical capacity – as well as the sheer press of events – there is, as one senior government policy advisor noted, 'inevitably some reliance on presumptions about what works best' (Interview, Chris Ham, 2007). As Jack Straw put the matter: all politicians need a 'framework of belief so that there is some template for the scores of individual decisions which they have to make every day' (Straw, 1998). To explicate the Blair government's 'framework of belief' and its 'presumptions about what works best' I shall draw upon Schon and Rein's concept of the frame. Frames, they contend, 'select for attention a few salient features and relations from what would otherwise be an overwhelmingly complex reality' (Schon and Rein, 1994, p 30). It may be possible, through assembling a body of data, to identify the most salient characteristics of a problem (say, uneven educational performance) but arriving at an agreed diagnosis of why it occurs, specifying the key variables and the relationships among them, defining causal sequences and so forth all presuppose the application of frames – whether explicitly or implicitly. 'The very task of making sense of complex, information-rich situations requires an operation of selectivity and organisation, which is what framing means' (Schon and Rein, 1994, p 30). By constructing analytical sequences and narratives illuminating why social ills or problems arise, frames indicate which types of policy responses are likely to be most effective. For analytical purposes, it is therefore useful to differentiate between the *diagnostic* and *prescriptive* aspects of frames. The *diagnostic* refers to the definition and elucidation of the causes of a problem and the *prescriptive* to the policy responses formulated to remedy it.

A major aim of this chapter will be to examine New Labour *reframing*, that is, the new ideas, concepts and modes of thinking it used to explicate to its own satisfaction the problems it confronted. A distinction is made between two sources of reframing, which will be called *policy learning* and *social narrative formation. Policy learning* has been defined 'as a deliberate attempt to adjust the goals or techniques of policy in response to past experience and new information' (Hall, 1993, p 278). Typically, it takes the form of an attempt to identify and draw conclusions from the experience of past policy failures. By *social narrative formation* I mean a particular way of understanding the new challenges posed by the process of social change, and therefore the type of policy responses required.

New Labour diagnostic frames

(1) Policy learning

The starting point for policy learning is the perceived inability of established policy recipes to resolve current policy problems. New Labour policy learning (we shall suggest) took place in two phases, with the assumption of power in 1997 as the dividing line. The initial phase took the form of drawing lessons from both the perceived *policy* failures in Labour government in the 1960s and 1970s and repeated *electoral* failures after 1979. Very briefly, the conclusions were that, in government, the party had been too attached to an archaic, musty and dogma-derived policy repertoire and too much in thrall to 'producer interests' – notably public sector unions, professional associations and public bureaucracies – while in opposition it had become wholly disconnected from public opinion and had lost touch with economic, social and political realties.

But if the new government, in 1997, had a sense of what had failed in the past, it lacked a clear programme of action. This was notably the case with the running of the public services. Later, key New Labour figures were to express regret that it had not been much bolder and more radical – by which they meant embarked more rapidly and energetically on the competition and consumer choice agenda (Interview, senior policy adviser, 2007). There were a variety of reasons for this. First,

Labour had for so many years campaigned against Tory 'marketisation' and 'privatisation' in the public services that it felt impelled to take such measures as 'abolishing the internal market' – though in fact the steps it took fell short of this. Second, a number of ministers (notably Frank Dobson at the Department of Health) would have resisted a market-oriented reform programme. Third, there was a widespread belief that a 'third way' could be found between the marketising approach favoured by the Tories and the tradition of centralised, top-down service delivery associated with Labour in the past, based on partnership and collaborative working. Fourth, public sector reform was not regarded as a top priority in Labour's first term. Hence, in general, the policy tone in both healthcare and education was, for most of Labour's first term, one of cautious incrementalism and limited experimentation.

But within a couple of years key policy actors – notably the prime minister himself and a coterie of senior health and education advisers in Number 10, such as Andrew Adonis, Michael Barber, Simon Stevens and Julian Le Grand – reached the conclusion that more drastic measures were needed. Until 2000 policy had been overshadowed by the commitment to abide by the Tories' very tight spending settlement, but with the new millennium the sluice gates of spending were opened. Would the new funds which flooded in be used to good effect, or would they – as Blair and his top aides feared – be squandered? If far more taxpayers' money was spent and there was little to show for it, in terms of policy outcomes, then the case for strong public services might well be irreparably damaged in the public eye. Simon Stevens, Downing Street's senior health policy adviser at the time, recalled:

> 'The terms of debate changed dramatically as the issue of getting value for money assumed decisive importance. The period between 2000 and 2002 was pivotal for it became increasingly clear that the additional resources made available were not being translated into more operations and falling waiting times. The system was absorbing cash without producing results. Hence new incentives were needed.' (Interview, 2006)

Key policy makers concluded that, while the 'command and control' regime that Labour reasserted in 1997 may have been necessary to offer immediate relief on such matters as incredibly long waiting times, it afforded no long-term solution. 'There was a perception', Julian Le Grand, Stevens' successor as Number 10 health policy adviser, recollected, 'that command and control had reached its limits' (Interview,

2006). 'There was only so much you could achieve', Health Secretary, Alan Milburn observed, 'by finger-wagging and instructions. We had to move to a system that was sustainable in its own right' (Interview, 2006). Indeed, keen Blairite reformers came to conclude that the real Tory failing was not that it had embarked on market-oriented reforms but that it had done so with insufficient verve and determination (Interview, Alan Milburn, 2006).

In effect, what was occurring was a major alteration in Labour's diagnostic frame. The way it defined the problem of public service underperformance – and hence the prescriptions it found more compelling – shifted. Central to traditional Labour thinking has been the concept of market failure – the inability of the market to meet social needs and distribute resources and life chances in an equitable manner. The Blair government agreed that this problem persisted but, equally, became convinced of the no-less-important dangers posed by *public sector failure* – a problem (it felt) that 'Old Labour' had so emphatically failed to acknowledge. For Blair, one top Downing Street aide observed, the party in the past had been too 'hung up about monopoly public provision, the close involvement of trade unions and public professional associations in the determining of public policy'; in his view, 'defending public service monopolies was simply … a category error' (Interview, 2007). Downing Street became convinced that, in their present form, the public services were incapable of making effective use of the additional funding. They were seen, as one senior policy adviser recollected, 'as lumbering, over-centralised and monolithic organisations incapable of responding with speed and flexibility and with no self-sustaining mechanisms of improvement' (Interview, Chris Ham, 2007).

New Labour's new diagnostic frame clearly bore the imprint of 'New Public Management' (NPM) theory: the language used in Osborne and Gaebler's seminal text constantly recurs in its pronouncements. The old-style 'bureaucratic model' of public services which 'delivered the basic, no-frills, one-size-fits-all services' was sorely wanting (Osborne and Gaebler, 1992, p 14). While the state should remain a crucial agency for the pursuit of public goals, it could only do so if it was radically reshaped, if it challenged bureaucratic feather-bedding and 'producer interests' and learned to be 'entrepreneurial'. Among the key characteristics of this 'entrepreneurial governance' were: the creation of markets or quasi-markets; the separation of purchaser from provider; the use of competition as a means for powering service improvements; accountability for performance against targets; and the reconstruction of service users (and the general public) as customers or consumers (Osborne and Gaebler, 1992, pp 19–20; see also Stewart, 2003, p 170).

All of these themes were to emerge as central motifs in New Labour-style 'modernisation'. Key features included curtailing the influence of supposedly self-interested service providers, a focus on outcomes or delivery and the creation of a 'performance culture' based on rewards for success and penalties for failure (Faulkner, 2008, p 233).

Underpinning NPM was the theory of 'public choice'. Public choice applied the principles of economic theory to the sphere of collective action. In their social interactions, it is assumed, people are driven principally by self-interest. Within the context of a market economy self-interest is reconciled with general welfare via the mechanisms of choice and competition. Because consumers can choose between alternative suppliers of goods, and service producers are under relentless pressure to satisfy their preferences, the consumer is 'sovereign'. Where, however, the supply of a service is monopolised by one single producer and where, further, this producer is highly organised (in trade unions and professional associations) and operates through a bureaucratic system of resource allocation, then a real problem of 'producer control' or 'producer capture' arises.

The thesis of producer capture occupied a central role in organising New Labour's diagnosis of what it saw as the perennial and endemic weakness of monopoly public sector service delivery. Bureaucratic monopolies delivering uniform services rendered public organisations unresponsive to shifting public preferences, and solidified structures in which producer interests took precedence over consumer needs. In the market sector, if private firms failed to respond to 'the immediate needs of demanding consumers', Blair pointed out, 'they go out of business. They know that poor service, lack of courtesy, massive delays, destroys their image and their success' (Blair, 2001). But where public monopolies prevailed, those offering 'a poor or a tardy service could continue to do so with impunity; for those badly treated had nowhere else to go' (Le Grand, 2006, p 5).

The conviction that, in the absence of choice and competition, the public services lacked 'self-sustaining mechanisms of improvement' – a recurrent and insistent Blair refrain (Barber, 2007, p 335) – reflected a major shift in thinking. In traditional Labour thinking the 'public service ethos' operated as precisely such a mechanism. Indeed, the notion of a deeply implanted 'public service ethos' regulating conduct in public sector organisations (especially in healthcare and education) permeated Labour thinking 'about the motivation, character and moral importance of the public sector within the political community' (Plant, 2003, p 561). Because adherence to the public service ethos – a combination of professional norms, respect for the public good and a sense of altruism

– was sufficiently strong among most professional people employed in the public services (teachers, nurses, doctors, probation officers and so forth) they could generally be trusted to do their best to help the people they served. They could be relied upon to deliver services more equitably, to a higher standard and with more concern with user need than people motivated primarily by self-interest and profit. They were 'knights' not 'knaves' (Le Grand, 1997, p 155).

The New Labour government by no means discounted the importance of a 'public service ethos'. It acknowledged that 'the public service ethos undoubtedly forms part of the motivation of professionals and others working in the public service', but – it was quick to add – 'it is only a part, with more self-interested or knavish concerns also playing a significant role'. Indeed, when 'self-interest and public spiritedness' conflicted for public sector providers, 'it is far from clear that public spiritedness always dominates' (Joint Memorandum from Ministers, 2005, para 3.3.5).[1] It readily conceded that public servants were driven by factors other than immediate self-interest – altruism, professionalism and so forth – yet, equally, it felt that the public service was invoked 'to a degree, as a cover for the producer interests of professional associations and public sector trade unions'. There was a tendency among the Blairites 'to see self-interest as a key determinant of behaviour within the public sector – they were [drawing upon the terminology used by Le Grand, 1997] knaves not knights' (Interview with government adviser, 2007; see also PMSU, 2006, p 59). As one former Downing Street aide crisply put it, despite much talk of the public service ethos, 'there was not much sense of service to the public' (Interview, Geoff Mulgan, 2006).

In the past, Labour had tended to contrast opportunistic, self-seeking behaviour in the private sector with public-spiritedness in the public sector. New Labour reframed the terms of the debate. The real challenge to effective public sector performance was no longer the threat of exposing it to market disciplines and pecuniary motivations but 'professional domination of service provision' (Blair, 2004). 'People in the public sector', Blair declared in a much-publicised speech, far from representing paragons of public virtue, were too cautious, unimaginative and too reluctant to experiment – at a time when 'the private sector, in its reward and motivation, has moved on apace' (Blair, 1999). Without the spurs of competition and relentless consumer pressure, public organisations lacked the incentive to modernise outdated work practices, use resources more economically and drive up standards of service. Reflecting upon his extensive governmental experience, Charles Clarke commented that professional associations had too often 'focused upon defence of their own short-term interests. ... Innovation and initiative have been rare and defensiveness and introversion are too often the norm' (Clarke, 2007, pp 134, 131; see also Hutton, 2007, p 171).

(2) Social narrative formation

If the notion of public sector failure was central to New Labour policy learning, it was also embedded in a broader narrative of social change. A narrative involves storytelling: 'We account for actions, practices and institutions by telling a story about how they came to be as they are and perhaps also how they are preserved' (Bevir and Rhodes, 2003, p 20). Social narratives, as the term is used here, are frames which depict social realities in such a way as to provide justification for a particular set of policies. Political actors 'use narrative story lines and symbolic devices to manipulate so-called issue characteristics' – while often claiming simply to be spelling out the facts. These narratives are important not only because they propel issues onto the political agenda, but also because of the way they assert the burden of action (Stone, 1989, pp 282–3).

The central motif in Labour's narrative was the relentless advance of the consumer society and consumer culture – terms apparently used interchangeably. Public services, in the formative period after the war, a leading New Labour strategist maintains, were created 'on the assumption of a uniform provision to a relatively compliant, homogeneous population' (Taylor, 2006, p 17). The old model of the welfare state was, for Tony Blair, 'the social equivalent of mass production, largely state-directed and managed, built on a paternalist relationship between state and individual, one of donor and recipient. Individual aspirations were often weak, and personal preferences were a low or non-existent priority' (Blair, 2002, pp 3–4). 'Old Labour' adhered to a 'one size fits all' model in which the task of determining people's needs could safely be left to public sector professionals. 'The public', Milburn observed, 'were supposed to be truly grateful for what they were about to receive. People expected little say and experienced precious little choice' (Milburn, 2003).

By a 'consumer society' New Labour appeared to mean a society in which a mass of often high-quality consumer goods and services offering multiple choices were readily available and highly competitive markets ensured that producers exhibited an acute sensitivity to consumer preferences. Its emergence was deemed to have fundamentally altered mass culture. The 'revolution in business', David Miliband observed, 'has found its way into social norms' (quoted in Cutler et al, 2007, p 848). With solidaristic or communal modes of thought and the collectivist forms of organisation which sustained them in irrevocable decline, the new spirit was one of individual aspiration and ambition, embodied in the concept of the confident, discriminating consumer. The experience of being able to choose between a wide range of goods and services proffered by rival suppliers, all vying for their custom, had raised popular expectations: 'Ordinary consumers are getting a taste for greater power and control in their lives. They expect services tailored to their individual needs. They want choice and expect quality' (Milburn, 2007, p 8).

As Vidler and Clarke point out, 'this conception of the modern world being dominated by the practices and experiences of a consumer culture is central to New Labour's articulation of the case for public service reform' (2005, p 21). Consumerism furnished the dominant frame of reference in which people defined and enacted their social roles. In the words of the PM's Strategy Unit, 'in light of their private sector experiences, the public want greater choice over the services provided to them by the state.... The public now expect services to be specifically appropriate to them' (PMSU, 2007, p 18). A second, related axiom was that the private sector was decidedly more effective than the public (as traditionally constituted) in supplying individual needs to a high standard of service. Hence the constantly reiterated observation that people wanted better public services because they were 'accustomed to high standards in commercial markets' (PMSU, 2007, p 16). Precisely why this should be regarded as axiomatic, given the serious cases of mis-selling of financial products (private pensions, endowment mortgages, high levels of bank overdraft charges), poor quality of rail services and often curt treatment of passengers by airlines is a matter of some puzzlement.[2]

A central New Labour proposition was that if the welfare state failed to adapt to the demands of the new consumer culture its very legitimacy would be jeopardised. People would only support schemes of collectively provided services if they could be shown to work to their advantage and that of their families. The welfare state – the satisfaction of needs through public services – could only continue to command popular support to the extent that it demonstrated sensitivity to increasingly powerful and pervasive individual aspirations and expectations (Interview, senior Downing Street adviser, 2007). Here a particular danger was that of the defection of sections of the middle class to the private sector (especially in healthcare and secondary education). This would, one Blairite minister declared, put at risk 'universal provision funded through general taxation' and ultimately lead to 'the break up of public service provision as we know it today' (Byers, 2003). The danger was especially pressing in the more highly populated – and marginals of – South-Eastern England. While it was estimated that 12% of the population had private health insurance, this figure rose to as high as 30% in the South-East (Mohan, 2003). The figures for private education were 7% in England, but three times that in parts of London. Middle-class flight to the private sector would thus, at one and the same time, damage the fiscal basis of the welfare state, delegitimate its institutions and erode Labour's electoral base. 'From this perspective, offering choice is one way in which we can bind into the public sector those that can afford to go private' (Byers, 2003).

New Labour's prescriptive frames

(1) Choice and empowerment

Such were the diagnoses. What policy prescriptions flowed from them? Blair summed up his broad credo for public service reform thus:

> We must develop an acceptance of more market-oriented incentives with a modern, reinvigorated ethos of public service. We should be far more radical about the role of the state as regulator rather than provider, opening up healthcare for example to a mixed economy under the NHS umbrella.... We should also stimulate new entrants to the schools market. (Blair, 2003)

We have already noted that many of the characteristic principles and motifs of NPM were assimilated into the Blair government's discourse and policies. This did not imply the adoption of a free market, New Right approach. The New Labour programme of public service reform was – to the contrary – grounded in a firm commitment to a large and vibrant sphere of collective activity where public goods such as healthcare and schooling were provided in an equitable fashion, according to need, free at the point of consumption and funded by progressive taxation (PMSU, 2007, p 10). But – in a sharp break with traditional Labour thinking – it *did* demand a recasting of the welfare state, through the injection of both consumer choice and competition. Though these constituted two faces of the same phenomenon, for purposes of analytical exposition, choice and competition will be treated separately.

Choice, the government explained, had two aspects. It was 'both a means of introducing the right incentives for improving services for users, and ... a desirable outcome in and of itself: that is, it is both intrinsically and instrumentally valuable' (Joint Memorandum from Ministers, 2005, para 1.2) because there was a strong and growing demand for choice. 'While people have become more empowered as consumers they have not as yet become empowered as citizens.... Ordinary consumers are getting a taste for greater power and control in their lives' (Milburn, 2007, pp 7–8). An older social democratic vocabulary which associated freedom and autonomy with the concept of self-development has here been subtly displaced by an emphasis on freedom as the extension of choice in competitive markets: 'the consumer exercises personal autonomy through the freedom to choose' (Needham, 2003, p 21). Choice was, equally, seen as indispensable to 'personalisation', which developed, from Blair's second term, as a major theme of policy. Personalisation was defined as 'the process by which services are tailored to the needs and preferences of citizens' (PMSU, 2007, p 34). This could be achieved by a range of means, including enhanced user voice (individual and collective), but the government's main emphasis was on extending choice on the grounds that 'it is difficult to see how personalisation can be implemented without choice' (Joint Memorandum from Ministers, 2005, para 3.6.2).

However, it was increasingly the 'instrumental' aspects of choice – 'acting as an instrument for achieving other desirable social ends' (Joint Memorandum from Ministers, 2005, para 3.3.1) – that received most attention. Choice would act as the spur to bolstering public service quality and efficiency and ensure much greater sensitivity to people's needs by fundamentally altering power relations between service users and providers. It imparted strong inducements for changes in provider behaviour. As Blair explained:

> choice isn't an end in itself. It is one important mechanism to ensure that citizens can indeed secure good schools and health services in their communities. Choice puts the levers in the hands of parents and patients so that they as citizens and consumers can be a driving force for improvement in their public services. (Blair, 2004)

But to have these effects, choice had to be yoked to competition.

(2) Consumer empowerment through competition

'On its own', the PM's Strategy Unit averred, choice would engender insufficient pressure for sustained service improvements 'but, coupled with competition, choice can provide powerful and continuing incentives for service providers to improve efficiency and raise service quality for all' (PMSU, 2006, p 66). One senior adviser was insistent on this point: 'the crucial point in generating sustained improvement in service quality is having competition, some from the private sector, most within the public sector' (Interview, Strategy Unit senior advisor, 2007). Another senior adviser observed: 'competition will promote an appetite for adopting best practice which has sadly been lacking until now. The policy of urging people to adopt best practice via information has had disappointing results. By linking failure ... with [financial] consequences a dynamic which will have a positive effect on the system as a whole has been created' (Interview, Strategy Unit senior advisor, 2006). Thus, where choice was coupled with competition and where, in addition, funding followed users' choices, providers would be under constant pressure to cut costs, avoid waste, raise quality and respond to individual preferences. Milburn put it this way:

> 'Where people can opt for a hospital where the waiting times are shorter and where money follows the patient then he is empowered. The hospital losing patients then has a choice – to continue to underperform or improve: getting doctors working as they should be and therefore getting patients back.' (Interview, 2006)

New Labour policy makers were genuinely attached to the precept that 'what matters is what works', but equally were convinced – as Michael Barber, highly influential head of the Downing Street Delivery Unit, put it – that, as 'competition drives productivity improvement in other sectors of the economy, so why not in the public services?' (Barber, 2007, p 335). For New Labour, a policy adviser commented, the 'presumption was that choice and competition operated as the most effective and reliable drivers of improvement, efficiency and innovation' (Interview, 2007). Choice within a competitive system, Health Minister John Hutton pointed out, would 'throw a spotlight on poor performance ... drive inappropriate costs out of the system and ... match capacity in the system to where people want it to be' (Public Administration Select Committee, 2005, evidence 150). To be effective, however, competition within existing public sector institutions would not suffice: what was needed was 'a broad base of suppliers' (PMSU, 2007, p 44). An essential aspect of a properly functioning market was the entry of new, innovative competitors who could provide additional capacity, inject new ideas, disturb cosy and established rhythms of behaviour and frighten existing producers, thereby forcing them to compete more fiercely for custom (Le Grand, 2006). New entrants, for the most part, could realistically only come from the private and (to a lesser degree) voluntary sectors. A central tenet of New Labour thinking was that public services did *not* have to be delivered by public organisations. What mattered was what worked, and what worked was intensified competition from new suppliers. Increased diversity of supply, one top prime ministerial aide emphasised, would 'prevent the damaging effects of monopoly' by facilitating new entrants to the market and thereby ensuring effective competition (Interview, top prime ministerial aide, 2007). The Office of Public Services Reform was confident that 'widening the market to create more suppliers of public services' – greater 'contestability', in the jargon – would 'drive up performance, improve the quality of management and secure more value for money'. It was vital for productivity growth, since, 'in the private sector as much as half of all productivity gains come from new entrants to the market, as opposed to incremental improvements from existing companies' (OPSR, 2002, p 24). All this constituted open defiance of one of Labour's traditional totems, but Tony Blair was absolutely adamant. 'Part of any reform package' had to be 'partnership with the private or voluntary sector' (quoted in Seldon, 2007, p 69).

Choice, one staunchly New Labour minister pronounced, 'should always be regarded as the default in public service delivery, because choice can promote equity as well as improve quality' (Hutton, 2007, p 171). But this was a contentious proposition. Much of the resistance within the party to the consumerist agenda revolved around its impact on equity. Critics argued that choice and competition mechanisms would inevitably skew services in favour of the more knowledgeable, educated and confident. 'The articulate and self-confident middle classes', Roy Hattersley contended, 'will insist on the receipt of the superior services. The further down the income scale a family comes, the less likely it is to receive anything other than the residue which is left after others have made a choice' (Hattersley, 2005). The government riposted that *monopoly* was a larger cause of inequality than was choice. The absence of choice, former Downing Street adviser Julian Le Grand reasoned, placed a premium on the ability to deploy 'voice' – in which the 'more articulate, more confident, and more persistent' middle class had a decided advantage (Le Grand, 2006a). Typically, lower-income groups were less able to navigate the system and less confident in dealing with professionals, ventilating their dissatisfactions and using complaints procedures. 'The voice of the poor is generally much quieter than that of the middle class' (Joint Memorandum from Ministers, 2005, para 3.5.3). Further, the more affluent sections of the middle class always enjoyed the option of choice by buying into privately supplied healthcare and education: the government was giving to all the opportunities of choice which had, until now, been the prerogative of the wealthier (Blair, 2003). This said, the government acknowledged that 'extending user choice of provider may create some problems for the exercise of choice by the less well off' but believed that these could be remedied by establishing choice advisers and mandating public authorities to ensure a steady flow of reliable guidance and information (Joint Memorandum from Ministers, 2005, para 3.5.6).

Consumer choice and the collective good

This final section considers some of the ambiguities and problems within New Labour's consumerist narrative. Choice, the PM's Strategy Unit opined, would 'allow users to become more *assertive customers* and help to ensure that public services respond more promptly and precisely *to their needs*' (PMSU, 2006, p 65, emphasis added). There are two key assumptions in this seemingly unremarkable statement. The first is that what people wanted and what people needed were broadly the same. Thus, one influential document called for services to be refocused on 'the needs of the patients, the pupils, the passengers and the general public' while also urging 'new ways of responding to customer demands' (OPSR, 2002, pp 8, 19). The second assumption was that what people wanted, on aggregate, could broadly be equated with social need, or the common good. Both suggest a growing permeation of New Labour thinking by market discourse, with its accent on needs as consumer preferences.

In reality, the government's position was more ambiguous. The public services have always pivoted around some notion of objective need, traditionally defined by a combination of professional judgement and democratic deliberation, and this remained the case with New Labour, as seen in its repeated avowals to ensure that key services such as healthcare and schooling remained free and available *according to need*. Indeed, one of the central distinctions between a quasi-market and a real market was that, in the former, priorities would be established by public authorities as agents for service users rather than by the users themselves acting as consumers in the marketplace.

But it was by no means always consistent, for there was a tendency to elide the distinction between wants and needs. Thus the government defended its drive to render the public services more consumer oriented on the grounds that allowing 'users to become more *assertive customers*' would 'help to ensure that public services responded more promptly and precisely to their *needs*' (PMSU, 2006, p 65, emphasis added). The more 'assertive consumer' with 'instant access to information' was, it was claimed, capable of making 'instant choices according to their own priorities' – assumed to correspond to their needs (PMSU, 2007, p 16). The passive 'pawn' (in Le Grand's terminology) of traditional, state-oriented, social democracy was being transformed into the 'queen' – the 'empowered user'.

There certainly was a considerable body of evidence indicating that people resented being treated as pawns, desired more personalised and sensitive forms of service delivery and experienced choice as empowering (Le Grand, 2007). But were there not more tensions between individual wants and needs, and even more between (aggregated) personal preferences and the social good than the government was prepared to concede? One can here identify a range of problems. The first arose from the fact of scarcity or relative inelasticity of supply. In the private sector supply could expand to meet rising demand, with price regulating the relationship between the two. But the price mechanism did not operate in the quasi-market and, with services free at the point of consumption, demand for high-quality services was more or less infinite: it will never be possible to satisfy all education and healthcare needs and expectations – the costs would be astronomical. Therefore some form of rationing is inevitable. Indeed, a central plank of the case for public services has always been that, in a situation of limited resources, availability should be determined by need rather than price, that this requires some criteria of priority and that what these should be would best be left to a combination of those with professional expertise and those with some form of democratic mandate. Inevitably, this meant that difficult decisions had to be taken. As Walsh pointed out, decisions over the allocation of public goods typically have to take account of 'problems of conflicting rights, differences between individual and collective rights, and differences of the long and the short-term impact of the exercise of rights' (Walsh, 1995, p 254). The result would always be an uneasy and contested equilibrium – but would this not be further unbalanced by a much-enlarged role for consumers?

Further, unlike in the conventional consumer market, in the resource-constrained public sector the exercise of choice by one set of individuals could have an adverse effect on others. This was particularly the case where services operated as position goods, that is, a matter of securing a competitive edge rather than being valued ends in themselves. As the Education and Skills Select Committee pointed out, 'in oversubscribed schools, the satisfaction of one person's choice necessarily denies that of another' (Education and Skills Select Committee, 2005, p 31). As parents sought to do their best for their children there would be an ever-more intense scramble for limited places in the more highly regarded and more effectively performing schools (in terms of league tables). As a result, as the Committee noted in an earlier report, 'far from being an empowering strategy the school admissions process, founded on parental preference, can be a time-consuming cause of much distress in the lives of many families' (Education and Skills Select Committee, 2004, p 3).

In addition, the aggregated preferences of sets of consumers may not necessarily conform to broader public purposes, or indeed may have negative social consequences, which individuals themselves may not favour. As Needham points out, 'a customer care ethos restricts public services to a mechanism for satisfying individual wants, ignoring the importance of such services in meeting collective goals' (Needham, 2006, p 857). For instance, it seems not at all unlikely that the impact of greater parental choice in the schooling system will be the intensifying of social, religious and ethnic segregation which may, in turn, weaken social cohesion and exacerbate social problems. The 'aggregate of individual choices' may not, in short, correspond to 'collective priorities' (Vidler and Clarke, 2005, p 35).

Finally, and paradoxically, the effect of policies which were avowedly designed to sustain the legitimacy of public services may actually undermine them – by unleashing the consumerist genie. Evoking a consumerist mentality may well raise expectations which cannot be realistically fulfilled. 'Rather than delivering a satisfied and pliable citizenry, consumerism may be fostering privatised and resentful citizen-consumers' (Needham, 2003, p 33). Would not the relentless emphasis on consumer rights – encouraging people to demand that *their* needs be met *as quickly as possible* irrespective of the impact upon others – legitimate a more or less exclusive concern with individual (or family) interests at the expense of any consideration of the community as a whole? Might it not give rise to 'consumption risk', whereby 'users may develop unrealistic and even improper demand of provision' and exhibit 'more demanding and display more assertive and even aggressive and bullying behaviour against providers' if their demands are not met (Gray, 2007, para 18)? Might not the effect of promoting what Bunting has called 'a pathology of individual entitlement' be to erode yet further sentiments and ties of social solidarity (*The Guardian*, 28 January 2008)?

Conclusion

This chapter has revolved around an examination of New Labour's consumer narrative – the way in which it has framed issues of public service delivery in terms of maximising individual consumer choice. Traditionally, Labour had viewed public services not only as a collective way of providing for individual material security but also as affording an institutional framework which would bring people together, strengthening social bonds. For New Labour, in contrast, the role of the consumer has increasingly come to define mass aspirations and expectations in all walks of life. A market-oriented programme of public sector reform is thus presented as a response to powerful social forces to which the government has to respond if the welfare state – understood here as public services universally delivered, free at the point of use and financed by progressive taxation – is not to forfeit its legitimacy.

The end here was not – as with the New Right – small government and an enlarged role for the market as supplier of public goods. Rather, it was big government reinvigorated by market mechanisms – by competition and choice. This meant repudiating what was dubbed 'one size fits all', that is, a system of monopoly public provision in which professionals are entrusted with considerable power to determine need and how it can best be met. For New Labour, consumer choice and competition were essential means for achieving more efficient and higher-quality service. They were also deemed to be inevitable, if the welfare state was to adapt to new social challenges: 'We live in a consumer age. Services have to be tailor-made not mass-produced, geared to the needs of users not the convenience of producers' (DH, 2000, p 26).

This chapter concluded with some observations suggesting that the equation of consumer demand with individual needs and the public good might be a little more problematic than the government had acknowledged. An approach which 'allows the user to shape services through expressing a preference and making a choice', as Needham points out, has 'potentially radical implications for public service provision' (Needham, 2006, p 853) and – one can add – for Labour's future as a party indelibly associated in the public mind with the collective provision of services. What these will be, only time will tell.

Notes

[1] As Robert Hill, a former senior Downing Street adviser, later recalled, 'the government has tended to talk as though professionals were knights.... But it has tended to act as though they were knaves' (Hill, 2007, pp 247–8).

[2] It was rare for this proposition to be queried. However, one former senior prime ministerial adviser did point out that 'many of the biggest private firms – such as the retail banks or cable companies, which operate in relatively oligopolistic markets – provide often dire standards of service that would be unacceptable in the public sector' (Mulgan, 2007, p 182).

References

Barber, M. (2007) *Instruction to deliver: Tony Blair, the public services and the challenge of delivery*, London: Politico's.

Bevir, M. and Rhodes, R. (2003) *Interpreting British governance*, London: Routledge.

Blair, T. (1999) Speech to the British Venture Capitalist Association, London, July.

Blair, T. (2001) Speech on Public Service Reform, London, October.

Blair, T. (2002) *The courage of our convictions: Why reform of the public services is the route to social justice*, London: Fabian Society.

Blair, T. (2003) Speech to the Progressive Governance Conference, London, July.

Blair, T. (2004) Speech at *The Guardian*'s public services summit, London, January.

Blair, T. and Schröder, G. (1999) *The third way/Die neue mitte* (www.socialdemocrats.org/blairandschroeder6-8-99.html).

Bunting, M. (2008) 'From buses to blogs, a pathologising individualism is poisoning public life', *The Guardian*, 28 January (www.guardian.co.uk/commentisfree/2008/jan/28/comment.society).

Byers, S. (2003) Speech to Social Market Foundation, London, May.

Clarke, C. (2007) 'Effective governance and the role of public service professionals', in P. Diamond (ed) *Public matters: The renewal of the public realm*, London: Politico's Publishing.

Clarke, J., Newman, J., Smith, N., Vidler, E. and Westmarland, L. (2007) *Creating citizen-consumers*, London: Sage.

Cutler, T., Wane, B. and Brehony, K. (2007) 'A new epoch of individualization? Problems with the personalization of public services', *Public Administration*, vol 85, no 3, pp 847–55.

DH (Department of Health) (2000) *The NHS Plan: A plan for investment a plan for reform*, London: The Stationery Office.

Education and Skills Select Committee (2004) *Secondary education: School admissions*, HC 58-I, London: The Stationery Office.

Education and Skills Select Committee (2005) *Secondary education*, London: The Stationery Office.

Faulkner, D. (2008) 'Government and public services in modern Britain: what happens next?', *Political Quarterly*, vol 79, no 2, pp 232–40.

Gray, A. (2007) 'Relationships of consumption: citizens, clients and customers of public services', Memorandum to Public Administration Select Committee (www.parliament.uk/documents/upload/PPFWrittenEvidence.pdf).

Hall, P.A. (1993) 'Policy paradigms, social learning and the state: the case of economic policy-making in Britain,' *Comparative Politics*, vol 25, no 3, pp 275–96.

Hattersley, R. (Lord) (2005) Memorandum to Public Administration Select Committee, Choice, Voice and Public Services, Volume III, Oral and written evidence, London: The Stationery Office.

Hutton, J. (2007) 'Economic inequality and public services' in P. Diamond (ed) *Public matters: The renewal of the public realm*, London: Politico's Publishing.

Joint Memorandum from Minister of State for Development of Health; Minister of State for Local and Regional Government; and Minister of State for School Standards (2005) *The case for user choice in public services*, London: Cabinet Office (http://archive.cabinetoffice.gov.uk/opsr/documents/pdf/the_case_for_extending_choice_in_public_services.pdf).

Le Grand, J. (1997) 'Knights, knaves or pawns? Human behaviour and social policy', *Journal of Social Policy*, vol 26, no 2, pp 149–69.

Le Grand, J. (2006) 'The Blair legacy? Choice and competition in public services', Public lecture, London School of Economics, 21 February.

Le Grand, J. (2006a) 'Equality and choice in public services', *Social Research*, vol 73, no 2, pp 695–710.

Le Grand, J. (2007) *The other invisible hand*, Princeton, NJ: Princeton University Press.

Milburn, A. (2003) Secretary of State for Health, Speech to Labour's local government, women's and youth conference, Glasgow, February.

Milburn A. (2007) 'A 2020 vision for the public services', Speech at London School of Economics, May.

Mohan, J. (2003) *Reconciling equity and choice? Foundation hospitals and the future of the NHS*, London: Catalyst.

Mulgan, G. (2007) 'Innovation, improvement and the empowered user in public services', in P. Diamond (ed), *Public matters: The renewal of the public realm*, London: Politico's Publishing.

Needham, C. (2003) *Citizen-consumers: New Labour's marketplace democracy*, Catalyst Working Paper, London: Catalyst.

Needham, C. (2006) 'Customer care and the public service ethos', *Public Administration*, vol 84, no 4, pp 845–60.

OPSR (Office of Public Services Reform) (2002) *Reforming our public services*, London: The Stationery Office.

Osborne, D. and Gaebler, T. (1992) *Reinventing government: How the entrepreneurial spirit is transforming the public sector*, London: Addison-Wesley.

Plant, R. (2003) 'A public service ethic and political accountability', *Parliamentary Affairs*, vol 56, no 2, pp 560–79.

PMSU (Prime Minister's Strategy Unit) (2006) *The UK government's approach to public service reform*, London: The Stationery Office.

PMSU (2007) *Building on progress: Public services policy review*, London: The Stationery Office.

Public Administration Select Committee (2005) Minutes of evidence to inquiry on choice, voice and public services, London: The Stationery Office.

Schon, D. and Rein, M. (1994) *Frame reflection*, New York: Basic Books.

Seldon, A. (2007) *Blair unbound*, London: Simon & Schuster

Shaw, E. (2007) *Losing Labour's soul? New Labour and the Blair government*, London: Routledge.

Stewart, J. (2003) 'Modernising government', in H. Tam (ed) *Progressive politics in a global era*, Cambridge: Polity.

Stone, D.A. (1989) 'Causal stories and the formation of policy agendas', *Political Science Quarterly*, vol 104, no 2, pp 281–300.

Straw, J. (1998) Speech to the Nexus Conference on Mapping out the Third Way, London, July.

Taylor, M. (2006) 'Empowerment: a Labour vision for public services', in L. Byrne, J. Purnell and M. Taylor *Power to the people: next steps for New Labour*, London: Progress.

Vidler, E. and Clarke, J. (2005) 'Creating citizen-consumers: New Labour and the remaking of public services', *Public Policy and Administration*, vol 20, no 2, pp 19–37.

Walsh, K. (1995) *Public services and market mechanisms: Competition, contracting and the New Public Management*, London: Macmillan.

THREE

Narratives of public service delivery in the UK: comparing central and local government

Catherine Needham

To disaggregate the 'differentiated consumer' of public services, it is important to consider how policy actors in central and local government talk about those who use key services: health, education, welfare, transport and policing. This chapter gives an interpretative account of public services in the UK, exploring how different words and narratives are used in government texts and the extent to which these vary between services and levels of government. Through measuring the frequency with which certain keywords appear it is possible to assess the emphasis that policy makers place on certain identities – such as citizen, taxpayer and customer – and to trace the importance of certain narratives – such as standardisation and differentiation.

Although a binary distinction between central and local government obscures the messiness of the networks that broker policy outcomes, it usefully focuses on two authoritative centres of state power (Marsh and Rhodes, 1992, p 264). The relationship between central and local government in the UK has been adversarial for several decades, as the centre has stripped powers away and enforced tighter control – often in the name of greater decentralisation. A range of new institutional forms has been created or expanded – quangos, foundation hospitals, academy schools, housing associations, business improvement districts – in which local authorities are sidelined (Jones, 2008). At the same time an elaborate apparatus of quality assurance and performance management has closely controlled resource allocation, management practice and policy priorities at the local level. Interest in 'localism' and decentred policy solutions, from across the political spectrum, more recently may be suggestive of a counter-trend, a willingness to delink centre/local narratives and priorities (Letwin, 2005; Brown, 2006; Campbell, 2006; Miliband, 2006). Given the ambivalence of national politicians about local government, it is interesting to trace how far integrated narratives are deployed at central and local levels.

In exploring the ways in which central and local government texts talk about service users, the chapter takes an interpretative approach that follows the work of Hay (1999, 2003), Bevir and Rhodes (2003, 2004) and Bevir (2005). In their discussion of British governance, Bevir and Rhodes explain, 'Interpretive approaches begin from the insight that to understand actions, practices and institutions, we need to grasp the relevant meanings, the beliefs and preferences of the people involved' (Bevir and Rhodes, 2003, p 1). A content analysis is the method used here, exploring how texts from central and local government construct the role of the public service user and develop distinctive narratives of service delivery. Narratives play a key role in interpretative analysis. They 'explain actions by reference to the beliefs and preferences of the relevant individuals ... [and] encompass the maps, questions, languages and historical stories used to explain British government' (Bevir and Rhodes, 2003, p 26).

Three textual sources are used, drawn from the period 1997–2005: the speeches of Tony Blair, command papers published by central government departments (encompassing White Papers, Green Papers and strategy documents), and local authority corporate plans. Details on the selection of texts are given in the appendix. The texts were uploaded into the content analysis software N6 to facilitate keyword searches. Although these texts do not share the same purpose or audience, they are all used to outline strategic approaches to the delivery of a range of services and are indicative of the assumptions of policy actors about those services. Together they allow comparison between the ways in which service user identities and narratives are employed by those working in central and local government. It should be noted that the speeches and White Papers cover the period from 1997 to 2005, whereas the local government documents are taken only from 2005, given that councils only make their most recent plan available. Thus, the local corporate plans provide a more static form of data than the other material, a point considered in the discussion of findings later.

Keyword searches were performed on the texts, exploring the references to public services and their users. Keywords are the 'manifest variables' which reveal 'latent variables' (Neuendorf, 2002, p 23). The keywords were selected to have face validity, 'the extent to which a measure "on the face of things," seems to tap the desired concept' (Neuendorf, 2002, p 115). They were also selected to be semantically valid, that is, '[w]ords or other coding units classified together need to possess similar connotations' (Weber, 1990, p 21). The measures were also designed to have construct validity, in the sense of meshing with other accounts of New Labour. Searches looked for stems of words, allowing for a range of word endings. Keyword-in-context lists were generated so as to ensure that inappropriate homonyms and negatives could be eliminated from raw totals. Although the percentage of keyword hits is low, with most of the results falling between 0% and 5% overall, low scores are to be expected in this kind of keyword searching, where the texts range over a variety of themes. Bara (2005, p 17), for example, uses 0.08% as a minimum measure of the importance of a keyword in a party manifesto. Here, since the emphasis is on the balance between the keywords, relative placings are more important than absolute placings, and no minimum is established.

Public service users

To explore the ways in which policy actors in central and local government talk about the service user across a range of services, three categories of keywords were identified, with three words in each. These nine words were selected as likely to be the most frequently used terms within each category, rather than as a comprehensive list. Limiting the selection to nine words ensured a manageable amount of data for analysis.

The first set of keywords contains terms that suggest an entitlement to services that is not conditional on service use: 'community', 'citizen' and 'taxpayer'. A range of authors have positioned these as key terms for New Labour's public service reform agenda, with a particular emphasis on community (Driver and Martell, 1999; Fairclough, 2000; Levitas, 2000; Lister, 2000; Clarke, 2004; Bevir, 2005). The second category of keywords contains terms that are conditional on service use, but not specific to any particular service. Three terms were selected that have been commonly invoked as synonyms for the users of public services: 'consumer', 'customer' and 'client'. In accounts of New Labour, the discursive importance of the consumer and the customer has been widely noted (Driver and Martell, 1999, p 68; Finlayson, 2003, p 132; Hall, 2003; Lister, 2003; Needham, 2003, 2007; Marquand, 2004, pp 118, 128, 135; Greener, 2005). It is also important to consider what role the client now plays in public services, the term which, more than any other, captured the position of the user in the post-war welfare state (Gower Davies, 1974, p 220; Gyford, 1991, p 15). A third category contains keywords that refer to the functional roles that people play in relation to services. Again, three keywords were selected so as to retain parity with the other categories, incorporating users of specific services ('patient' and 'pupil') and a range of services ('parent').

Together these nine words were used as indicators of the ways in which authors of the speeches and documents frame members of the public. Clearly, the terms are overlapping and in practice people perform all of these roles, often on a daily basis. Their exact meanings are disputed and they have often been used interchangeably. However, the terms are indicative of different entitlements of the service user and responsibilities of the state. The citizen stands in a different relationship to the state than does the community or the taxpayer. Patients, parents and pupils all play distinctive, if not uniform, roles which are narrower than those of the consumer, customer or client. These latter three terms are sometimes used synonymously, but a range of authors have highlighted the differences between them (Gower Davies, 1974, p 220; Williams, 1988, p 7; Gyford, 1991, p 168; Lusk, 1997, p 69; Aldridge, 2003, pp 35–6). An assumption is made here that the selection of one of these terms rather than another in a speech or policy document contributes to an understanding of the ways in which policy actors conceive the roles and status of that type of service user.

Three public service narratives

To understand the differentiated consumer it is also important to explore the sets of expectations and responsibilities that policy actors ascribe to service delivery. These can be characterised as different narratives of public service which set out overarching normative frameworks, clarifying what users and providers will contribute. Three narratives can be identified in secondary literature on New Labour's public service reforms. These can be broken down into keywords to allow comparison across services and between levels of government.

The first is a standardisation narrative, where public services are as consistent as possible, with an emphasis on fairness and equity. Legal or procedural mechanisms are put in place to secure users' rights and ensure that they have access to information and to services. In this narrative the consumer need not play an active role in shaping services; user agency may be weakly developed. This narrative has been linked to New Labour's approach to public services, given the target and audit apparatus introduced since 1997 (Kelly, 2003; Barber, 2007). Keywords selected as likely to be indicative of uniform public services are as follows:

- access   • inform
- standard   • target
- convenient • right

The second is a differentiation narrative, where services are tailored to meet the individual needs of users. In this narrative users must be active, although forms of activity may vary from making a choice of provider to communicating with a monopoly supplier to agree a personalised form of service. In *The Blair Revolution*, Mandelson and Liddle describe New Labour's welfare state as 'universal in its reach but no longer uniform in what it offers' (1996, p 143, quoted in Bevir, 2005, p 89). The growing significance of choice and personalisation to New Labour's service delivery since 1997 has been widely noted (Greener, 2003; Leadbeater, 2004; Clarke et al, 2007). Again, six keywords were identified which were likely to tap into efforts to provide differentiated public services:

- choice
- individual
- personal
- responsive
- diverse
- tailor

Whereas these first two narratives emphasise the provision of services to users as consumers, a third narrative can be identified that has more to say about the active and co-productive role of the service user. This co-productive narrative gives users responsibilities as well as rights and choices in public services, an assumption commonly linked to New Labour's approach to service reform (Clarke et al, 2000; Lister, 2000; Finlayson, 2003; Clarke, 2004; Newman, 2006; Needham, 2008). The co-productive approach 'views citizens not as the passive targets or beneficiaries of government programs but as a vital element in their ultimate success or failure' (Brudney, 1984, p 466). Keywords selected here were those that indicated an active role for the service user:

- opportunity
- engage
- involve
- empower
- participate
- responsible

Together, these sets of keywords allow for an exploration of the narratives used in public service delivery across levels of government and between services.

Communities, customers and parents

Using the first set of keywords it was possible to explore the balance between the language used in Blair's speeches, the command papers and the corporate plans. Tables 3.1, 3.2 and 3.3 show the number of text units (sentences) which included the keywords, with the result as a percentage of total text units for that type of text, given in parentheses. The dominance of 'community' is evident. It is the most commonly used keyword in the central government command papers and the local plans (found in 6.3% and 8.7% of sentences respectively). 'Community' is Blair's second most frequently used term (after 'parent'), found in 3.1% of sentences. This dominance of 'community' is consistent with many interpretations of New Labour.

The speeches and reports from national government make frequent use of the functional terms – parent, patient and pupil. Blair uses the term 'parent' more than any other (in 3.4% of sentences) and the central government command papers use the language of parents and patients more than any other, aside from community (in 2.7% and 2.6% of sentences respectively). The more abstracted roles – citizen, taxpayer, consumer, customer and client – are invoked relatively little by national government. The pattern is different in local government – patients, parents and pupils get less attention, whereas the term 'customer' is much more frequently used. It is found in 3.5% of sentences in the local government plans, compared to 0.2% for Blair and 0.6% for the command papers.

Table 3.1: Service user keywords in Blair's speeches

	General	Education	Health	Welfare	Transport	Law/order	**Total**
	Units (%)	Units (%)	Units (%)	Units (%)	Units (%)	Units (%)	**Units (%)**
Community	35 (2.8)	62 (2.5)	7 (0.6)	25 (2.7)	0 (*)	95 (8.0)	**224 (3.1)**
Taxpayer	5 (0.4)	2 (0.1)	1 (0.1)	3 (0.3)	0 (*)	0 (*)	**11 (0.2)**
Citizen	6 (0.5)	6 (0.2)	1 (0.1)	2 (0.2)	0 (*)	12 (1.0)	**27 (0.4)**
Client	0 (*)	0 (*)	0 (*)	4 (0.4)	0 (*)	0 (*)	**4 (0.1)**
Consumer	22 (1.8)	0 (*)	5 (0.4)	0 (*)	0 (*)	0 (*)	**27 (0.4)**
Customer	2 (0.2)	0 (*)	1 (0.1%)	4 (0.4)	4 (1.5)	0 (*)	**11 (0.2)**
Patient	19 (1.5)	0 (*)	142 (12.6)	0 (*)	0 (*)	0 (*)	**161 (2.2)**
Pupil	7 (0.6)	123 (5.0)	1 (0.1)	1 (0.1)	0 (*)	2 (0.2)	**134 (1.9)**
Parent	19 (1.5)	133 (5.4)	2 (0.2)	78 (8.5)	3 (1.2)	11 (0.9)	**246 (3.4)**
Total hits	**115 (9.3)**	**326 (13.3)**	**160 (14.2)**	**117 (12.8)**	**7 (2.7)**	**120 (10.1)**	**845 (11.8)**
Total text units	**1,243 (100)**	**2,455 (100)**	**1,125 (100)**	**914 (100)**	**261 (100)**	**1,193 (100)**	**7,191 (100)**

Note: Percentages show keyword usage as a proportion of total text units, ie sentences, in Blair's speeches. The 'general' column refers to parts of the speeches that refer to more than one public service or services in general. * Indicates less than 1%.

Table 3.2: Service user keywords in national command papers

	Education	Health	Welfare	Transport	Law/order	Total
	Units (%)	Units (%)	Units (%)	Units (%)	Units (%)	Units (%)
Community	247 (3.0)	616 (6.1)	587 (5.2)	119 (2.1)	1,119 (15.4)	2,688 (6.3)
Taxpayer	9 (0.1)	7 (0.1)	25 (0.2)	15 (0.3)	5 (0.1)	61 (0.1)
Citizen	20 (0.2)	41 (0.4)	47 (0.4)	1 (*)	37 (0.5)	146 (0.3)
Client	0 (*)	14 (0.1)	22 (0.2)	3 (0.1)	5 (0.1)	44 (0.1)
Consumer	3 (*)	38 (0.4)	15 (0.1)	17 (0.3)	5 (0.1)	78 (0.2)
Customer	4 (*)	9 (0.1)	143 (1.3)	45 (0.8)	56 (0.8)	257 (0.6)
Patient	0 (*)	1,077 (10.6)	41 (0.4)	0 (*)	6 (0.1)	1,124 (2.6)
Pupil	596 (7.2)	29 (0.3)	8 (0.1)	1 (*)	11 (0.2)	645 (1.5)
Parent	666 (8.0)	98 (1.0)	243 (2.2)	12 (0.2)	110 (1.5)	1,129 (2.7)
Total hits	1,545 (18.7)	1,929 (19)	1,131 (7.7)	213 (3.8)	1,354 (18.6)	6,172 (14.5)
Total text units	8,277 (100)	10,145 (100)	11,203 (100)	5,609 (100)	7,273 (100)	42,507 (100)

Note: Percentages show keyword usage as a proportion of total text units, ie sentences, in the command papers. There is no 'general' column for the command papers as each one could be allocated to a particular service area. * Indicates less than 1%.

Table 3.3: Service user keywords in local government corporate plans

	General	Education	Health	Welfare	Transport	Law/order	Total
	Unit (%)	Unit (%)	Unit (%)	Unit (%)	Unit (%)	Unit (%)	Unit (%)
Comunity	119 (13.8)	20 (3.2)	18 (14.5)	124 (6.5)	7 (1.3)	113 (21.8)	401 (8.7)
Taxpayer	1 (0.1)	0 (*)	0 (*)	0 (*)	0 (*)	0 (*)	1 (*)
Citizen	26 (3.0)	1 (0.2)	2 (1.6)	21 (1.1)	3 (0.5)	3 (0.6)	56 (1.2)
Client	7 (0.8)	0 (*)	1 (0.8)	21 (1.1)	0 (*)	2 (0.4)	31 (0.7)
Consumer	4 (0.5)	0 (*)	2 (1.6)	0 (*)	0 (*)	2 (0.4)	8 (0.2)
Customer	142 (16.5)	1 (0.2)	1 (0.8)	11 (0.6)	2 (0.4)	2 (0.4)	159 (3.5)
Patient	0 (*)	0 (*)	2 (1.6)	1 (0.1)	0 (*)	0 (*)	3 (0.1)
Pupil	3 (0.3)	76 (12.1)	2 (1.6)	10 (0.5)	3 (0.5)	2 (0.4)	96 (2.1)
Parent	0 (*)	15 (2.4)	3 (2.4)	21 (1.1)	0 (*)	2 (0.4)	41 (0.9)
Total hits	302 (35.0)	113 (17.9)	31 (25.0)	209 (10.9)	15 (2.7)	126 (24.3)	796 (17.3)
Total text units	862 (100)	630 (100)	124 (100)	1915 (100)	552 (100)	519 (100)	4,602 (100)

Note: Percentages show keyword usage as a proportion of total text units, ie sentences, in the corporate plans. The 'general' column refers to parts of the plans that refer to more than one public service or services in general. * Indicates less than 1%.

Since local authorities have only indirect responsibility for healthcare, the low usage of the term 'patient' is to be expected, although it is less evident why parents and pupils feature little in the corporate plans. The high rate of frequency for the term 'customer' may be explained by the time frame, since the local government texts are taken from 2005. As the national document analysis gives an average usage of keywords in the 1997 to 2005 period, distinctive features of the 2005 period are hidden. Indeed, time series analysis of the Blair documents and government White Papers conducted elsewhere does show that usage of the term 'customer' intensifies over time, occurring more in Labour's second term in government than in the first (Needham, 2007). Thus the higher frequency in the corporate plans may be indicative of a more general increase in the use of customer terminology over time.

The term 'client' was somewhat more frequently used in the local government corporate plans than in Blair's speeches and the command papers, being found in 0.7% of local government sentences, compared to 0.1% at the national level. This finding indicates that local authorities retain more of a place for the traditional terminology of client than national policy makers allow, although the rate of frequency is low as compared to customer. The term 'consumer' is used little in any of the documents, perhaps confirming that it has a generalised role with less applicability than 'customer' to the mechanics of service delivery (Lusk, 1997, p 69).

The citizen has a higher profile role in the local documents than in the national texts, the term being used in 1.2% of sentences, compared with 0.4% in Blair's speeches and 0.3% in the command papers. With its broader connotations as a mark of democratic status, it is unclear why the term 'citizen' would be more commonly invoked in relation to local rather than national services. Local government suffers from low electoral turnout and weak democratic legitimacy, and it may be that in this context local policy actors feel a need to reassert the civic role.

Given that the tension between taxpayers and consumers was an important theme of public services under the Conservatives – and of neoliberalism more generally (Clarke, 2004) – it is interesting to see how little the documents refer to public services from the perspective of the taxpayer. The need to strengthen the relationship between those using and those paying for services, central to the rationale for the poll tax, for example, is not evident here.

Breaking the results down by service area reveals the way in which policy makers' vocabulary shifts between services. By far the most 'community'-oriented service in all three types of texts is law and order. Given the collective impact of policing services, and the difficulty of identifying specific beneficiaries, the use of this term is unsurprising. It is also in the context of law and order that Blair and the command papers make most frequent reference to citizens. The use of 'citizen' in relation to criminal justice may be an attempt to make explicit the civic contract – it is a service which is associated with deviation from the role of the good citizen – or indicative of the need to protect law-abiding citizens from the failed citizens involved in criminality. Within local government, the term 'citizen' is most often invoked in the general category, relating more holistically to the role of the individual in relation to multiple services.

In Blair's speeches and the national command papers the language of 'customer' is most commonly used in relation to transport and welfare. Its application to public transport as a service paid for, in part at least, at the point of use, is unsurprising. It is more surprising to find it used in the welfare context, given that welfare users lack many of the features commonly applied to the customer, particularly payment for a service and choice of provider (Williams, 1988, p 79; Gyford, 1991, p 181). 'Customer' appears to have replaced 'client' as the general term used to refer to the users of welfare services. Blair clarifies his meaning of the term in a speech on welfare reform, when he says: 'Instead of the old benefit mentality, individuals are treated as customers and potential employees – given high quality advice and support by professional advisers in a business-like environment' (Blair, 2002). Thus he suggests that the term 'customer' forms two purposes: first, marking an obvious break with the past, and, second, making the service more closely analogous to a business.

Blair uses the term 'parent' in the context of welfare more often than in relation to education. This finding highlights the important role that parents play in Blair's revised conceptions of welfare entitlement and responsibility. At the local level, parents are just as likely to be evoked in the context of health as in education, suggesting an emphasis on encouraging children to adopt active and healthy lifestyles.

Comparing the narratives

The second set of keyword searches explored the relationship between the three narratives. Findings are shown in Tables 3.4, 3.5 and 3.6. All of the narratives are used within the texts, occurring in 18.0% of Blair's sentences, 28.5% of sentences in the command papers and 33.2% of sentences in the local corporate plans. This high level of frequency suggests that the narrative categories are central to the ways in which policy makers position public services and makes them a useful tool for unpacking policy makers' assumptions about those services.

All three types of documents give most emphasis to the standardisation narrative. For local government, the dominance of standardisation is pronounced, with keywords occurring in one in five sentences (20.1% of text units), whereas in Blair's speeches and the command papers

Table 3.4: Narrative keywords in Blair's speeches

	General	Education	Health	Welfare	Transport	Law/order	**Total**
	Units (%)	Units (%)	Units (%)	Units (%)	Units (%)	Units (%)	**Units (%)**
Stand-ardi-sation	89 (7.2)	267 (10.9)	76 (6.8)	36 (3.9)	17 (6.5)	40 (3.4)	**525 (7.3)**
Differ-enti-ation	78 (6.3)	156 (6.4)	29 (2.6)	51 (5.6)	3 (1.1)	34 (2.8)	**351 (4.9)**
Co-produc-tion	63 (5.1)	157 (6.4)	22 (2.0)	104 (11.4)	2 (0.8)	68 (5.7)	**416 (5.8)**
Total hits	230 (18.5)	580 (23.6)	127 (11.3)	191 (20.1)	22 (8.4)	142 (11.9)	**1,292 (18.0)**
Total text units	1,243 (100)	2,455 (100)	1,125 (100)	914 (100)	261 (100)	1,193 (100)	7,191 (100)

Note: Percentages show keyword usage as a proportion of total text units, ie sentences, in Blair's speeches. The 'general' column refers to parts of the speeches that refer to more than one public service or services in general. * Indicates less than 1%.

Table 3.5: Narrative keywords in national command papers

	Education	Health	Welfare	Transport	Law/order	Total
	Units (%)	Units (%)	Units (%)	Units (%)	Units (%)	Units (%)
Stand-ardi-sation	1,067 (12.9)	1,388 (13.7)	1,087 (9.7)	728 (13.0)	765 (10.5)	**5,035 (11.8)**
Differ-enti-ation	780 (9.4)	1,139 (11.2)	1,151 (10.3)	294 (5.2)	449 (6.2)	**3,813 (9.0)**
Co-produc-tion	696 (8.4)	716 (7.1)	844 (7.5)	229 (4.1)	768 (10.6)	**3,253 (7.7)**
Total hits	2,543 (30.7)	3,243 (32.0)	3,082 (27.5)	1,251 (22.3)	1,982 (27.3)	**12,101 (28.5)**
Total text units	8,277 (100)	10,145 (100)	11,203 (100)	5,609 (100)	7,273 (100)	42,507 (100)

Note: Percentages show keyword usage as a proportion of total text units, ie sentences, in the command papers. There is no 'general' column for the command papers as each one could be allocated to a particular service area. * Indicates less than 1%.

Table 3.6: Narrative keywords in local government corporate plans

	General	Education	Health	Welfare	Transport	Law/order	**Total**
	Units (%)	Units (%)	Units (%)	Units (%)	Units (%)	Units (%)	**Units (%)**
Stand-ardi-sation	198 (23.0)	161 (25.6)	40 (32.3)	321 (16.8)	131 (23.7)	75 (14.5)	**926 (20.1)**
Differ-entia-tion	71 (8.2)	23 (3.7)	16 (12.9)	79 (4.1)	17 (3.1)	11 (2.1)	**217 (4.7)**
Co-produc-tion	103 (11.9)	51 (8.1)	18 (14.5)	158 (8.3)	17 (3.1)	40 (7.7)	**387 (8.4)**
Total hits	**372 (43.2)**	**235 (37.3)**	**74 (59.7)**	**558 (29.1)**	**165 (29.9)**	**126 (24.3)**	**1,530 (33.2)**
Total text units	862 (100)	630 (100)	124 (100)	1915 (100)	552 (100)	519 (100)	4,602 (100)

Note: Percentages show keyword usage as a proportion of total text units, ie sentences, in the corporate plans. The 'general' column refers to parts of the plans that refer to more than one public service or services in general. * Indicates less than 1%.

standardisation keywords are used somewhat less (7.3% and 11.8% of sentences respectively). Blair and the local government texts have least to say about differentiation, with relevant keywords occurring in 4.9% of Blair's sentences and 4.7% of local government sentences. In contrast, the command papers use differentiation keywords in 9.0% of text units, making it the second most frequently used narrative. Thus it appears that an approach to service delivery based on enhancing choice for the individual user, associated with the second half of Blair's premiership (Clarke et al, 2007, p 34; Needham, 2007, p 137), is most fully established in the detail of national policy, rather than in prime ministerial speeches or local implementation. This suggests that the service departments are pushing forward the detailed implementation of the choice agenda, rather than demonstrating resistance to a prime ministerially imposed model.

Again, the time difference may be relevant in explaining the differences between the local and national levels. Analysis of change over time in the national texts reveals that Blair and the command papers focused more on differentiation and co-production relative to standardisation during Labour's second term in government than they did during the first (Needham, 2007). However, if local authorities were mirroring this pattern it would be expected that standardisation would be less important in 2005 than in earlier documents. Given the dominance of the standardisation narrative in local authorities, it is striking that this lead should be so strong in 2005, when central government's attachment to a discourse of targets and standards was waning.

In all three types of text, the standardisation narrative is most often deployed in relation to education, health and transport. At the national level, welfare and criminal justice are to be co-produced services, emphasising an active role for the user, whereas for local government these too are to be standardised services. The impact of New Labour's 'rights and responsibilities' agenda is evident in such national policy. Service users previously characterised as passive or unwilling are expected to take responsibility for removing themselves from deviancy or dependency.

The importance of the three narratives in the texts raises questions about the relationship between them. It is possible to see the narratives as layered, each contributing to a different aspect of public service excellence, with access, choice and participation combining. Alternatively, tensions can be found between them: services that are standardised cannot easily be differentiated; services delivered on the basis of convenience may struggle to emphasise user responsibility. The keyword counts give an indication of how policy makers rank the importance of the narratives, suggesting here that access, rights and the other standardisation keywords are more important than choice, responsibility, empowerment and the other words associated with differentiation and co-production.

Conclusion

Keyword searching is a rough tool for understanding the assumptions that policy actors hold about services and their users, but it allows comparison between service areas and levels of government, disaggregating general claims about the growth of consumerism in public services and uncovering the narratives that are used in relation to service delivery. The findings highlight important differences between services, many of which are not compatible with expected features of those services as types of public good – the welfare user as customer, for example. They also show differences of emphasis between types of document, such as the tendency for local government to emphasise standardised services to a greater extent than national government. Different narratives are deployed in relation to particular services. Welfare, for Blair, is primarily a co-produced service, emphasising what users put in as well as what they get out. In the command papers welfare is, in the main, a differentiated service, with an emphasis on choice and individualisation. Only in local government is welfare primarily talked about as a standardised service, with particular focus on targets and information.

The textual analysis underlines the importance of the term 'community' in discussions of New Labour's public service agenda and the sidelining of other terms that have traditionally been associated with the welfare state, such as 'client' and 'taxpayer'. 'Community' is particularly important in the command papers and corporate plans, where it is by far the most frequently used of the nine keywords. For Blair, although 'community' is a frequently used keyword, it comes second to 'parent'. This finding is unexpected, given how closely the New Labour project and Blair himself have been associated with communitarian approaches. It may be that the parent is a more tangible version of the community, a rooted role that suggests responsibilities to children and a stake in a range of public services. It is clearly consistent with the 'political communitarianism' of Etzioni, to which Blair is sympathetic (Etzioni, 1994). 'Parents' receives less attention in the command papers and the term is used much less often than 'community' in the local corporate plans. At local government level it is the customer that comes second to community in frequency of usage, perhaps reflecting the closer links between local government and the front line of service delivery.

That local authorities should differ from central government in their narratives of public service delivery is, in some ways, unsurprising, since the Labour Party does not have political control over most of the local authorities in the sample. However, given the tight audit regime that directs local government service provision and, indeed, which mandates the writing of corporate plans, it might be expected that closer integration with national public service narratives would be observed. Local authorities are more strongly wedded to the language of standardisation than are national government actors. This may suggest a commitment to the universalist aspirations of the traditional welfare state long denounced by New Labour as 'one-size-fits-all' (Blair, 1999). In this interpretation, local governments remain resistant to micro-management from the centre. Alternatively, and perhaps more plausibly, the high frequency of standardisation keywords indicates the ascendance of quality assurance techniques and performance measures which homogenise local vocabularies.

Recent debates around 'localism' and 'double devolution' provide ambiguous signals about likely future developments. There are promises of (conditional) freedoms for local authorities to develop innovative approaches to service delivery, matching the needs of the local community (CLG, 2006). The government's *Communities in control* White Paper sets out how local communities can have more influence over local service delivery (CLG, 2008), suggesting that localities will have the power to develop their own, divergent, narratives. However, elsewhere the government has positioned local authorities as the conduit for its own choice and personalisation agenda (CLG, 2006). Initiatives such as direct payments in social care, choice-based lettings and trust schools place choice at the core of local authorities' service responsibilities. Such trends indicate the continued ascendance of a choice-based narrative, suggesting that the future for local government will be homogeneity rather than heterogeneity. Local service users may experience differentiated services, but they will choose from a nationally mandated menu of options.

The relationship between the three narratives is complex and warrants further discussion (on this see Needham, 2007). Each narrative has profound consequences for the individual citizen as well as for intergovernmental relations. The emphasis on co-production in the national speeches and documents highlights New Labour's insistence on the active user, but raises questions about how far rights and choices become conditional on what the user puts in. If co-production entails users managing their own conditions and bearing the risks associated with them, they may find their rights and choices curtailed. Instead of being empowered, the freedoms granted by the state may simply facilitate ever-more subtle forms of self-regulation (Rose, 1996).

Appendix: selection and coding of texts

A corpus of Blair's speeches as prime minister between May 1997 and December 2005 was constructed from the archive of speeches on the 10 Downing Street website, comprising 193 speeches. Those sentences in the speeches that related to public services were coded by theme: education, health, welfare (including social care and housing), criminal justice, transport and a 'general' category for sentences referring to services in general or more than one service. A dictionary of policy categories was developed inductively by reading through the speeches to extract key themes. The speeches were then coded using the dictionary as a code book. Sentences that did not relate to public services were excluded from the data set.

A quota sample of central government command papers (White and Green Papers and strategy documents) was developed to cover the period from May 1997 to the end of 2005. To generate a manageable number of texts, five key documents were selected in five public service areas (education, health, welfare, transport and law and order), generating 25 documents overall. The first two texts included in each category were the earliest and latest documents for that service area.

Since most departments published five-year plans around the summer of 2004, it was decided to include these as the third document in the set, to maximise comparability across service areas. The fourth and fifth documents for each service area were selected on the basis of perceived importance. Expert collections of New Labour policy were mined to identify the most regularly cited papers (Powell, 1999; Savage and Atkinson, 2001; Ludlam and Smith, 2004; Dorey, 2005; Seldon and Kavanagh, 2005). Reference to a document in one or more collection was taken to indicate that it made an important contribution to policy in that area. Sentences in the documents were coded by public service (education, health, welfare, law and order and transport) according to the overall theme of the document. Since the texts were focused primarily on a single service area, there was no need for a general category.

To obtain the corporate plans, a quota sample of English local authorities was devised to identify 18 councils – again ensuring a manageable number of texts for analysis. The sample was designed to be broadly proportional of councils by authority type and political control, and to include councils from across England's regions. The quota also includes councils that scored high, medium and low on the Comprehensive Performance Assessment conducted by the Audit Commission. The most recently available corporate plan was taken (produced around June 2005 to cover the period 2005–06) from each of the 18 councils. Sentences in the plans that referred to public services were again coded by theme, using the coding dictionary.

References

Aldridge, A. (2003) *Consumption*, Cambridge: Polity.

Bara, J. (2005) 'With a little help from our friends: comparing British and American party manifestos', Paper presented to the American Political Science Association Annual Meeting, Washington, DC.

Barber, M. (2007) *Instruction to deliver: Tony Blair, the public services and the challenge of meeting targets*, London: Politico's.

Bevir, M. (2005) *New Labour: A critique*, London: Routledge.

Bevir, M. and Rhodes, R.A.W. (2003) *Interpreting British governance*, London: Routledge.

Bevir, M. and Rhodes, R.A.W. (2004) 'Interpretation as method, explanation and critique: a reply' in 'The interpretive approach in political science: a symposium', *British Journal of Politics and International Relations*, vol 6, no 2, pp 156–61.

Blair, T. (1999) Speech at the opening of the Central Middlesex Ambulatory Care Centre, 2 December.

Blair, T. (2002) Speech on Welfare Reform, Jobcentre Plus Office, Streatham, London, 10 June.

Brown, G. (2006) Speech to the Fabian Society, London, 14 January.

Brudney, J.L. (1984) 'Local coproduction of services and the analysis of municipal productivity', *Urban Affairs Quarterly*, vol 19, no 4, pp 465–84.

Campbell, M. (2006) Speech to the Spring Conference of the Liberal Democrats, Harrogate, 5 March.

Clarke, J. (2004) 'Dissolving the public realm? The logics and limits of neo-liberalism', *Journal of Social Policy*, vol 33, no 1, pp 27–48.

Clarke, J., Gerwirtz S. and McLaughlin, E. (2000) 'Reinventing the welfare state', in J. Clarke, S. Gerwirtz and E. McLaughlin (eds) *New Managerialism, New Welfare*, London: Open University Press in association with Sage Publications, pp 1–26.

Clarke, J., Newman, J., Smith, N., Vidler, E. and Westmarland, L. (2007) *Creating citizen-consumers: Changing publics and changing public spaces*, London: Sage.

CLG (Department of Communities and Local Government) (2006) *Strong and prosperous communities – The Local Government White Paper*, Cm 6939, London: HMSO.

CLG (2008) *Communities in control: Real people, real power*, Cm 7427, London: HMSO.

Driver, S. and Martell, L. (1999) *New Labour: Politics after Thatcherism*, Cambridge: Polity.

Dorey, P. (ed) (2005) *Developments in British public policy*, London: Sage.

Etzioni, A. (1994) *The Guardian*, 24 July.

Fairclough, N. (2000) *New Labour: New language*, London: Routledge.

Finlayson, A. (2003) *Making sense of New Labour*, London: Lawrence and Wishart.

Gower Davies, J. (1974) *The evangelistic bureaucrat*, London: Tavistock.

Greener, I. (2003) 'Who choosing what? The evolution and impact of "choice" in the NHS, and its importance for New Labour', in C. Bochel, N. Ellison and M. Powell (eds) *Social Policy Review 15*, Bristol: The Policy Press, pp 49–68.

Greener, I. (2005) 'The role of the patient in healthcare reform: Customer, consumer or creator?', in S. Dawson and C. Sausman (eds) *Future health organisations and systems*, Basingstoke: Palgrave, pp 227–45.

Gyford, J. (1991) *Citizens, consumers and councils: Local government and the public*, London: Macmillan.

Hall, S. (2003) 'New Labour's double shuffle', *Soundings*, Issue 24, pp 10–25.

Hay, C. (1999) *The political economy of New Labour*, Manchester: Manchester University Press.

Hay, C. (2003) 'How to study the Labour Party: contextual, analytical and theoretical issues', in J. Callaghan, S. Fielding and S. Ludlam (eds) *Interpreting the Labour Party: Approaches to Labour politics and history*, Manchester: Manchester University Press, pp 182–96.

Jones, G. (2008) *The future of local government: Has it one?* London: Public Management and Policy Association.

Kelly, J. (2003) 'The Audit Commission: Guiding, steering and regulating local government', *Public Administration*, vol 81, no 3, pp 459–76.

Leadbeater, C. (2004) *Personalisation through participation*, London: Demos.

Letwin, O. (2005) 'With Cameron we can win', *Daily Telegraph*, 3 July.

Levitas, R. (2000) 'Community, utopia and New Labour', *Local Economy*, vol 15, no 3, pp 188–97.

Lister, R. (2000) 'To RIO via the third way: Labour's "welfare" reform agenda', *Renewal*, vol 8, no 4, pp 9–20.

Lister, R. (2003) 'Investing in the citizen-workers of the future: transformations in citizenship and the state under New Labour', *Social Policy and Administration*, vol 37, no 5, pp 427–43.

Ludlam, S. and Smith, M. (eds) (2004) *Governing as New Labour: Policy and politics under Blair*, Basingstoke: Palgrave.

Lusk, P. (1997) 'Tenants' choice and tenant management: who owns and who controls social housing?', in C. Cooper and M. Hawtin (eds), *Resident involvement in community action*, Coventry: Chartered Institute of Housing, pp 65–79.

Mandelson, P. and Liddle, R. (1996) *The Blair Revolution: Can New Labour deliver?* London: Faber and Faber.

Marquand, D. (2004) *Decline of the public*, Cambridge: Polity.

Marsh, D. and Rhodes, R.A.W. (1992) 'Policy communities and issue networks: beyond typology', in D. Marsh and R.A.W. Rhodes (eds) *Policy networks in British government*, Oxford: Clarendon Press, pp 249–68.

Miliband, D. (2006) 'Putting people in control', Speech to the National Council of Voluntary Organisations, London, 21 February.

Needham, C. (2003) *Citizen-consumers: New Labour's marketplace democracy*, London: Catalyst.

Needham, C. (2007) *The reform of public services under New Labour: Narratives of consumerism*, Basingstoke: Palgrave.

Needham, C. (2008) 'Realising the potential of co-production: negotiating improvements in public services', *Social Policy and Society*, vol 7, no 2, pp 221–31.

Neuendorf, K. (2002) *The content analysis handbook*, Thousand Oaks, CA: Sage.

Newman, J. (2006) 'A politics of "the public"', *Soundings*, Issue 32, pp 162–76.

Powell, M. (ed) (1999) *New Labour, new welfare state?*, Bristol: The Policy Press.

Rose, N. (1996) 'Governing "advanced liberal democracies"', in A. Barry, T. Osborne and N. Rose (eds) *Foucault and political reason: Liberalism, neo-Liberalism and rationalities of government*, London: UCL, pp 37–64.

Savage, S. and Atkinson, R. (eds) (2001) *Public policy under Blair*, Basingstoke: Palgrave.

Seldon, A. and Kavanagh, D. (eds) (2005) *The Blair effect, 2001–5*, Cambridge: Cambridge University Press.

Weber, R. (1990) *Basic content analysis*, London: Sage.

Williams, R. (1988) *Keywords: A vocabulary of culture and society* (2nd edn), London: Fontana.

FOUR

Understanding the 'differentiated consumer' in public services

Richard Simmons

Introduction

As we have seen, 'choice' and 'voice' have become watchwords of current policy and provision in the public services. Current debates often focus on notions of 'choice'. Alongside these debates, 'voice' is often acknowledged as being related and of certain value, although it has been claimed to be a less influential driver of change:

> Evidence points to choice serving as an important incentive for promoting quality, efficiency and equity in public services – and in many cases more effectively than relying solely or largely upon alternative mechanisms such as 'voice'. (Cabinet Office, 2005, p 3)

We argue here and elsewhere that both choice and voice have their merits (Simmons et al, 2006a), based on the need that users identify for ensuring that providers listen to what they have to say. While notions of choice invite images of public service users 'shopping around' for the best provider, the best appointment time, the best housing and so on, there are different elements to people's relationships with the public services they use, which mean that it is 'not like shopping' (Clarke, 2005; this volume, Chapter Nine). Recognising this, Hoggett (2003, p 2) argues that the public sector has two unique characteristics:

> It is the site for the continuous contestation of public purposes and it is an essential means of containing social anxieties. Such characteristics serve to remind us that the public sector is primarily a site for the enactment of particular kinds of social relations rather than a site for the delivery of goods and services. To reduce it to the latter is to

commodify such relationships, to strip them of their moral
and ethical meaning and potential.

Given these conditions of 'contestability', in addition to the relative
unavailability of 'exit' that is widely recognised in public services, voice
may also be seen as important if people's interests are to be adequately
taken into account. Voice provides a mechanism through which users
can *negotiate* – either as individuals or collectively. This is particularly
important for public services, where the extent to which collective
as well as individual benefits are provided is generally acknowledged
to be high.

For some, voice could be used in an attempt to extend the menu of
choices available to service users, or to argue for choice where it is not
currently available (what we might call 'voice about choice'). Yet, as we
argue below, voice often goes beyond the confines of choice altogether,
allowing people to express things such as the depth of feeling on an
issue, or a sense of 'membership'/solidarity/support. These differences
reflect a variety of perspectives on the kinds of 'public purposes' and
'social anxieties' that people may emphasise at different times. In short,
different kinds of users have different things to say, and wish to say them
in different ways. If we are to better understand the ways in which
choice and voice are valuable, we therefore argue that there is a need
to find ways to understand the 'differentiated consumer' in today's
public services. Using empirical data gathered as part of the £5m
ESRC/AHRC 'Cultures of Consumption' Programme,[1] we devise a
typology of users, suggest how each perceives the opportunities and
barriers to their expression of choice and voice, and suggest the kinds
of prescriptions that might follow on from this for public services.

Current approaches to public service users

It used to be thought that users of public services had relatively universal
needs that could be met by 'one-size-fits-all' public services. Nowadays
it has been recognised that people's needs and expectations of public
services are diverse, and that this kind of one-size-fits-all approach is no
longer appropriate. A number of reasons have been offered for this, from
a growth in individualism and social pluralism, to greater affluence for
some that sharpens social divisions, a breakdown in traditional structures
and centres of authority, and a greater willingness on the part of service
users to challenge professionals (Policy Commission on Public Services,
2004). Yet, as ideas of a 'universal public' recede, those who run public
services have not always found it easy to understand the ways in which

people differ, or how these affect their expectations and experiences of modern public services. This has often made it harder for them to understand how to respond appropriately to 'what users want'.

Many contemporary attempts to differentiate between people on this basis compare models of citizenship with those of consumption. Hence, ideals of 'citizens' (as universalised members of a political community with rights accrued under the social contract) and 'consumers' (as individualistic, utility-maximising, rational actors) are offered as opposing models for understanding the modern public service user. However, we suggest that neither of these models is sufficiently robust. In one sense the public is seen as *impossibly universal*, with similar needs that can be served by a standardised approach. If this was ever true, it certainly is not true today. Taking a 'universalist' viewpoint may be conducive to overall service planning and coordination, but it carries the risk of inflexibility and insensitivity to individual service users, even where mechanisms are put in place for them to raise their 'voice'. In the second sense, however, the public is seen as *impossibly particular* – everybody is seen as having their own specific and personal needs that lead to demands for their own individualised service packages. In this view, public services must respond, tailoring the service from a range of choices on a menu.

While both of the above scenarios have some basis in empirical evidence, we suggest that it is inappropriate to characterise public service users according to simplistic stereotypes (such as those of the citizen or the consumer). Almost certainly, people take on characteristics commonly associated with each of these stereotypes at different times and in different contexts. Other stereotypical caricatures (such as the largely passive 'client', solidaristic 'member of the community' and so on) also capture only elements of service users and their relationships with the services they use. If today's public service users can be stereotyped in these different ways, the question arises as to 'who' it is that presents themself when they use a public service. The question of 'Who chooses?' has possibly received more attention in the recent literature (eg Greener, 2003; Le Grand, 2006) than that of 'Who speaks?'. In this chapter we therefore focus particularly (although not exclusively) on the latter question.

The research upon which this chapter is based examined the level of involvement users have with different public services; how service users want to be consulted and to have their voices heard; and whether the 'culture' of different public services helps or hinders user voice. Three public services were studied: day care services in health/social care, tenant management organisations in housing, and local leisure services.

In a first phase of data collection, in-depth interviews were undertaken with 80 service users, and with 30 service providers: members of staff, managers, local authority officers and elected representatives. Key documents such as policy statements, information for the public and the minutes of public meetings were also analysed. This analysis included the 'complaints files' in each organisation (including both communications from users and the providers' replies). Material gathered in these ways was then used to inform a second phase of data collection across our three services, in a face-to-face survey. The survey was used to measure the distribution of consumer attitudes and behaviour about 'voice', and sampled 543 users.

In our in-depth interviews we were consistently told by service providers that a lack of user voice simply meant that service users must be happy with the service. Yet we did not have to press them far before they accepted that there might be other alternatives:

> 'We tend not to get many complaints, and perhaps because of that you get a bit complacent and think "Oh well, everything must be alright". But I think its ... maybe we do need to stand back from time to time and just think about it a bit more carefully.'
>
> *(Senior housing manager, M, 40s)*

Our results indicate a need to move beyond ideas of the 'universal' public service user and the moribund notions of 'consensus' around service provision that this suggests. Our research supports that of the previous chapter, showing that public service users are more differentiated in their views about public services than ideas of a universal public allow, making one-size-fits-all solutions untenable. However, there is also a need to move beyond simplistic notions of individualised public service users with their personal 'axe to grind', creating a cacophony of 'noise' from their numerous demands. This was another common fallacy among service providers. Our findings again support those of other recent studies, showing very clearly that users often see beyond their own needs, having a desire to share with others in decent public services (eg Leadbeater, 2004; Policy Commission on Public Services, 2004).

So, how do we draw a balance between these 'universalistic' and 'individualistic' positions? Herein lies a difficulty for modern public services. For while there are problems in thinking of the public as either a single mass or a constituency of individuals all seeking to maximise their own advantage, it is perhaps even more problematic to think of them as falling between these two positions. Yet this is the reality. What is needed is better ways to understand the complexity of today's constituency of public service users, so that we may better meet their needs and expectations.

The 'differentiated consumer' in public services

Public service users differ in a number of important ways. As discussed at length in our previous work, one important factor concerns people's resources. Some users have greater levels of personal resources such as time, money, education, skills and confidence. These generally support the exercise of voice (and, presumably, choice) (Simmons and Birchall, 2005). However, two further sets of factors emerge from our current findings as important, which we have termed 'subjective' and 'objective' factors. Subjective factors concern how people see themselves as public service users. Objective factors concern how 'connected' people feel to the service itself.

'Subjective' factors: how people see themselves

Subjective factors concern people's identities and identifications as public service users. Some of these identifications are more personal and individual, others are more social and collective. The relationship people have with public services will depend to some extent on which part of them dominates at a given moment. This makes it difficult to pigeonhole people according to many of the terms that are often applied to service users: citizens, consumers, customers, clients, members of the public, members of the community and so on. Indeed, for some users, such terms are seen as abstract and superfluous:

> I: (*Showing respondent list of terms*) 'How do you think the service providers see you?'
>
> R: 'They just call me John.'
>
> (*Day care service user, M, 30s*)

Of those users who did identify with the various terms we asked them about, a large proportion held a mix of both individual and collective identifications (eg customer and member of the community; service user and member of the public). This serves to confirm that users have complex identities that are unsuited to simplistic 'either–or' notions of universalism or individualism. We believe attempts to pigeonhole public service users as citizens, consumers, clients (or whatever term) are likely to prove unreliable and unrewarding. In any case, public service users seem relatively unmoved by such debates. More important than the terms themselves are the positive or negative associations that people hold of them. This is usually related to people's perceptions of their ability to have their say and make a difference. Hence, in what follows we examine two sets of issues that our research suggested to be of particular relevance, but that sometimes get hidden behind the above 'labels':

1. The balance between individual and collective identifications.
2. The sense of control that is associated with different identifications.

Balancing collective and individual identifications

The balance between individual and collective identifications is important. First, this balance is reflected in the different values, norms, beliefs and attitudes that people hold. People's backgrounds and socialisation have important effects on how they interpret the world. For example, some people will tend to value their personal independence most highly, while others will tend to place greater value on their solidarity with a particular group or community. Second, the balance between individual and collective identifications is important in defining people's motivations for action. In our previous work we have shown how people's individualistic motivations to participate in collective action are often outweighed by collectivistic motivations such as a sense of community, shared values and shared goals (Simmons and Birchall, 2005).

People's individual and collective identifications often interact when they give their views. A prominent 'default assumption' of many service provider representatives was that service users raised their voices when they wanted something; that they were making additional claims on resources, based on their own personal preferences. Sometimes user communications are indeed about the expression of preferences, for example arguing for the extension of choice:

> 'When I started, what you did in the morning or afternoon, that was you. Day in, week out, month out, year out. And I thought about it, and I said "No, this is wrong – people are bored doing the same thing every day".... Over the years they began to realise that wasn't what people wanted, they wanted a service that was geared to providing something that would challenge service users, give them an interest. So now we have, like, shopping trips, we have trips to museums, there's fishing groups during the summer (they're quite popular), there's the chess group that I run, there's woodwork.... So there's usually something for a service user to do although, as I say, you'll get the odd one that won't ... but that's their choice too.'
>
> *(Day centre user, M, 40s)*

Yet our findings show that it would be inaccurate to see voice as exclusively (or even predominantly) about extending choice. We found that voice is used at least as regularly to express things other than preferences, such as the depth of feeling on an issue, or a sense of 'membership'/solidarity/support. In the following quotation, for example, it is difficult to reconcile the ideas of 'obligation' and speaking for others with notions of 'choice':

> I:'When you first attended a user meeting, what made you think, "Yes, I would like to be part of that meeting"?'
>
> R:'I support the pool and I thought this would be a good way of expressing my support ... I also felt that I could communicate the views of the other people I know who didn't have time to go. So I did use an opportunity to say, "I don't happen to feel this but a lot of people do feel that".'
>
> *(Leisure services user, M, 60s)*

Balancing both individual and collective identifications, the above respondent wanted to make a public expression of his personal support for the pool at a user meeting, where he spoke explicitly about not only what he thought but what others thought as well. The latter point is important. Our findings show a clear and significant body of feeling among service users that they do not want their own preferences to take priority over those of others if this is going to lead to an 'unfair' outcome:

'I was swimming for seven years and I loved it. And then suddenly they started to play music in the pool. I really blew my stack – I couldn't bear it. So I went to one of the lifeguards and said "I really don't like this". And then he went and turned it off. And I felt terrible because I thought, you know, "What about everybody else .... how does he know [what they think]?". So there I was, I felt really embarrassed. And then I asked a couple of people, you know, in the pool, and said did they mind the music? And they said "No". So I felt I had exercised disproportionate influence.'

(Leisure services user, F, 50s)

A sense of control – having a say and making a difference?

We also found that more important than the use of terms such as citizen, consumer, customer, client, member of the public, member of the community and so on are the meanings that people attach to them. Of particular importance, we found, was the sense of control users associated with each of these labels – whether or not they felt able to have a say and make a difference. These associations were dependent on people's experiences of how they were treated, and could not be read off simply from the terms themselves. For example, some people saw the term 'client' very positively, as someone who issued instructions for others to carry out:

'Being a client ... it's like when you go to the hairdresser's: you tell them what you want and they do it for you. They treat you properly, you get respect.'

(Leisure services user, F, teenager)

Others, however, saw the same term as objectifying them; as someone who was simply 'administered to':

'[It means] taking what's offered, and there's not much choice in what you're offered.'

(Tenant, M, 50s)

> '[It means] they think they're better than you.'
>
> *(Tenant, F, 30s)*

Similarly, being treated as a 'consumer' was seen as a double-edged sword. Some saw it as being able to make demands, with expectations that these demands would be met, while others thought that as a consumer you would be treated as 'just a number'. As one tenant put it, being treated as a consumer means 'it's your money they're after – once they've got it they don't want to know'. In fact, each of the terms and categories we explored with service users was seen by some as having positive associations, and by others as having negative associations. Positive associations tended to reflect users' ability to have their say and make a difference, and negative associations vice versa.

We found a common tendency for service providers to stereotype users, with some stereotypes held more positively than others. For example, leisure service providers were often disparaging about 'early-morning swimmers' as being somehow radical and subversive. Because these swimmers typically share the facilities together on a regular basis, they tend to get talking to one another about matters of common interest. This can lead to requests being made to managers for changes and improvements to the pool from what might be seen as a fairly legitimate group. However, this is often regarded by service managers as challenging, which tends to make them wary and unresponsive. They therefore prefer to treat early-morning swimmers as separate individuals rather than as a collective entity, even where the swimmers have deliberately organised collectively.

Patterns of stereotyping are rarely accurate or benign in the context of public service delivery. Stereotypes are usually inaccurate because, as we have already identified, service users tend to stand simultaneously in a number of different relationships with public service organisations (see Hirschmann, 1999; Alford, 2002). They are usually malign, because stereotypical terminology tends to signify particular attitudes from public service providers towards those who are stereotyped:

> I: 'When you first moved in and reported the situation with the toilet, what kind of response did you feel you got?'
>
> R: 'Oh the response was as if I was an idiot: "Well, it has been inspected and the inspector said it was alright."'
>
> *(Tenant, F, 50s)*

> 'Because they can't see you face to face and you are at the other end of the phone they must think we are stupid, that's the impression I get.'
>
> *(Tenant, F, 30s)*

> 'I'm not a village idiot by any means, at least I don't think so [laughs] but, you know, they're treating me like one.'
>
> *(Tenant, M, 50s)*

In sum, our research shows that producers routinely construct users according to their own perspectives and interests. For their part, users may accept these constructions, negotiate, or contest them.

Colleagues on the ESRC/AHRC 'Cultures of Consumption' programme have suggested that people's sense of connection with public services is based on the relationships they build with service providers (Clarke, 2005). We agree. However, despite the fact that many users see these relationships as relatively positive and are willing to share their views with providers in the best interests of the service, there are mixed views about the extent to which providers are interested in making available genuine opportunities for this. Our research indicates a relationship between the positivity of these relationships and whether or not there are considered to be good opportunities to express one's views (Table 4.1).

Table 4.1: Nature of user–provider relationships vs 'good opportunities' to express views

	Day care (N=116)		Leisure (N=318)		Housing (N=109)	
Good opportunities? Relationship?	Yes (%)	No (%)	Yes (%)	No (%)	Yes (%)	No (%)
Very positive	88.5	11.5	79.2	20.8	77.8	22.2
Quite positive	78.1	21.9	43.8	56.2	58.3	41.7
Neither positive/ negative	42.9	57.1	18.8	81.3	40.6	59.4
Quite negative	0	100.0	7.7	92.3	9.1	90.9
Very negative	0	100.0	0	0	0	100.0

Overall, then, our findings support those of other recent research, that 'the way in which individuals negotiate the role of consumer is clearly relevant to their propensity to get involved' (Lupton et al, 1998, p 114). However, the different identifications and associations held by public service users represent the 'subjective' components of their relationship with the service. Our research showed that this was important, but that there is another 'objective' component that also needs to be considered.

Objective factors: a sense of connection?

Not all users 'connect' with public services. Some are happy to simply take what they are given, good or bad, engaging uncritically with the service and its providers. Others are so disconnected that they barely engage with the service at any level; it is something to be tolerated, endured or shut out completely. The sense of alienation and/or detachment in this latter group is associated with notions of 'withdrawal' that we have discussed at length elsewhere (Simmons et al, 2006b).

However, there is good evidence that large numbers of users do have a sense of connection with the public services they use. In our research, over 70% of survey respondents reported that they had expressed their views at some point in time about the service in question. Voice is therefore extremely commonplace, reflecting people's sense of attachment to public services. Why do people feel this way? In short, it is because they often see public services as being important and care about them being done well. Evidence for people caring about their public services was widespread in our interviews with both users and providers:

'I look after my premises. Can't you see? I'd like the council office up the road to realise: "Oh, there is a tenant in that premises ... someone who does care for the premises, who does care for the area and not just anybody who's paying rent."'

(Tenant, M, 40s)

'There will always be a certain amount of people that will complain because of personal circumstances or how they are feeling that day. But there are genuine people that will say: "Look, that is not good. I like coming here, I want to keep coming here. Can you do something about it?" And I think it is because they care. I know that sounds quite deep but I think generally they do, otherwise they wouldn't bother.'

(Leisure services manager, M, 20s)

This was backed up in our survey, where 96.5% of day care users, 89.8% of leisure service users and 66.1% of tenants said they care either 'a great deal' or 'quite a lot' about the service. For the many people who do connect with the service, there are different levels at which this happens. This reflects the kinds of relationships people have with the services they use, and the kinds of concerns they develop. It also reflects the importance people attach to the service. In practice, this can be quite a complex set of conditions to pull apart. We have represented some of the key aspects in Table 4.2, where we divide users' connection with public services into 'higher' and 'lower' levels.

Table 4.2: What 'caring about' public services involves for users

Level at which people 'connect'	What is involved?	Level of interaction	Relationship with service	Nature of user concerns	Judgements made over
'Lower' level	Service attributes and their consequences for the user experience	Personal and temporal characteristics of service situation	Specific user roles/ behaviours temporal in nature	Technical (*although may become political*)	Service attributes
'Higher' level	Service-related values and their consequences for the user experience	Personal versus service-related values	Stakeholder/ co-contributor/ 'partner' ongoing in nature	*Both* technical *and* political	*Both* service attributes *and* service-related values

When users connect at a lower level, it does not mean that their concerns are insignificant. It simply means that their concerns tend to address issues of a 'lower order' than do the concerns of those who connect at a higher level. Users' concerns here focus on the *attributes* of the service and their consequences for how they experience using the service. At this lower level, people's relationship with the service tends to be limited in time and space to a particular 'processing situation' (Laaksonen, 1994). It is also limited to the specific roles and behaviours directly associated with their use of the service. This leads them to focus on 'technical' concerns – for example, whether something is 'working' or not:

> 'It was just, you know, when you do something that's slightly silly and you do it every day and it slowly annoys you. And you say "Well, why don't we do it that way?" ... That's what happened with this particular system.'
>
> *(Leisure services user, M, 20s)*

Connecting at a higher level introduces an extra dimension. Here, users' concerns also focus on the *values* that underpin the provision of the service, how these compare with their own personal values, and the consequences for how they experience using the service. In practice, we found that many users felt a sense of 'ownership' in relation to public services; of having a stake. This led them to see their relationship with the service as one of 'co-contributor' or even 'partner'. In addition to technical concerns, at a higher level people also focus on the more 'political' (with a small 'p') concerns of what the service *should* be doing.

Amid a growing perception of the disconnection of service users from the means of public service 'production', alternative methods for the inclusion of user voice at this higher level have been widely promoted – for example in notions of 'citizen governance' (Home Office, 2005; ODPM, 2005; Simmons et al, 2007b). Implicitly, this suggests a rejection of previous assumptions that people are only interested in 'lower-level' involvement. Our evidence suggests that this is entirely appropriate. However, there is a difference in people's sense of 'caring about' the service (which they generally see as a shared responsibility) and notions of responsibility for 'caring for' the service (which is generally seen as being that of service providers). In this way, there is a sense that people want providers to take the lead – but crucially *not before* they have listened appropriately to what users have to say. Hence, while in general service users tend to trust providers to take the lead in running public services, this trust is limited and conditional, not absolute. Users often feel a need to keep their eye on the ball and to make sure that important matters do not go unchallenged. The need to strike a balance between 'leadership and listening' has recently been recognised in the public sector (eg Needham, 2001; Simmons, 2008), and this is a matter to which we shall return.

Differentiating public service consumers: combining 'subjective' and 'objective' factors

People have different ways of relating to the public services they use. To categorise these different relationships, we believe it is useful to combine the 'subjective' aspects of user identity with the 'objective' aspects of users' relationship with the service itself. In Figures 4.1a and 4.1b we have therefore taken our 'individual–collective' dimension and put it against our 'connected–disconnected' dimension to produce a 2 x 2 matrix.

Figure 4.1a: Combining positive 'subjective' and 'objective' aspects of user involvement

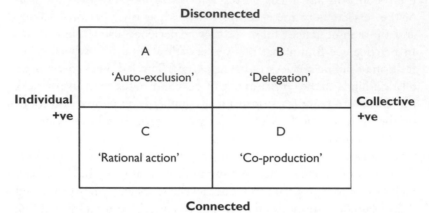

Figure 4.1a shows how 'positive' user identifications (ie where users feel able to have a say and make a difference) combine with a sense of connection or disconnection with the service itself. Users' identifications may be individual or collective.

In cell A, users identify themselves as individuals and able to 'have a say and make a difference'. However, they feel disconnected from the goals and aims of the service itself. These users could be seen as 'apathetic', not caring enough about the service to engage with it further. However, they may also lack understanding about the significance of the choices that are available to them. This amounts to a kind of 'auto-exclusion', or 'refusal of agency'. Here the prescription for public services might be a programme of 'public engagement'; drawing in individual members of the public, building more substantial relationships with them and creating the more connected consumers found in cell C.

In cell B, users see themselves as members of a collectivity. This identification is seen positively, as one that is able to have a say and make a difference. However, they do not feel a strong sense of connection to the service itself. The users' role here is limited to 'delegation': giving their allegiance (and deference) to political representatives in arbitrating between different demands on collective resources in the 'public interest' and periodically voting for different political representatives if they perceive the incumbents to be failing in this task. Users' influence is one step removed from the actual provision of services – hence the prime minister's assessment of voting as a 'blunt tool' (PASC, 2004). Where users have an issue, the leading expectation is that redress will be sought via politicians representing the collectivity – anything more being regarded as undue influence. In this environment, trust in politicians and senior administrators to effectively coordinate public services is a key commodity.

In cell C, users are directly connected to the service as individuals. The users' role here is to make service choices so as to support their private needs and wants and then negotiate the best package of services for themselves in terms of cost and quality. Again, their expectation is of organisational responsiveness to their demands – this time as individuals – with a system of complaint and personal redress if things go wrong. At 'higher' levels of discourse, users may argue for modes of coordination that promote individualistic values such as personalisation and autonomy.

In cell D, users are connected collectively to the coordination and 'co-production' of the service. The users' role here is to involve themselves in deliberative and participative processes that are specific to the service or service issues. Collective action therefore takes in a range of processes that include user groups, peer advocacy and campaigns. Users have an expectation of responsiveness to their demands, which are derived through collective processes ('collective choice') and/or expressed through collective channels to demonstrate solidarity. At 'higher' levels of discourse, users may argue for services to be organised in ways that promote mutualistic values such as equality, solidarity and association.

By contrast, Figure 4.1b shows how 'negative' user identifications (ie where they do not feel able to have a say and make a difference) combine with a sense of connection or disconnection with the service itself. Again, users' identifications may be individual or collective.

Figure 4.1b: Combining negative 'subjective' and 'objective' aspects of user involvement

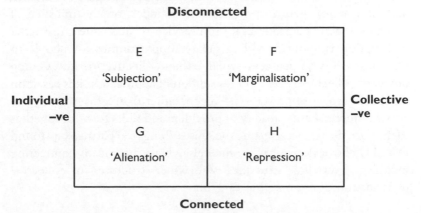

In cell E, users feel both disconnected from the coordination of service provision and unable to have a say and make a difference. As isolated individuals, their role is to chart the best course they can through their use of public services – not an easy task since they feel they have little control. In this way, they tend to feel that they are simply 'subjected' to whatever the service provides.

In cell F, users identify themselves as members of a collectivity. These, however, are 'marginalised communities'. They feel their group to be at the bottom of the pile, both disconnected from the goals and aims of the service and powerless to have a say and make a difference. Their solidarity with other group members is their only resource, which they may (or may not) use for mutual support. Engagement with these groups/communities must both reiterate the importance of the service in their lives and persuade them that viable opportunities are available to express their views as group members.

In cell G, users identify themselves as individuals. This time, however, they are 'connected'; they do care. The problem here is that they do not feel able to have a say and make a difference. These users could be described as 'alienated'. Their sense of personal agency is denied. The prescription here differs: it is more about providing greater opportunities for individuals to participate. Voice is important here: 'empowerment begins by finding that voice which provides the truth to one's experience' (Hoggett, 2001, p 46). However, as Le Grand (2006, p 2) also argues, 'choice gives power to voice'. At this individualistic level, adding choice to voice is an appropriate means of empowering users.

Finally, in cell H users again identify themselves as members of a collectivity. They feel connected with the goals and aims of the service, but powerless to have a say and make a difference. Collectively, they form a 'mobilisation potential' within their communities. However, collective action here may be focused as much on the injustice of being excluded as a group as it is on service-related issues. Again, the prescription is about providing greater opportunities for people to participate in ways that acknowledge their collective identity. Giving power to collective voice requires a different approach, as it is based on a different aspect of power – 'power to' rather than 'power over'. The aim is to increase the capacity of providers and users to work together to improve the service, creating the sense of 'engaged partnership' found in cell D above. As we have argued elsewhere, this means connecting inclusive governance structures with wider structures for collective participation (Simmons et al, 2007b).

For service providers, as we suggested earlier, meeting this challenge means that it is necessary to demonstrate the extent to which they are 'listening' as well as 'leading'. However, we recognise the importance of context; elsewhere we have argued that some contexts demand that the balance falls more towards leadership, while others demand it falls more towards listening (Simmons et al, 2006c). In terms of the listening component, we reiterate here that both choice and voice are important. However, the differentiated nature of public service consumers means that different types of choice (individual choice, interactive choice, collective choice) and voice (hierarchical, individualistic, group based) will be required (Simmons et al, 2006c). In other words, no one of these different models of choice or voice provides a panacea in today's public service environment. We found strong demand among users for being listened to in each of these different ways.

Meeting people's increasingly diverse expectations as to how they should be treated provides a key challenge for public service providers. Other evidence collected in the course of our research shows that the majority of people want services to move in a direction that makes them feel (1) more positive about their identifications as service users (both individually *and* collectively) and (2) more 'connected' to the service itself (Simmons et al, 2007a). In particular, this has implications for how they want to be treated, in terms of:

- courtesy and respect
- how knowledge is valued
- how fairness and equity issues are resolved
- how rules are set and policed.

Failure to recognise value pluralism and to 'welcome rather than fear conflict' (Hoggett, 2003) is likely to result in increasing levels of negativity and disconnection.

Importantly, providers can themselves become disconnected in a number of ways. First, they can fail to understand the service attributes and consequences that are important to service users. Second, they can differ in their judgements of the service's performance in relation to these key attributes and consequences. Third, they can differ in the values, beliefs and attitudes they hold. This can be a key site of 'contestation' between users and providers. However, a fourth way concerns the exercise of choice and voice. Different types of choice and voice provide different ways for messages to be communicated and accommodations to be reached. Where different types of choice and voice are stifled, problems can eventually be expected – even if there appear to be short-term gains. The need to balance leadership and listening has therefore never been clearer – but more work is needed to create the kind of listening culture that users want.

People know a listening culture when they see it. Generally it reflects greater congruence between users' perceptions of how they *actually are* treated by the service, and their expectations of how they *should be* treated (Simmons et al, 2007a). Two things are necessary in order to achieve greater levels of congruence:

- institutional design that recognises value pluralism and promotes the provision of a range of 'spaces' for users to exercise choice and voice;
- the investment of institutional effort to make these spaces work, providing listening as well as leadership.

The first provides the 'organisational architecture' to ensure that effective means are provided for organising the inputs people (whether users or providers) want to put into an organisation – and the outputs that they want to get out. The second provides the commitment necessary to 'reconnect' and strengthen the ties between public service organisations and their 'differentiated' public.

Note

[1] This is based on research conducted for the ESRC/AHRC 'Cultures of Consumption' Programme between 2003 and 2006 (Grant no: RES 143250040). Three public services were studied: housing, social care and leisure services.

References

Alford, J. (2002) 'Defining the client in the public sector: a social exchange perspective', *Public Administration Review*, vol 62, no 3, pp 337–46.

Cabinet Office (2005) *Choice and voice in the reform of public services: Government response to the PASC report – choice, voice and public services*, London: Cabinet Office.

Clarke, J. (2005) 'Competitive choice or relational reasoning?', Paper to Cultures of Consumption Seminar, *Choice and Voice in Public Services*, HM Treasury, London, 24 June.

Greener, I. (2003) 'Who choosing what? The evolution of the word "choice" in the NHS and its implications for New Labour', *Social Policy Review 15*, Bristol: The Policy Press, pp 49–67.

Hirschmann, D. (1999) '"Customer service" in the United States Agency for International Development', *Administration & Society*, vol 31, no 1, pp 95–119.

Hoggett, P. (2001) 'Agency, rationality and social policy', *Journal of Social Policy*, vol 30, no 1, pp 37–56.

Hoggett, P. (2003) 'Why public is not the same as private', Paper to International Society for the Psychoanalytic Study of Organizations Symposium, *Power and Politics*, Boston, June 19–21.

Home Office (2005) *Together we can: A government action plan led by the Home Office*, London: Home Office.

Laaksonen, P. (1994) *Consumer involvement*, London: Routledge.

Leadbeater, C. (2004) *Personalisation through participation: A new script for public services*, London: Demos.

Le Grand, J. (2006) 'Choice and competition in public services', *Research in public policy*, Summer 2006, p 2.

Lupton, C., Peckham, S. and Taylor, P. (1998) *Managing public involvement in healthcare planning*, Buckingham: Open University Press.

Needham, C. (2001) *Listen and lead – the challenge from the women of Worcester* (www.opendemocracy.net/people-worcesterwomen/article_329.jsp).

ODPM (Office of the Deputy Prime Minister) (2005) *Vibrant local leadership*, London: ODPM.

PASC (Public Administration Select Committee) (2004) *Choice, voice and public services: An issues and questions paper*, London: PASC.

Policy Commission on Public Services (2004) *Making public services personal*, London: National Consumer Council.

Simmons, R. (2008) 'Leadership and listening: striking the balance in today's public services', Paper to Social Policy Association Conference, Edinburgh, June.

Simmons, R. and Birchall, J. (2005) 'A joined-up approach to user participation in public services: strengthening the "participation chain"', *Social Policy and Administration*, vol 39, no 3, pp 260–83.

Simmons, R., Birchall, J. and Prout, A. (2006a) *Cultural tensions in public service delivery: Implications for producer-consumer relationships*, Working Paper 026, ESRC/AHRC 'Cultures of Consumption' Programme.

Simmons, R., Birchall, J. and Prout, A. (2006b) 'Choice about voice', Paper to Social Policy Association Conference, Birmingham, July.

Simmons, R., Birchall, J. and Prout, A. (2006c) 'Facilitation of constraint?', Paper to Public Administration Committee Conference, Durham, September.

Simmons, R., Birchall, J. and Prout, A. (2007a) 'Hearing voices? User involvement and public service cultures', *Consumer Policy Review*, vol 17, no 5, pp 234–40.

Simmons, R., Birchall, J., Doheny, S. and Powell, M. (2007b) '"Citizen governance": opportunities for inclusivity in policy and policy making?', *Policy & Politics*, vol 35, no 3, pp 455–75.

FIVE

Differentiating consumers in professional services: information empowerment and the emergence of the fragmented consumer[1]

Angus Laing, Gill Hogg, Terry Newholm and Debbie Keeling

Introduction: politics, information and empowerment

Arguably one of the most provocative theoretical accounts of consumer sovereignty was articulated more than half a century ago by the economist L.E. von Mises (quoted in Gonse, 1990). At the heart of his argument lay the notion that consumers are empowered through 'catalytic, or indirect, power', where markets operating free from political or sectoral interests ensured that organisations and professionals were responsive to the needs of consumers. However, Gonse (1990, p 138), articulating what has now become a familiar critique of this highly theoretical position, posed the question of whether this perspective could be:

> convincing in the face of externalities, imperfect consumer rationality, variations in the distribution of income of consumers, real costs, monopoly, mass production of standardised products, and [producers'] selling efforts?

These issues still form the basis of contemporary debate around consumer empowerment, not least in professional service settings. However, in the past two decades significant changes have occurred in the relationship between producers and consumers, across a range of professional service settings from healthcare to financial services, which have served to reinvigorate the debate around consumer empowerment.

Two interconnected sets of developments lie at the core of this renewal of the consumer empowerment debate.

First, the articulation by the New Right in the 1980s of the primacy of markets, anchored in neoclassical economic theory, witnessed, inter alia, the transferral of responsibilities from the state to the individual, the liberalisation of markets and radical change in the organisation of public services (Laing and Hogg, 2002). At the core of this shift was a fundamental change in the relationship between service providers and users. From relationships being couched in terms of citizenship, with myriad mutual commitments and obligations, from being dominated by respect for professional status, and from being expressed in the use of terms such as 'patients' and 'clients', relationships are increasingly articulated in consumerist terms, with emphasis placed on the rights of service users as sovereign individuals (Walsh, 1994; Keaney, 1999). The promotion of an overtly consumerist culture in public services, together with changes in the regulation of financial and, subsequently, legal markets, has generated an environment in which concepts of consumer empowerment have gained renewed relevance and power.

Second, the rise of the knowledge society on the back of the internet-enabled information revolution has fundamentally affected the relationship between consumers, service organisations and professionals responsible for the delivery of services (Laing et al, 2005). In particular, the information revolution has impacted on the consumption and provision of what have widely been framed as 'knowledge-based services', that is, professional services such as health, legal and financial services where the core of the service is knowledge and expertise (Mills and Moshavi, 1999). Central to this shifting relationship was the idea that the internet offered the consumer the opportunity to challenge professionals through the acquisition of information which had previously been the preserve of the professional. The patient confronting the doctor with information downloaded from the internet has become symbolic of the perceived changes in consumer behaviours and roles in such settings. Although providing a powerful image of the renegotiation of the professional service encounter, such anecdotes run the risk of simplifying the complexities inherent in any renegotiation of the consumer–professional encounter, as well as the uniformity of such information-based empowerment.

Context: professional services and the information society

Professional services, whether located in the public or private sectors, have traditionally been characterised by an inbuilt power imbalance where the consumer engages with the professional from a position of dependency and the professional determines what is in the consumer's best interest on the basis of professional judgement (Friedson, 1986). The professional–consumer relationship in this context has, however, undergone unprecedented change in the last two decades, with an increasingly confident consumer culture coming into conflict with conventional professional establishments (Laing and Hogg, 2002). Driven by the intersection of socio-economic and technological trends, this has raised a debate about the relationship between professionals and society. The debate has been set against an apparent increase of high-profile service failures. Ranging from the mis-selling of investment products to the disregarding of patient rights, such publicised negligence has, at least in popular consciousness, been viewed as symbolic of the failure of the professions at a policy level, as well as of individual professionals at an operational level, to address the needs of contemporary consumers.

Conventionally, certain categories of services, for example medicine and the law, have been protected from overtly consumerist behaviours by the acceptance of the concept of professionalism by a majority of service users. This notion of professionalism was characterised by a number of key features. First, an esoteric discourse which generated the perception of homogeneity across qualified practitioners; second, a rational scientifically anchored rhetoric of reliability; third, the restricting of entry into a profession through vocational education and accreditation; fourth, a domineering approach to alternatives that simulated a knowledge monopoly; and, last, an asymmetry of information between the profession and its consumers that largely suppressed debate (Vermaak and Weggeman, 1999). However, in contemporary western societies, professional services have increasingly been exposed to scrutiny driven by a number of interconnected trends:

- *Occupational parity*: in a post-industrial economy many occupations acquire professional or quasi-professional status. Many service consumers present the same confidence, if not disciplinary knowledge, as their professional advisers in dealing with previously esoteric information (Abercrombie, 1994).

- *Informed consumers*: increasing access to information of a highly specialised nature from within, and in opposition to, the dominant discourse results in service consumers becoming more able to explore professional opinion (McKean, 1999).
- *Consumer culture*: consumers are less accepting of a homogeneous professional product, given their increasing awareness of the proliferation of alternative service offerings (Gabriel and Lang, 1995).
- *Questioning of science*: challenging of the claims of scientific knowledge, and indeed the basis of knowledge and expertise. There is an associated acceptance of 'alternative' frameworks and approaches to addressing underlying service needs (Elam and Bertilsson, 2003).
- *Pervasive media*: media presentation of extreme characterisations of professions and professional behaviour. Publicising and exploiting professional disagreements leads to perceptions of heterogeneity (Petts et al, 2000).
- *Risk society*: service consumers simultaneously strive to, and it is demanded of them that they, take control of their lives. At the same time, risks increasingly become the subject of debate, because major risks are ascribed to human activity (Beck, 1992).

In these circumstances, patterns of user behaviour and resultant relationships change, in some cases radically. Consequently, the apparent continuing stability of the established professional–client relationship format can no longer be taken for granted. Increasingly, contemporary consumer cultures come into conflict with conventional professional establishments. Thompson (2003), in exploring consumption of healthcare services within the context of private sector healthcare delivery in the United States, encapsulates this tension:

> The patient as consumer desires to produce his/her own medico-administrative identity through interaction with physicians, nurses and technologies. This has contributed to the diminution of medical authority as well as increased expectations (and incidences of dissatisfaction) regarding the quality of service. Yet these post-modern currents inevitably collide with the more intractable, modernist features of the medico-administrative system. (p 103)

That is, consumer expectations of flexibility and interaction cannot, or at least cannot easily, be accommodated within services that were conceived to protect dependent consumers. In the particular context of healthcare services in the United Kingdom, the rigidity of the professional establishment is compounded by the inflexibility of prevailing public sector governance regimes.

Underpinning the rise of such consumer expectations of active participation is the internet-driven information revolution. Although the interconnected socio-economic trends outlined have collectively created the conditions which have led to such seismic social change, the revolution in access to information has been the trigger for this change. The internet has effectively been the vehicle through which the emergent consumerist culture has been articulated and has found its fullest expression. Politically, the internet has been characterised as a resource through which citizens can become more self-reliant, being viewed by parts of the political spectrum as a liberating medium, a mechanism by which users of public sector services have been able to challenge the authority of professional and political establishments. The work of David (2001) in relation to healthcare exemplifies this notion that unprecedented access to information via the internet has empowered consumers and radically altered consumption relationships:

> One of the main forces within the e-environment is *consumer empowerment*. With greater access to more readily available sources of information than their forefathers, consumers are assuming an increasingly active role. … Instead of being passive recipients of judgements and treatments handed out by the medical community, consumers will be actively involved in managing their own healthcare. They will demand a better quality of life, better care, personalized treatment, convenience, choice, and value for money. (pp 6–7, emphasis in original)

Against such a backdrop the description of the impact of the internet on medical services by Ham and Alberti (2002) as 'being akin to the translation of the Bible from Latin into English' is a powerful analogous image of the potential disruptive capabilities of the internet and, in turn, of the implications for the professional priesthood. For services such as medicine and law, traditionally characterised by professional authority, what Foucault refers to as a 'regime of truth' (1980, p 84), in part based on informational asymmetries and exclusive possession of specialist skills (Friedson, 1986), this implies a fundamental challenging of established monopolistic patterns of organising and delivering services, as well as of the dominant professional discourse.

David (2001) suggests such a breaking of professional monopoly when he refers to the ending of judgements being 'handed out by the medical community' (p 7). In parallel, increased competition among established service suppliers, together with the entry of new service suppliers, operating within or outside of the established professional discourse, is the assumed consequence of such information-based consumer empowerment in legal services (McKean, 1999; Port, 1999). Adopting this somewhat absolutist perspective, Peppard (2000, p 318) argues that 'competition in the market place returns power to the consumer'. This is mirrored in the context of healthcare, where Heritage (2001) argues that, within prevailing policy and organisational settings, 'the "consumer movement" in medicine has evidently changed the ways in which doctors normally deliver diagnoses' (p 54). In reviewing the literature on this much-vaunted transference of authority from the producer to the consumer, Abercrombie (1994) sounded a note of caution. While Abercrombie accepted that the scope for consumer empowerment has opened up during times of producer restructuring and increased competition, the opportunity for increasing consumer empowerment requires to be framed in social as well as narrow economic terms. Specifically, the social capital of individual consumers is central to any understanding of patterns of consumer empowerment (Wathieu et al, 2002). This social capital perspective challenges the prevailing economic conceptualisation of empowerment, arguing that not all consumer aspirations towards empowerment are equal. Henry (2005) argues that 'distinctive self-perceptions' (p 775) imbued within 'class positions' impact on the *expectations* of empowerment. Thus, some individuals 'self-restrict already limited opportunities' (p 767) even where markets are open to consumer empowerment, highlighting the prospect of uneven empowerment and diversity of consumerist behaviours.

Looking beyond the drivers and facilitating conditions for consumer empowerment, even where the necessary informational and market conditions exist, and where individual consumer-will towards empowerment is present, it has been argued that the debate on empowerment should not simply assume only benefits arising from increasing consumer empowerment (Starkey, 2003). Approaching this issue from a similar perspective, MacStavic (2000) specifically identifies a number of potential disadvantages accruing to consumers through greater empowerment. First, they make choices that, in spite of their greater knowledge, they might be ill-prepared to make, as a result both of limited expertise and of emotional vulnerability. Second, they take risks of which they may only have a limited grasp and they bear the unameliorated responsibility for the consequences. Third, they spend more time than previously in making decisions, thereby incurring significant opportunity costs. Consequently 'the fact that consumers have more choice means the onus is on them to make them [sic].' (MacStavic, 2000, p 30). That is, for consumers, this may be viewed as generating new uncertainties, anxieties and challenges in terms of negotiating or resisting a new settlement with professionals. Thus, the plurality of the internet as a space for opportunity or as a space of challenge (Laing et al, 2008) has the potential to destabilise traditional consumer 'certainties'. This plurality is reflected in the extensive debate among professionals and their representative bodies as to whether such information-based consumer empowerment may ultimately undermine consumer autonomy and reinforce dependence on professionals, albeit in a very different form (Newholm et al, 2006). The central thrust of this debate is around the quality of information available to consumers in an unregulated environment such as the internet, and the capacity of consumers to handle the available information.

Reflecting these multiple perspectives, there is a risk in periods of rapid socio-economic change of characterising such change as paradigmatic. The danger is of overstating the extent of such shifts and inferring generalisations from the behaviour of subsets of distinctive, innovative consumers. Although it potentially represents emergent trends, caution is required in extrapolating the distinctive behaviour of particular clusters of consumers to the broader population (Laing et al, 2005). The pattern of patient behaviour described by Thompson (2003) within a North American context, although sporadically evident within the NHS, is by no means universal in healthcare settings in the United Kingdom. The identification and analysis of trends in consumption behaviours in professional services is complicated by the plurality and complexity of service expectations, as well as of usage behaviours, that are increasingly apparent among consumers. The core challenge confronting service organisations and professionals may consequently be less about responding to a paradigm shift in consumption behaviour and more about responding to increasing diversity of consumption behaviours.

Methodology: service consumption in the knowledge economy

Forming part of a broader research programme examining the impact of the internet-driven information revolution on professional service consumption, the data reported in this chapter focus on the attitudes of healthcare consumers to internet-derived information and experiences of service utilisation. The research was structured around interconnected qualitative and quantitative phases. In each phase participants had consulted a qualified healthcare professional and made related use of the internet within the last 12 months. Each phase focused on consumers' experiences of interaction with healthcare professionals and associated use of health information.

In the qualitative phase, 10 focus groups (n=53) were conducted in six locations in the UK and comprised a mixed population of healthcare consumers encompassing a range of ages, socio-economic backgrounds and levels of experience of healthcare services. None of the participants was employed in healthcare services. Participants were asked to relate experiences they had had with relevant professionals, and in particular their use of information in both addressing the underlying need which prompted the use of the professional and in their subsequent dealing with that professional. Following transcription, the focus group data sets were analysed using template analysis (King, 1998), identifying influential factors in the use of health information from the internet and the impact of such information on relationships with professionals.

In the quantitative phase, a telephone-based survey (n=333) was conducted using a professional data collection agency. The sample was structured to ensure an appropriate demographic mix and spectrum of service experience and utilisation. Survey items regarding use of and approaches to healthcare, as well as issues relating to the use of internet-based health information, were based on the preceding qualitative phase. Where appropriate, established and validated measurement scales were used. Results were analysed using K-means cluster analysis to elicit profiles of groups with respect to their beliefs and behaviour in healthcare services and health information use, and cross-tabulations to identify patterns of, and differences in attitudes to, health information use. The sample consisted of 29% (n=96) non-internet users and 71% (n=237) internet users.

Discussion: internet and fragmenting consumer behaviours

The internet represents a new forum, a new environment within and through which consumers can contest the service domain with professionals. For some consumers this will offer valued opportunities to assert power over professionals and set the terms of engagement; for others it will pose questions as to the nature of their role; and for some it will generate doubts and uncertainties. There is a fundamental danger in implicit assumptions that consumers will exhibit similar views in relation to the disruption of the 'established church' of professionalism arising from the internet, or at least will be facing in a common direction. Rather, the underlying nature of the internet suggests increasing fragmentation among consumers and a growing diversity of patterns of behaviour in engaging with professional services. Such fragmenting of behaviours can be linked to divergent patterns of internet information usage, with differing usage of the internet in terms of the types of forums and infomediaries being exploited (or not) by different groups of consumers, by the same consumers on different occasions and by consumers in different circumstances.

Categorising consumers: attitude and behaviour

Drawing on the survey data to explore the way in which consumers use the internet in shaping their interaction with healthcare professionals, it is possible to categorise contemporary healthcare consumers into four coherent and discrete behavioural clusters. The twin dimensions around which these clusters are constructed are, first, consumer attitude towards healthcare professionals, and, second, behaviour in the service encounter, ie within the consultation. Independently, these two variables do not provide a viable explanation for the fragmentation of behaviours witnessed in contemporary healthcare settings. Taken together, however, they provide an empirically robust categorisation and explanation of patterns of healthcare consumption behaviours in the knowledge society. In terms of attitudes towards healthcare professionals, the continuum extends from convinced through to sceptical. Among 'convinced' consumers there is an acceptance of the basis of conventional medical practice and of the integrity of the medical profession in delivering the appropriate services. By contrast 'sceptical' consumers question the tenets of conventional medical practice and are ambivalent about the integrity and objectivity of the medical profession, at both individual and group level.

With regard to behaviour in the service encounter, the spectrum ranges from compliant to active. The active end of the spectrum is characterised by assertive challenging of professionals within the service encounter. By contrast, at the compliant end of the spectrum, behaviour could, at the extreme, be parodied as the 'yes Doctor, no Doctor' ethos presented in traditional *Dr Finlay's Casebook* representations of patient behaviour. These two dimensions reflect that the internet-driven information revolution, together with the connected socio-economic trends, has impacted on patterns of professional service consumption at two levels: first, at a superficial level, in terms of learned behaviours regarding appropriate ways of engaging with professional service providers; second, and more fundamentally, in terms of shifts in underlying values and beliefs regarding expertise and experts. In considering the specific characteristics of each cluster it is instructive to explore the occasionally contradictory intersections of attitude and behaviour and the resultant tensions. The clusters are outlined in Figure 5.1.

Figure 5.1: Consumer clusters

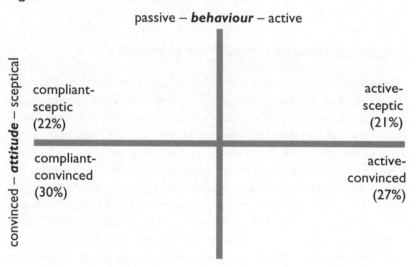

There are a number of striking differences across the clusters in terms of the demographic profile of each group. For example, consumers within the compliant-sceptic cluster are typically less educated, while active-sceptics are predominantly female and, interestingly, the majority are in the over-45 age group, suggesting that experience of service use rather than technological socialisation is a key driver influencing information usage and behaviour. This is reinforced by qualitative evidence suggesting that younger consumers exhibit a comparative absence of interest in the delivery of healthcare services and perceive that time spent acquiring information on healthcare services would be wasted. The specific demographic characteristics of the clusters are outlined in Table 5.1.

Active consumers described themselves as ranging from 'learners' to 'addicts' in using the internet for health-related information. Health information was broadly used for two major goals: health promotion and illness management. Illness management was particularly strongly

Table 5.1: Demographic profile of clusters

Cluster: Demographic	Active-convinced	Compliant-sceptic	Compliant-convinced	Active-sceptic
Gender (M:F) (%)	42:58	44:56	31:69	23:77
Age (18–44:45+) (%)	47:53	40:60	39:61	33:67
Education (degree level or above: A level or below) (%)	48:52	27:73	33:67	60:40

Note: n=333 (internet and non-internet users). Shading represents significant differences.

emphasised, with health information perceived as assisting consumers in taking control of their illnesses and ultimately improving the quality of the service experience. The use of information to assist in illness management can be split into two subcategories: those consumers using information for self-diagnosis prior to consulting a health professional, and those using it to verify professional advice post-consultation. In both cases, consumers can be viewed as adopting what may be termed 'confirmatory behaviour' in that, respectively, independently gathered information is confirmed by the professional, or information provided by the professional is confirmed (or not) by independently gathered information (Laing et al, 2005).

Unpacking the rationale behind the information usage behaviour of active consumers, it is evident, arguably unsurprisingly, that the primary driver for such behaviours is a perceived inadequacy of information provision on the part of healthcare professionals. However, this disguises a range of views as to why information provision is inadequate and reflects prevailing consumer attitudes towards professionals (the attitudinal dimension of the matrix), and, given the public sector setting of healthcare in the United Kingdom, attitudes towards policy makers and the perceived rationing of service provision. The differences in the rationale for and goal of independent information acquisition across the four clusters are illustrated in Table 5.2.

In comparing the relative frequency of information acquisition across the clusters, two key themes emerge. First, the propensity for members of clusters to seek health information in relation to illness management forms a continuum. Active-sceptics at one pole represent consistent, and indeed perhaps habitual, information-seeking behaviour. Compliant-convinced consumers at the opposite pole represent consistently, again perhaps habitually, low levels of information seeking. Active-convinced and compliant-sceptic consumers are located in the middle of the continuum. Second, the timing of seeking health information differs according to cluster. Active consumers tend to seek information prior to the consultation, while sceptical consumers predominantly search for

Table 5.2: Percentage of consumers using health information (often or very often)

Cluster: Consultation stage	Active-convinced	Compliant-sceptic	Compliant-convinced	Active-sceptic
Seek information before seeing the healthcare professional ($\chi2=31.114$, df=12, p=0.002)	50.9	40.4	24.2	75.5
Understand professional terminology ($\chi2=23.710$, df=12, p=0.022)	56.4	57.5	37.9	71.1
Find information on professional's recommended course of action ($\chi2=33.938$, df=12, p=0.001)	43.6	55.3	31.7	66.7
Lack of information from healthcare professional ($\chi2=29.937$, df=12, p=0.003)	16.4	29.6	10.3	44.5
Dissatisfaction with information from healthcare professional ($\chi2=24.182$, df=12, p=0.019)	20.0	31.9	8.6	44.4
Curiosity ($\chi2=14.548$, df=12, p=0.267)	69.1	66.0	62.1	71.7

Note: n=237 (internet users only). Shading represents significant differences.

information following the consultation. All groups are likely to search for information to confirm and/or understand information provided by the healthcare profession. The differentiation across clusters comes in terms of how the consumers use this post-consultation information to manage their relationships with healthcare professionals. This is consistent with recent medically oriented research around this theme (Murray et al, 2007).

An individual's position on the continuum from active-sceptic through to compliant-convinced will determine the application of what has been termed central (effortful) information processing or peripheral (less-effort) information processing (Rucker and Petty, 2005). Positioning on the continuum in terms of approach to information processing is dependent on motivation and ability. Motivation comprises two dimensions: first, cues to action, and, second, approach to healthcare. At one end of the continuum the active-sceptic is highly motivated and applies an effortful central processing of information throughout the healthcare encounter. At the other end, the compliant-convinced consumer is less motivated and resorts to peripheral (low-effort) information processing.

The level of ability can be explained by technology-acceptance factors (Venkatesh et al, 2003). Two factors can be viewed as particularly important in explaining different patterns of information usage and subsequent behaviours, namely, the role of social influence and facilitating conditions. The idea of social influence centres on whether important social figures encourage use of the internet and, in turn, respect the individual consumer for acquiring and using information. Within healthcare this not only includes family and peer groups, but also professionals. The perceived attitudes of healthcare professionals, alongside previous experience of using healthcare services, can profoundly impact on the integration of internet-based health information into the healthcare encounter. Table 5.3 provides an overview of the perceived attitudes of professionals towards consumer information acquisition.

Table 5.3: Perceived attitudes of professionals to 'informed' patients

Cluster: Perceived attitude	Active- convinced	Compliant- sceptic	Compliant- convinced	Active- sceptic
Healthcare professionals encourage patients to use the internet for medical information ($\chi 2=8.545$, df=12, p=0.741)	23.7	21.3	10.3	13.3
Healthcare professionals dislike being challenged by well-informed patients ($\chi 2=26.915$, df=12, p=0.008)	56.3	80.9	55.1	71.1

Note: n=237 (internet users only)

The majority of consumers in all clusters disagree that healthcare professionals encourage use of the internet. Sceptical consumers, in particular, feel that healthcare professionals dislike being challenged. The perceived norm is one of professional discouragement. In terms of to what extent clusters differ in the degree to which they are influenced not to search the internet for information because of this perceived lack of encouragement, it is reasonable to assume that active-sceptics are not influenced by this to the same degree as consumers within other clusters. Compliant-sceptics, for example, may search for information on the internet but not discuss this with their doctor, although it will inevitably impact on their expectations and subsequent evaluation of service provision.

Facilitating conditions encompass two core elements, first, whether resources are available to support use of the internet for health information, including the characteristics of the healthcare system and personal social support systems, and, second, whether individuals feel they have the requisite knowledge to find and use that information

(Pavlou and Fygenson, 2006). Associated with having the knowledge and social support required to use internet-derived information is the attitude towards the veracity of that information and consumers' ability to evaluate this information. Table 5.4 highlights the patterns of perceived accessibility and trustworthiness across the clusters.

Table 5.4: Perceived accessibility and trustworthiness of information

Cluster: Accessibility and trustworthiness	Active- convinced	Compliant- sceptic	Compliant- convinced	Active- sceptic
Find doctor's advice easier to understand than the internet ($\chi2$=12.754, df=12, p=0.387)	51.0	44.7	56.9	31.2
Taking advice from healthcare professional is less risky than internet ($\chi2$=13.603, df=12, p=0.327)	67.3	78.7	69.0	55.5

Note: n=237 (internet users only)

In terms of the comparative ease of use of professional advice versus internet-based advice across the clusters, it is evident that at either end of the information-seeking continuum there is a tendency for the active-sceptic to be more comfortable with advice from the internet and for the compliant-convinced consumer to be more comfortable with the doctor's advice. Such behaviour is entirely consistent with the broader profile of consumers in these clusters. A recurring theme noted by consumers was the potential for confusion in using medical information from the internet because of the complexity of that information, the existence of apparently conflicting information, and doubts over the origin and veracity of information (Laing et al, 2008). In terms of trust, the active-sceptic cluster is more trusting of internet-based health information than are the other three clusters; the other clusters perceive the healthcare professional to be more trustworthy than internet-derived information. This is reflected in their relative uses of the internet for health information.

Drawing these individual strands together through the use of qualitative data, it is possible to develop a behavioural typology of healthcare consumers. Although offering a coherent and credible representation of emerging behaviours, such a typology inevitably presents a simplified interpretation of consumer positions in that, within each cluster, consumers will vary and may adopt complex and sometimes contradictory attitudes. Table 5.5 presents a detailed interpretation of the characteristics of each cluster.

Table 5.5: Service consumer typology

Compliant-sceptic	Active-sceptic
These consumers question authority and are sceptical of professionals and professional knowledge. However, the embedding of the medical profession in the public sector results in a perception of use as a right. Within that setting there is little perceived choice if the service fails them, and knowledge will be acquired only as necessitated by perceived service failure. They are distrustful of authority but see little alternative to consulting professionals and lack a sense of informational empowerment.	These consumers are dissatisfied with the profession and not convinced it has the necessary knowledge. Consequently, they are ambivalent about placing trust in the profession. Nevertheless, they want professionals to serve consumers' interests. In this situation consumers see it as necessary to be informed, proactive and to make their own decisions regarding treatment options. They move within and between conventional and alternative medicine and gather information from both.
Compliant-convinced	Active-convinced
These convinced consumers see no need to acquire knowledge because they trust the professional's knowledge, judgement and commitment to pursue consumers' best interests. No need to change professionals is recognised, because they are all similarly qualified. Information is not sought on performance or treatment options. They will expect to be directed by the doctor because of the professional's acknowledged superior knowledge and experience.	These consumers see society as well served by the medical profession. If, however, a particular professional fails, these consumers are perfectly prepared to change to another. There is a strong focus on independent information gathering about professional performance rather than about treatment options. They accept conventional medicine but are interested in locating the best practitioner within that discourse.

Understanding fragmented behaviours: balancing paradoxes

Confronted with the breadth of information available via the internet, all consumers face comparable choices and challenges in using such information. The challenges are not only in assessing and assimilating information, but also in understanding the nature and dynamic of particular online spaces (Kozinets, 2002), as well as in balancing socio-political pressures for empowerment (Newholm et al, 2006) with the need for reassurance in the face of individual vulnerability. At the heart of these balances is the issue of the trustworthiness and credibility of different sources of information and the challenges confronting even highly internet-socialised consumers in evaluating the claims of competing sources of information (Hogg et al, 2004). The 'balancing paradigm' of consumer satisfaction posits that consumers constantly try to address a number of paradoxes in any consumption environment (Mick and Fournier, 1998). Satisfaction derives from the degree to which they are successful in that ongoing process of balancing. Using this perspective, consumers need to resolve a number of paradoxes arising from the use of online information. Figure 5.2 shows that these can be typified in healthcare as balancing between the following.

Figure 5.2: Balancing health paradoxes

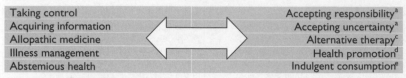

Taking control		Accepting responsibility[a]
Acquiring information		Accepting uncertainty[a]
Allopathic medicine		Alternative therapy[c]
Illness management		Health promotion[d]
Abstemious health		Indulgent consumption[e]

Notes: [a] See Elwyn et al (1999)
[b] See Elwyn et al (1999)
[c] See Cantillon (2004)
[d] Kravitz and Melnikow (2001)
[e] Kravitz and Melnikow (2001)

Thus, taking control of one's medical biography also implies taking greater responsibility. Holding professionals to account implies that any failure is a failure to meet otherwise acceptable practices. Acquiring information both widens the scope of possibilities and increases the consumer's uncertainty. Any given service sets boundaries around its product: allopathic medicine, for example, will not prescribe homeopathy, and vice versa. More generally in respect of internet-derived information, Shankar et al (2006) note that, confronted by hyper-choice, consumers have to balance between empowerment and paralysis arising from information overload. Similarly, the greater use of information by consumers is seen as empowering consumers but also '*harnesses the productive capacity of consumers*' in the service delivery process (Giddings and Robertson, 2003, p 102, emphasis added). Thus, as they take control, they also, paradoxically, produce more of the service themselves, with consequent significant implications for the service experience and the potential for service failure.

Given this balancing act, the internet not only offers potential opportunities for seizing control of, and hence customising, the professional service encounter, but equally confronts the consumer with the challenges of accepting risk and personalised responsibility. The internet thus can be characterised as offering the opportunity and freedom which have not only been central to the contention of David (2001), among others, of driving unprecedented consumer empowerment, but which also confront consumers with uncertainty and risk. Critically, the nature of internet-based information may disable users' ability to form adequate judgements regarding the credibility of participants, the affiliation of sites and the veracity of the information (Laing et al, 2005). For consumers engaging with the internet, this ongoing tension between the internet as a source of support and as generating uncertainty requires a personalised balancing of these countervailing forces, reflecting the circumstances and characteristics of the individual consumer. Table 5.6 sets out the ways in which each consumer cluster could view these paradoxes as being addressed.

Clearly, these conditions create challenges in designing services at the strategic or policy level, at the organisational level and at an operational, service-delivery level. The increasingly fragmented population of healthcare consumers have diverging expectations of the consumer–professional interaction. While current service frameworks within the medical profession, as a disciplinary community, and the NHS, as a strategic entity, may be acceptable to the convinced majority, the sceptics are unlikely to be assuaged by initiatives to engage consumers through processual changes. The core of the task of re-engaging compliant-sceptics is embedded in wider arguments about the legitimacy of authority – both that of medical professionals and that of policy makers – for this group. The active consumers will

Table 5.6: Handling paradoxes

Compliant-sceptic	*Active-sceptic*
A. Reluctantly cedes responsibility and control to the professional. B. Remains ambivalent about trusting professionals and authority in general but expects professional behaviour to be maintained. C. Conventional medical information may be sought but, being within the medical paradigm, it opens limited choice and does not produce significantly more uncertainty than is already experienced. D. The boundaries of conventional medicine are not necessarily perceived.	A. Takes control and accepts a degree of responsibility within the parameters of the selected discipline. B. Remains ambivalent about trusting professionals, but expects professional behaviour to be maintained. C. Sees the need to be informed. This opens choices with which the consumer will engage and a degree of uncertainty. D. Options are not bounded because the consumer may choose among alternative disciplines on the bases of perceived needs.
Compliant-convinced	*Active-convinced*
A. Cedes responsibility and control to the professional. B. In the (unlikely) event that failure is perceived, holding to account against a professional standard implicitly accepted by the consumer is perfectly possible. C. The consumer sees no need to seek additional information and is therefore likely to enjoy a degree of perceived certainty. D. Options are bounded by the profession but this is the discipline the consumer accepts.	A. Takes control in terms of seeking an appropriate practitioner but mostly cedes responsibility to that professional thereafter. B. In most normal circumstances, does not need to hold the professional to account because the consumer accepts conventional medicine and changes practitioner if dissatisfied with the performance of a particular service provider. C. There is little need for additional information to be sought because of the acceptance of the professional discourse. As a result, uncertainty does not arise. D. The issue of service restriction rarely arises because choice is exerted where necessary within an already accepted paradigm.

expect to exercise choice, whether or not this increases their uncertainty, with uncertainty being an accepted and acknowledged part of the contemporary consumer society. The active-sceptics present the biggest challenge, since the expectation of choice of alternatives is coupled with an expectation of disciplinary engagement that extends beyond the boundaries of the conventional medical discourse. Active-sceptics will, for example, seek egalitarian collaboration with professionals. They are likely to want to confirm the information they are given by a professional and to confirm other information they find with that professional, expecting them to engage beyond their core professional discourse and raising in turn fundamental questions about the nature of the 'profession'.

Conclusion: understanding the fragmented consumer

It is evident that there is logic to the idea of the fragmentation of healthcare consumers. There is an evident move from a position where consumers were, with some notable exceptions, characterised as passive and compliant, accepting the authority not only of medical science but also of the professional as decision maker. In contemporary society it is increasingly valuable to think in terms of a range of consumption behaviours in respect of such professional services. Expectations of the service encounter vary from compliant acceptance of both medical science and authority, to the active challenging of medical science as a paradigm and the medical professional as decision maker. Although the picture is inevitably more complex than such a typology suggests, this characterisation of 'ideal types' provides a means for exploring, first, the design of the service delivery process, and, second, the regulatory challenges inherent in the evolving environment within which contemporary professionals operate. The challenge lies in balancing the competing, and occasionally contradictory, perspectives of all the parties involved within a context in which the consumerist discourse has gained primacy.

For professionals, healthcare organisations and policy makers, the challenge is to ensure that the process of service delivery as well as regulation evolve in terms of both information provision and consumer engagement to meet the expectations of this fragmenting population. Given this trajectory of evolution, the retention of a unitary 'one-size-fits-all' model of service provision would seem unlikely to be effective in meeting these expectations and in ensuring consumer satisfaction. However, the development of a portfolio of service formats structured around such divergent behaviours raises a number of fundamental issues. First, at an operational level, professionals face the challenge of identifying the mode of engagement sought by this increasingly fragmented consumer population within a diversity of service settings, and framing the encounter accordingly. For these professionals this poses profound challenges over the parameters of the professional discourse and the extent to which consumer empowerment can be accommodated by the profession. Second, at a strategic level, in publicly funded healthcare systems, where equity and public benefit are central principles and resource constraint a reality, the justification for designing services around individual consumers must be questioned. This latter issue raises fundamental questions over the very nature of public service provision in contemporary societies and, ultimately, the boundaries to consumer sovereignty.

Note

[1] The research on which this chapter is based is funded by the ESRC/ AHRC under the 'Cultures of Consumption' Programme. Project title: 'Consuming services in the knowledge society: the internet and consumer culture' (Award reference: RES 143-25-0009).

References

Abercrombie, N. (1994) 'Authority and consumer society', in R. Keat, N. Whitley and N. Abercrombie (eds) *The authority of the consumer*, London: Routledge, pp 43–57.

Beck, U. (1992) *Risk society: Towards a new modernity*, London: Sage.

Cantillon, E. (2004) 'Is evidence based patient choice feasible?', *British Medical Journal*, no 329, pp 39–40.

David, C. (2001) 'Marketing to the consumer: perspectives from the pharmaceutical industry', *Marketing Health Services*, vol 21, no 1, pp 65–73.

Elam, M. and Bertilsson, M. (2003) 'Consuming, engaging and confronting science: emerging dimensions of scientific citizenship', *European Journal of Social Theory*, vol 6, no 2, pp 233–52.

Elwyn, G., Edwards, A., Gwyn, R. and Grol, R. (1999) 'Towards a feasible model for shared decision making: focus group study with general practice registrars', *British Medical Journal*, no 319, pp 753–6.

Foucault, M. (1980) *Power and knowledge*, Brighton: Harvester.

Friedson, E. (1986) *Professional powers: A study of the institutionalisation of formal knowledge*, Chicago, IL: University of Chicago Press.

Gabriel, Y. and Lang, T. (1995) *The unmanageable consumer: Contemporary consumption and its fragmentations*, London: Sage.

Giddings, J. and Robertson, M. (2003) 'Large-scale map or the A–Z? The place of self-help services in legal aid', *Journal of Law and Society*, vol 30, no 1, pp 102–19.

Gonse, R.A. (1990) 'L.E. von Mises on consumer sovereignty', in D.E. Moggeridge (ed) *Perspectives on the history of economic thought, vol 3*, Cheltenham: Edward Elgar Publishing, pp 136–46.

Ham, C. and Alberti, K. (2002) 'The medical profession, the public, and the government', *British Medical Journal*, no 324, pp 838–42.

Henry, P. (2005) 'Social class, market situation, and consumers' metaphors of (dis)empowerment', *Journal of Consumer Research*, vol 31, no 4, pp 766–78.

Heritage, J. (2001) 'Goffman, Garfinkel and conversation analysis', in M. Wetherall, S. Taylor and S. Yates (eds) *Discourse theory and practice*, London: Open University Press/Sage, pp 48–56.

Hogg, G, Laing, A.W. and Newholm, T.J. (2004) 'Talking together: exploring consumer communities and healthcare', *Advances in Consumer Research*, no 31, pp 67–74.

Keaney, M. (1999) 'Are patients really consumers?', *International Journal of Social Economics*, vol 26, no 5, pp 695–706.

King, N. (1998) 'Template analysis', in G. Symon and C. Cassell (eds) *Qualitative methods and analysis in organizational research*, London: Sage, pp 217–31.

Kozinets, R.V. (2002) 'The field behind the screen: using netnography for marketing research in online communities', *Journal of Marketing Research*, vol 39, no 1, pp 61–72.

Kravitz, R. and Melnikow, J. (2001) 'Engaging patients in medical decision making', *British Medical Journal*, no 323, pp 584–5.

Laing, A.W and Hogg, G. (2002) 'Political exhortation, patient expectation and professional execution: Perspectives on the consumerisation of health care', *British Journal of Management*, vol 13, no 2, pp 173–88.

Laing, A.W., Newholm, T.J. and Hogg, G. (2005) 'Crisis of confidence: re-narrating the consumer-professional discourse', *Advances in Consumer Research*, no 32, pp 514–22.

Laing, A.W., Hogg, G. and Newholm, T. (2008) 'Space for change or changing spaces: exploiting virtual spaces of consumption', in M. Goodman, D. Goodman and M. Redclift (eds) *Consuming space: Placing consumption in perspective*, Aldershot: Ashgate, pp 128–52.

MacStavic, S. (2000) 'The downside of patient empowerment', *Health Forum Journal*, Jan/Feb, pp 30–1.

McKean, J. (1999) *Information masters: Secrets of the consumer race*, New York, NY: Wiley.

Mick, D.G. and Fournier, S. (1998) 'Paradoxes of technology: consumer cognizance, emotions, and coping strategies', *Journal of Consumer Research*, no 25, pp 123–43.

Mills, P. and Moshavi, D. (1999) 'Professional concern: managing knowledge–based service relationships', *International Journal of Service Industry Management*, vol 10, no 1, pp 48–67.

Murray, E., Lo, B., Pollack, L., Donelan, K., Catania, J., White, M., Zapert, K. and Turner, R. (2007) 'The impact of health information on the internet on the physician-patient relationship', *Archives of Internal Medicine*, no 163, pp 1727-34 (July 28).

Newholm, T.J., Laing, A.W. and Hogg, G. (2006) 'Assumed empowerment: consuming professional services in the knowledge economy', *European Journal of Marketing*, vol 40, nos 9/10, pp 994–1012.

Pavlou, P. and Fygenson, M. (2006) 'Understanding and predicting electronic commerce adoption: an extension of the theory of planned behaviour', *MIS Quarterly*, vol 30, no 1, pp 115–43.

Peppard, J. (2000) 'Customer Relationship Management (CRM) in financial services', *European Management Journal*, vol 18, no 3, pp 312-27.

Petts, J., Horlick-Jones, T. and Murdock, G. (2000) *Social amplification of risk: The media and the public*, London: Health and Safety Executive.

Port, O. (1999) 'Consumers move into the driver's seat', *Business Week*, no 4, pp 58–60.

Rucker, D. and Petty, R. (2005) 'Increasing the effectiveness of communications to consumers', *Journal of Public Policy and Marketing*, vol 25, no 1, pp 39–52.

Shankar, A., Chyerrier, H. and Canniford, R. (2006) 'Consumer empowerment: a Foucauldian interpretation', *European Journal of Marketing*, vol 40, nos 9/10, pp 1013–30.

Starkey, F. (2003) 'The empowerment debate: consumerist, professional and liberational perspectives in health and social care', *Social Policy and Society*, vol 2, no 4, pp 273–84.

Thompson, C.J. (2003) 'Natural health discourses and the therapeutic production of consumer resistance', *Sociological Quarterly*, vol 44, no 1, pp 81–107.

Venkatesh, V., Morris, M., Davis, G. and Davis, F. (2003) 'User acceptance of information technology: toward a unified view', *MIS Quarterly*, vol 27, no 3, pp 425-78.

Vermaak, H. and Weggeman, M. (1999) 'Conspiring fruitfully with professionals: new management roles for professional organisations', *Management Decision*, vol 37, no 1, pp 29-44.

Walsh, K. (1994) 'Marketing and public sector management', *European Journal of Marketing*, vol 28, no 3, pp 63–71.

Wathieu, L., Brenner, L., Carmon, Z., Chattopadhyay, A., Wertenbroch, K., Drolet, A., Gourville, J., Muthukrishnan, A., Novmsky, N., Ratner, R. and Wu, G. (2002) 'Consumer control and empowerment: a primer', *Marketing Letters*, vol 13, no 3, pp 297–305.

SIX

The healthcare consumer

Martin Powell and Ian Greener

Introduction

Conceptualising users of health services remains a contentious issue. On the one hand, some authors have claimed that 'the essential problem with the healthcare industry is that it has been shielded from consumer control – by employers, insurers and the government' (Herzlinger, 2002, in Spiers, 2003, p 6). On the other hand, however, writers such as Titmuss (1968) and Stacey (1976) argued that the consumer has no place in healthcare (see Clarke et al, 2007; Le Grand, 2007; Needham, 2007).

In practical terms, there has often been little evidence of NHS organisations adopting a patient-centred approach to the delivery of care. Sir Patrick Nairne, a former Permanent Secretary at the Department for Health and Social Services (DHSS), noted in 1988 that no public service thought less about the public (in Smee, 2005, p 133). In this sense, both the critique of Herzlinger and the concerns of Titmuss can claim that there is evidence to support their perspectives; consumerism has not often been very apparent in healthcare, regardless of whether particular commentators regard it as a good thing or not.

This chapter focuses on the consumer of healthcare. It first briefly examines the terms of 'client', 'citizen' and 'consumer' that were introduced in Chapter One with respect to healthcare. It then examines the 'consumer' in the NHS, before discussing the mechanisms of healthcare consumption and the different faces of health consumerism.

Citizens, consumers and clients in healthcare

The term most familiar to those using healthcare services is the 'patient', and Coulter (2002, p 7) argues that none of its alternatives is entirely satisfactory. There is no word that everyone may comfortably use to describe the individual receiver of health or social care. However, the terms 'patient', 'client', 'customer', 'consumer' and 'user' are all used, and each has different implications (Hogg, 1999, p 2) even if 'patient' is still regarded as a good label by staff and users (Clarke et al, 2007, pp 126–8) and is still widely used in policy documents (Needham, 2007).

Client

Most associated with the term 'patient' is the client role. Clients are often located in the context of professionalism. Talcott Parsons' 'sick role' sums up the relationship between professional and client: the professional has expert knowledge and the passive client should be compliant (see, eg, Sheaff, 2005, pp 90–1). Coulter (2002, p 31) cites the advice of Oliver Wendell Holmes to American medical students in 1871: 'Your patient has no more right to all the truth you know than he has to all the medicine in your saddlebags. He should get only just so much as is good for him.' Hogg (1999, p 2) writes that, until the 1968 Medicines Act, patients did not have the right to know the names of drugs prescribed for them. The word 'patient' implies a compliance and passivity that reflects but also reinforces the unequal power between patient and professional. Clients are often portrayed as relatively passive figures in thrall to a professional's expertise, as 'pawns' in Le Grand's typology of welfare service users. However, this does not have to be the case; a client could also be the principal in a principal–agent relationship, for example. However, the NHS has often been extremely poor at dealing with the complaints of health users (Allsop and Jones, 2008), suggesting that the more passive role has been more common.

Citizen

The NHS is essentially a nationalised industry owned by citizens and funded by taxpayers. It can be argued that most of the time the public are 'well' citizens rather than 'ill' clients. As such, healthy taxpayers may wish to minimise NHS expenditure, but wish treatment with unlimited cost when unhealthy. The classic mechanism of citizens is (collective) 'voice', but it can be argued that the NHS has always suffered from a 'democratic deficit', and that it is one of the most undemocratic services in Britain. In principle, the public can vote politicians out of office at national and local level, but most people do not know the 'grey suits' who run their local health services, let alone have any idea of how to influence local decisions. Foundation Trusts now have in place attempts to extend democracy through the use of membership schemes, but the extent to which they become more influenced by their local populations as a result remains to be seen (Klein, 2003). Citizenship also carries conceptions of equality, but it is clear that the *National* Health Service shows differential levels of local provision and that where you live influences what treatment you receive, which has been termed 'postcode prescribing' (Powell, 1998).

Consumer

The term 'healthcare consumer' is contested. Some writers regard it as inappropriate (see Baggott et al, 2005; McDonald et al, 2007). For example, Titmuss (1968, p 145) critically examined four assumptions, most famously 'that social services in kind, particularly medical care, have no characteristics which differentiate them from goods in the private markets'. In response to Lees' (1965) claim that medical care would appear to have no characteristics which differentiate it sharply from other goods in the market, Titmuss produced 13 characteristics which differentiated medical care; Stacey (1976) regards the healthcare consumer as a 'sociological misconception'. However, there is also an extensive literature on patient or health consumer groups (Wood, 2000; Baggott et al, 2005); but in many ways the main activities of these groups is lobbying on behalf of their members, giving them a citizen role as much as consumer role. In other words, the line between 'citizen' and 'consumer' is blurred, rather than their being polar opposites (see Clarke et al, 2007).

Consumers in the NHS

The NHS was born in an era when doctors' authority and expertise was revered and their decisions were rarely challenged. There was no need to seek patients' views because doctors knew what was best (Coulter, 2002, p 106; Smee, 2005, p 131). According to Spiers (2003, p 76), in 1948 the government abolished the individual consumer when it founded the NHS. However, we will show that the 'consumer' appeared earlier than the conventional wisdom of about the last 25 years (see Smith, 2005, p 13), but that the dimensions of choice and faces of consumerism have varied.

Choice was not entirely absent in the creation of the NHS. On the 'appointed day' of the creation of the service the public were given lists of GPs with whom they could register to receive 'family doctor' services, but this carried an assumption that, once registered, they were likely to remain with the same GP unless they moved from the area.

The choice of GP was an 'associational' one rather than one where 'exit' was a possibility (Greener and Powell, 2009). In addition, those with independent means or private health insurance could always afford to receive healthcare from private providers.

In theory, GPs had a free choice of the secondary provider to whom they could refer a patient, but in practice patients were probably unable or unwilling to travel very far, and the vast majority of patients were referred to the local hospital or community health service. Indeed, the NHS attempted to develop a 'rational' planned system based on 'functional union' in 1948, and on 'hierarchical regionalism' under the Hospital Plan of 1962, which aimed to ensure that most patients went to their local district general hospital (Powell, 1997; Mohan, 2002; Klein, 2006).

The period leading up to the 1974 reorganisation of the NHS was a long and tortuous one that involved changes of government from Labour to Conservative and back to Labour again. There was little mention of consumerism, even if a Conservative government suggested that it was 'right for people to have an opportunity to exercise a personal choice to seek treatment privately' (DHSS, 1972, s 23). NHS patients were also told that they should receive 'services best suited to [their] needs, [their] convenience and, as far as practicable, [their] choice' (s 48), but without any explanation of how this was to be achieved.

Community Health Councils (CHCs) were introduced in the 1974 reforms as 'bodies to represent the views of the consumer' (Klein and Lewis, 1976), but both the membership and efficacy of CHCs varied considerably from one locality to the next, with some being made up predominantly by appointments of 'the great and the good' or the 'usual suspects' who, although caring a great deal about local healthcare, probably did very little to demand better services or to support individual patients wishing to complain. In other areas, however, CHCs often became effective lobbying organisations, campaigning, often with the local media, to change the way local health services were provided. They were not consumer organisations in that, compared with the Consumers' Association, they failed to provide the public with detailed information or to pursue national campaigns to improve health services, and compared with specialist health consumer groups associated with particular conditions, they often provided very little support or lacked the resources to represent individual patients in their complaints. However, depending on their local membership, they did often provide a means for holding local health providers to account, at least through the media, and so had the potential to occupy a useful role.

The health 'consumer' appeared in the evidence and discussion of the Royal Commission on the NHS (Merrison, 1979), where it was claimed that: 'the present climate of opinion is in favour of consumers of any service being able to influence the direction, provision and quality of that service' (TNA BS6/2661, 1979, p 12). Again, however, this does not appear to be the same conception of consumerism as is present in current policy – not referring to health consumers as having a choice of GP or hospital, and not using that choice to try to drive up responsiveness. Instead, this appears to be more the health consumer as citizen (direction) or principal (provision and quality).

The Conservative governments of the 1980s are strongly associated with the drive to introduce markets into the public sector and to give public service users more choice. However, very few mechanisms were put in place to make the NHS more consumerist, with the most significant change perhaps being the growth in private medicine (Higgins, 1988; Calnan et al, 1993; Powell, 1997). It is debatable, however, whether this was a direct consequence of policy, with rises in incomes in the 1980s being just as much responsible, and the growth in private medicine slowing in the 1990s, when the Conservative reforms were at their peak.

In 1987 the White Paper *Promoting better health* (DH, 1987) made it easier for patients to change GP, and increased the proportion of GP income coming from capitation fees. It was hoped that the possibility of patients 'voting with their feet' would provide incentives to 'knavish' GPs to provide better services. The 1989 White Paper *Working for patients* (WFP) broadly continued this theme. One of its objectives was 'to give patients ... greater choice of services' (DH, 1989, para 1.8). The rhetoric was that the money would follow the patient (ie a quasi-voucher scheme), but it introduced few mechanisms to achieve this. It aimed to make the choice of going private cheaper by introducing tax relief on private medical insurance for certain population groups. It also increased the proportion of GP income from capitation from 46% to at least 60%, and made it easier for patients to choose and change their GP (Clarke, in *Hansard*, 1989, cols 166–7). Clarke (*Hansard*, 1989, col 188) claimed that when confronted with the choice of either speedy treatment 30 miles down the road or a long wait for the patient in the local hospital, it would be for the patient and his or her GP to decide whether the inconvenience of travel was worth the speedier treatment. However, this described the *old* system that WFP ended. WFP reduced choice, as it abolished the *theoretical* right to be referred to any hospital within the NHS (Klein and Millar, 1995), but at the same time extended it by trying to make referrals decisions count by attaching resources to them – money should 'follow the patient'. 'Choice' continued only through General Practitioner Fund Holding (GPFH) and individually agreed Extra Contractual Referrals (ECRs). As the Labour spokesperson, Robin Cook, put it, Clarke had a 'brass neck to claim that the White Paper will increase patient's choice' (*Hansard*, 1989, cols 170–1). This policy was not money following the patients; this was patients following the money. Choice was made 'wholesale' by managers, through block contracts, rather than 'retail' by individual consumers.

In 1989, patients were not seen as consumers, but as principals who put their trust in agents to perform a particular role for them, effectively delegating decisions and then making a decision about the service they had received as a result (Scott and Vick, 1999). Alain Enthoven, sometimes credited or blamed for the internal market, considered that on the scale from Soviet planning (0) to the textbook free market (10), the 'internal market' was about a '2' (Powell, 2003). The internal market was criticised by the Right for giving competition a bad name. Despite the name of the Conservative White Paper that began the reform process (DH, 1989), there was little in the internal market that got the NHS 'working for patients' (Ham, 2000; Witness Seminar, 2006).

With John Major replacing Margaret Thatcher as prime minister, the Conservatives quickly alighted upon a new approach to public reform, based upon the use of Charters (Prime Minister, 1991). *The patient's charter* (DH, 1991) aimed to specify standards of service for 'the rights and standards' patients could expect to receive. New rights were granted across a whole range of areas, from receiving prescriptions, to receiving notice of being referred to a mixed-sex ward and to having complaints investigated.

Critics argue that the apostrophe in the 'Patient's Charter' is important, stressing its individual rather than collective nature, and its being more consumerist than citizen-oriented. However, it was not a strong consumer mechanism. Despite the language of rights and their careful differentiation from those elements patients could only 'expect', charter rights were not legally enforceable (Powell, 1997, p 83; Coulter, 2002, p 90; Needham, 2007, p 58), perhaps leaving patients wondering exactly what their purpose was. This was less consumerism than an attempt to introduce a basic level of customer focus, a supermarket-type model, which did little to empower patients or challenge producers (Winkler, 1987; Powell, 1997, p 88). Little was heard of 'choice' (Ham, 2000; Witness Seminar, 2006), and in 1992 the National Health Service Management Executive (NHSME) stressed 'voice' in suggesting that health authorities should be the 'champions of the people' and listen to 'local voices' (NHSME, 1992).

Consumerism was present in New Labour's discourse on its election in 1997 (Crinson, 1998), but at the fringes, not as a central focus for policy. New Labour's White Paper *The new NHS: Modern, dependable* (DH, 1997) claimed to have abolished the internal market, with collaboration replacing competition, but rather recast it onto a longer-term basis, with the purchaser–provider split still very much in place. Patient choice was almost entirely omitted from the document. Labour's alternative was to revive the Patient's Charter, with Greg Dyke being asked to reformulate it. Coulter (2002, p 92) claims that all mention of 'rights' had been expunged, to be replaced by 'commitments', 'responsibilities' and 'expectations'. The new approach was intended to look more like a contract between the NHS and its users than a charter, and seems more designed to reassure staff than to empower patients, and it smacks strongly of a return to paternalism.

The replacement of Frank Dobson by Alan Milburn as secretary of state for health in 1999 seems to mark a change of direction (see Greener, 2004). The rhetoric of consumerism sharply increased. The classic NHS was dismissed as a monolithic, 'one-size-fits-all' organisation (Clarke et al, 2007; Needham, 2007). 'In 1948, deference and hierarchy defined the relationships between citizens and services. In an era of mass production needs were regarded as identical and preferences were ignored' (DH, 2000, para 2.1). Now, health is being developed for the 'consumer age' (DH, 2000) and the 'consumer society' (DH, 2004a) in which we live (Needham, 2007, pp 115–17).

The NHS plan (DH, 2000) reminded patients that they had 'the right to choose a GP' (para 10.5) and that 'to make an informed choice of GP, a wider range of information about GP practices will be published' (para 10.5). However, as in 1989, this was essentially a principal–agent approach in which patients chose GPs and GPs chose care on behalf of their patients. Patients were given new choices about the way they accessed health services, they were 'to have choice emailing or phoning their practice for advice and booking appointments online' (para 1.11) and the right to 'treatment at a time and hospital of the patient's choice' (para 10.20) in cases where their scheduled operation had been cancelled.

The idea of responding to the 'individual' patient is ubiquitous in *The NHS plan*; 'today successful services thrive on their ability to respond to the individual needs of their customers' (para 2.12). There was a drive to improve complaints procedures, in which 'the government will act to reform the complaints procedure to make it more independent and responsive to patients' (para 10.21), giving patients not only the ability to be heard in their interactions with health professionals, but a reassertion of their right to complain if they were not. There would be a national patient survey. Smee (2005, p 135) writes that 'for the first time in the history of the NHS there will be systematic evidence to enable the health service to measure itself against the aspirations and experience of its users'. However, this is still market research rather than individual 'exit' or 'voting with your feet'. Patients still largely placed their trust in medical professionals and managers to make decisions on their behalf rather than being expected to make decisions for themselves. With the concordat with private medicine, the Conservative 'internal market' changed to an 'external market', although it still limited choice for individual consumers (Powell, 2003).

The 2001 Labour election manifesto stated that 'we will give patients more choice' (Smee, 2005, pp 137–8), and Labour's second term saw a number of consumerist initiatives. The Director of Patient Experience and Public Involvement ('czar') was appointed in 2001 (Baggott et al, 2005, p 41). *The expert patient* initiative (DH, 2001) has engaged those with chronic ill-health in managing their own conditions, noting that patients can become key decision makers in the treatment process (Greener, 2005). In 2003, the government announced the beginning of a journey towards an NHS 'where patients can choose how, when, and where they get treated' (DH, 2003, p 10). Documents stressing choice and consumerism appeared thick and fast. *Choosing health: Making healthier choices easier* (DH, 2004a) stressed 'putting people at the heart of public services'. This was followed by *Creating a patient-led NHS* (DH, 2005a), and *Independence, well-being and choice: Our vision for the future of social care for adults in England* (DH, 2005b).

The London Pilot Scheme offered choices to patients who had already waited six months for treatment: they were then offered a guaranteed appointment with the option even of public transport, with two thirds to three quarters of patients taking the choice of provider offered to them (Coulter et al, 2005). The project was judged to be a success and extended to the rest of the country, but was implemented in an entirely different way, with patients generally (whether they had waited for six months or not) being expected to make choices of secondary providers, without public transport help, and often either with their GP or even by telephoning a call-centre.

A programme to increase choice in hospital appointment booking was rolled out in stages under the 'Choose and Book' scheme. From August 2004 people waiting more than six months for surgery were offered faster treatment at an alternative hospital. By December 2005 patients requiring surgery were offered a choice of four or five providers at the point of referral. 'Free choice' (of all hospitals, including private hospitals) has been fully introduced from April 2008 for all patients who require an elective referral, allowing patients technically to choose whichever hospital they wish, regardless of whether it lies within the locality or not.

GPs found themselves not as agents purchasing care, but in new roles where their competitive relationship with other practices was stressed. Practices were to 'redesign care pathways to match patients' needs and wishes' (DH, 2006, para 6.8), with the relationship between GPs presented as a competitive one: 'To ensure that there are real choices for people, we will introduce incentives to GP practices to offer opening times and convenient appointments which respond to the needs of patients in their area' (DH, 2006, para 1.9).

The *NHS Next Stage Review* (Darzi, 2007) sets out a vision for 'personalised care', tailored to the needs and wishes of each individual, providing access at the time and place of their choice. However, the Darzi vision of 'polyclinics' may centralise services and reduce choice for many patients. The *Final Report* (Darzi, 2008) argues that patients will be offered more choice of GP practices, with high-performing practices receiving better rewards. Everyone with a long-term condition will have a personalised care plan and personalised budgets will be piloted (see Chapter Ten).

The NHS *Operating framework for 2008–9* (DH, 2007, p 7) states that 'at the heart of our strategy for the NHS is listening and responding to what matters to our patients, public and staff'. It continues, under the heading 'Empowering patients – choice, information and personalisation', that 'Choice is an important way of building public confidence in the NHS, as well as empowering individual patients' (p 24).

Brown (2008) argues for 'even deeper and wider' reform of the NHS. It will not be the NHS of the 'passive patient'. The NHS of the future will be one of patient power, patients engaged and taking greater control over their own health and healthcare. It will be a preventive and 'personalised' NHS. He advocates 'informed users' and 'active patients', 'real empowerment' and 'real control and power for patients': 'more than today's new choice of where and when you are treated, a new choice tomorrow – in partnership with your clinician – about your treatment itself'. In this sense, patients will be 'more than consumers', by becoming partners. Where it is appropriate – just as with personal care budgets for the 1.5 million social care users – this could include the offer of a personal health budget, giving patients spending power and thus a real choice of services (see Le Grand, 2007). Finally, a new strategy of July 2008 aims to give patients and the public a stronger voice, enabling them to make informed decisions and have greater choice and control in managing their health and healthcare (DH, 2008). This claims that by 2010 everybody with a long-term condition will have their own personalised care plan, and those with complex health needs will have a care coordinator. Individual health budgets will be piloted so as to allow patients to have greater control over how NHS funding is used to support their care.

This chronological review has shown that some terms associated with consumerism have been around since the start of the NHS, but have seen a sharp rise in recent years. Indeed, New Labour's discovery of choice has been relatively recent (Greener, 2004; Smee, 2005; Needham, 2007). Ironically, there appear to be few signs of a 'third way', but there is broadly a movement from an initial 'command and control' system towards a 'divisive internal' (and external) market (but with uniform prices), more radical than the one criticised by Labour in the 1990s. However, as the next sections show, a greater consumer discourse does not necessarily translate into more consumer mechanisms, and the consumer has different 'faces'.

Mechanisms of consumerism

As we saw in Chapter One, 'choice' has a number of different dimensions (Hood et al, 1996; 6, 2003; Greener, 2003; Leadbeater, 2004; Le Grand, 2007). Propper et al (2006, p 538) suggest that, 'despite the simple appeal of "choice", the term is actually used in many different ways and can refer to quite different institutional settings'. Table 6.1 summarises the changes in choice in the NHS using Le Grand's (2007) dimensions.

In the classic NHS, patients could choose GPs, and GPs could – in theory – choose to refer to any hospital in the NHS. Those with money have always had the choice of exit or 'going private' (eg Higgins, 1988; Calnan et al, 1993). However, in practice, patients generally chose their nearest GPs and rarely changed unless they moved home (Cartwright and Anderson, 1983). GPs tended to refer to their nearest hospitals, and few people went private (Higgins, 1988; Calnan et al, 1993). However, the numbers in the 'private welfare class' have always been fairly low (Burchardt and Propper, 1999). Patients queued patiently for GPs and for hospital appointments, largely chosen to suit the producer. A few people were referred to complementary therapies, such as the homeopathic hospitals.

Table 6.1: Le Grand's dimensions of choice applied to healthcare

Dimension	Classic welfare state	Conservatives (1979–97)	New Labour (1997–)
Choice of provider (where?)	(Associational)	Choice of GP	Choice of GP
	Choice of GP	1991: GP referral for GPFH, and ECR	2004: choose and book 4–5 choices
	GP referral to hospital		2008: free choice of NHS or private
Choice of professional (who?)	Choice of GP	Choice of GP	Choice of GP
			NHS Walk-in Centres
			NHS Direct
Choice of service (what?)	Limited	Limited	Limited
Choice of appointment time (when?)	GP: appointment time and 'wait'	GP: appointment time and 'wait'	GP: appointment time and 'wait', but constrained by 48-hour rule
	Hospitals: block booked	Hospitals: appointment time	Choose and book
Choice of access channel (how?)	Limited	Limited	NHS Direct (telephone and www)
			Text messages for results
			Choose and book to set appointment times
Choice of additional services	Limited	Possibility of private room	Private rooms
			Telephones and TVs
			Food choice

The Conservative governments of the 1980s wished to encourage people to 'shop around' for GPs and to 'go private'. However, the internal market of the 1990s was largely a 'mimic market' (Klein, 2006), where patients followed the money rather than money following the patients. The theoretical freedom of referral was reduced for most GPs, and the only patients with choice were those with GPFH and ECRs.

John Major's Patient's Charter saw some 'soft' consumerism, such as moves towards individual hospital appointment times, and some limited guarantees on waiting times at hospitals and for those whose treatment was cancelled.

New Labour, however, has introduced choice in a number of dimensions in the NHS. Its prime concern has been with waiting times and with reducing waiting lists, culminating in the 18-week waiting target. However, it has also given choices over the professional and access channel (NHS Direct; NHS Walk-In Centres). It has moved from schemes giving choice to those waiting for certain lengths of time (London Pilot Scheme) to a restricted list of 'free' choices, including private hospitals. *The NHS improvement plan* (DH, 2004b) claims that:

> With much shorter waiting times for treatment, 'how soon?' will cease to be a major issue. 'How?', 'where?' and 'how good?' will become increasingly important to patients. Patients' desire for high-quality personalised care will drive the new system. Giving people greater personal choice will give them control over these issues, allowing patients to call the shots about the time and place of their care, and empowering them to personalise their care to ensure the quality and convenience that they want.

It should also be noted that there are strict limits on some choices, such as the choice of single rather than multiple (eg MMR) vaccines. Some choices, such as complementary and alternative medicine, appear to have declined under New Labour (Stopp, 2002). Moreover, there are tensions between choice and evidence-based medicine. Should health services with little or no evidence base be paid for from public funds (Toynbee, 2008), and should public services be organised as efficiently as possible, based on the scarce resource of health professional time, or for the convenience of patients?

In short, choice is not the only reform lever and 'choice' has a number of different dimensions. The most radical form of consumerism is individual budgets/vouchers (Le Grand, 2007). However, most choice has tended to be, primarily, choice of location of hospital treatment.

Faces of the healthcare consumer

Much of the academic literature and policy debate has been limited to a discussion of the consumer as chooser (Gabriel and Lang, 2006) or 'queen' (Le Grand, 2007), and the polarised view of whether the consumer is a 'king' (Milburn, 2004) or a 'victim' (Schwartz, 2004).

A number of writers sympathetic to New Labour feel that the focus on 'the consumer' in too narrow. Leadbeater (2004) argues that choice cannot provide a sole organising principle for a reform strategy. Users of public services want to be treated well, as customers, but that does not necessarily mean that they want to become consumers, shopping around for the best deal or even threatening to do so. We need to find a way to make public services responsive without turning the public sector into a shopping mall (p 52). Diamond (2007) claims that we need to empower citizens and communities through public services, including extending individual and collective choice, but states that 'there has been a simplistic faith in individual choice as a lever for diffusing power in public services' (p 9).

It is possible to go beyond the consumer as chooser ('king' or 'victim') debate to examine other faces: communicator, rebel, identity seeker, hedonist or artist, victim, activist, citizen and explorer (Gabriel and Lang, 2006). Gabriel and Lang (2006, p 173) write that some see the notion of the consumer as being too individualistic and restrictive – in short, irrecoverably hijacked by the political Right – and have resurrected an older idea propounded by the founder of the UK's *Which?* (formerly the Consumers' Association [CA]) and the National Consumer Council, Michael Young, who has envisaged organised consumers as a third force for the citizenry, alongside labour and capital (p 173). Hilton (2007, p 124) points out that the current historiography of consumer politics, a US-based literature, has largely assumed that 'consumerism' – that is, an organised movement often associated with Ralph Nader – has been edged aside by its second meaning, the more pejorative 'consumerism', referring to those economic and cultural forces promoting a shallow materialism and individual acquisitiveness.

Some commentators have stressed consumers as activists (Kroen, 2004; Hilton, 2005; Gabriel and Lang, 2006). Hilton (2005, p 313) points to the wider social-democratic vision of consumerism associated with Michael Young. For Young, consumers connected to the CA were seen as progressive, socially aware and committed to their duties as well as their rights as citizens, holding a wider vision of consumerism; not acquisitive and materialist, but broad-minded internationalists, Eurocentric, benevolent and in favour of the liberal lifestyles earlier set out by the Labour revisionist politician, Tony Crosland (Crosland, 1964). Similarly, some commentators have pointed to 'responsible' or 'ethical' consumers. Malpass et al (2007, pp 238–9) point out that 'citizenly consumers' may choose, but not necessarily on narrowly self-interested grounds. 'Choice' can be reconfigured as a dimension of civic engagement. They conclude that it is 'actually quite difficult to find the archetypal individualized, rational egotistical consumer idealized by rational choice theorists and bemoaned by critics as an unwelcome sociological fact' (p 252). McDonald et al (2007) discuss identity construction in order to discuss other faces of the consumer. They write that 'We now risk drawing opprobrium from other social scientists by challenging the view that the label "consumer" should not be used in relation to healthcare' (p 447).

The parameters of consumerism therefore appear unclear, but it is possible to see beyond the narrow 'charm school' (Potter, 1988) or 'supermarket model' (Winkler, 1987) varieties of consumerism to more collective and progressive types (that we may term, after Michael Young, 'Young consumerism').

Conclusion

Health documents talk about the consumer more than any of the other policy texts (Needham, 2007, p 115). Although there has been a significant increase in the use of the term 'consumer' by policy makers, they still use the term 'patient' much more frequently (Needham, 2007), and the public and professionals do not tend to use the term to any great extent (Clarke et al, 2007).

More significantly, although there has been a large increase in the discourse of consumerism and choice, this does not necessarily mean that users have more consumer mechanisms. For example, despite the consumerist discourse, the Conservatives' internal market reforms saw a reduction in choice for most people. Perri 6 (2003, p 248) states that there is very limited direct consumer choice in the NHS. The 1990 reforms appear not to have greatly increased choice. The inconsistencies in the Conservative approach to the consumer, and continued resistance to strands of consumerism, suggests that the citizenship regime promoted by the Conservatives was not fully consumerised (Needham, 2007, p 61).

Moreover, there are many different dimensions of choice, and the most frequently used is choice of location of treatment. Choice is not necessarily the same thing as health consumerism. Even though it can easily be disputed whether patients want greater choice, especially when they face complex or life-threatening conditions, it is possible to give patients choices without their having to adopt a full consumer role. Health consumers are expected to be informed about the choices before them, as well as being both willing and capable of making those choices. However, offering patients choices between appointment times, for example, is relatively straightforward and does not require patients to acquire specialist knowledge or to try to compare the merits of providers – doctors and other healthcare professionals are overwhelmingly more qualified to make these decisions in most cases. Expecting patients to be active, empowered agents in the healthcare marketplace requires a great deal of them. Moreover, the consumer has different faces, and the 'consumer as chooser' is only one possible face of consumerism.

There are many potential problems with choice in the public sector. 'Market mavens' can send signals to producers in the private sector, such as lower salt in the food on sale at supermarkets, which can benefit all. However, if 'public progessives' send signals that 'X' is the best hospital, will that lead to increased capacity or to stimulating better quality in competitors, which might lead either to greater public benefit or to increased inequality? The most significant debate is over whether or not choice increases inequality (Clarke et al, 2007; but see Le Grand, 2007).

Choice is unlikely to be the only, or perhaps the main, reform stream in healthcare. Choice and consumerism is unlikely to supply the only or necessarily the best answers in healthcare, not least because there are different dimensions of choice and different faces of consumerism. Indeed, it is not always clear what is the problem to which consumerism is the answer.

References

6, P. (2003) 'Giving consumers of British public services more choice', *Journal of Social Policy*, vol 32, no 2, pp 239–70.

Allsop, J. and Jones, K. (2008) 'Withering the citizen, managing the consumer: complaints in healthcare settings', *Social Policy and Society*, no 7, pp 233–43.

Baggott, R., Allsop, J. and Jones, K. (2005) *Speaking for patients and carers: Health consumer groups and the policy process*, Basingstoke: Palgrave Macmillan.

Brown, G. (2008) Speech on the NHS, 7 January (www.number10. gov.uk/Page14171).

Burchardt, T. and Propper, C. (1999) 'Does the UK have a private welfare class?', *Journal of Social Policy*, vol 28, no 4, pp 643–65.

Calnan, M., Cant, S. and Gabe, J. (1993) *Going private: Changing expectations about healthcare?*, Buckingham: Open University Press.

Cartwright, A. and Anderson, R. (1983) *General practice revisited*, London: Tavistock.

Clarke, J., Newman, J., Smith, N., Vidler, E. and Westmarland, L. (2007) *Creating citizen-consumers*, London: Sage.

Coulter, A. (2002) *The autonomous patient: Ending paternalism in medical care*, London: The Stationery Office.

Coulter, A., le Maistre, N. and Henderson, L. (2005) *Patients' experience of choosing where to undergo surgical treatment: Evaluation of London Patient Choice Scheme*, Oxford: Picker Institute.

Crinson, I. (1998) 'Putting patients first: the continuity of the consumerism discourse in health policy', *Critical Social Policy*, vol 18, no 2, pp 227–39.

Crosland, C.A.R (1964) *The future of socialism* (revised edn), London: Jonathan Cape.

Darzi, A. (2007) *Our NHS, our future: NHS Next Stage Review – Interim Report*, London: Department of Health.

Darzi, A. (2008) *High quality care for all, NHS Next Stage Review – Final Report*, London: Department of Health.

DH (Department of Health) (1987) *Promoting better health*, Cm 249, London: HSMO.

DH (1989) *Working for patients*, London: HMSO.

DH (1991) *The patient's charter*, London: DH.

DH (1997) *The new NHS: Modern, dependable*, London: The Stationery Office.

DH (2000) *The NHS plan*, London: The Stationery Office

DH (2001) *The expert patient*, London: The Stationery Office.

DH (2003) *Building on the best: Choice, responsiveness and equity in the NHS*, London: DH.

DH (2004a) *Choosing health: Making healthier choices easier*, Cm 6374, London: The Stationery Office

DH (2004b) *The NHS improvement plan: Putting people at the heart of public services*, Cm 6268, London: DH.

DH (2005a) *Creating a patient-led NHS*, London: DH.

DH (2005b) *Independence, well-being and choice: Our vision for the future of social care for adults in England*, London: The Stationery Office.

DH (2006) *Our health, our care, our say: A new direction for community services*, London: The Stationery Office.

DH (2007) *The NHS in England: Operating framework for 2008–9*, London: DH.

DH (2008) *Our vision for primary and community care*, London: DH.

DHSS (Department of Health and Social Security) (1972) *The National Health Service reorganisation: England*, London: HMSO.

Diamond, P. (ed) (2007) *Public matters: The renewal of the public realm*, London: Politicos.

Gabriel, Y. and Lang, T. (2006) *The unmanageable consumer* (2nd edn), London: Sage.

Greener, I. (2003) 'Who choosing what?', in C. Bochel, N. Ellison and M. Powell (eds) *Social Policy Review 15*, Bristol: The Policy Press, pp 49–68.

Greener, I. (2004) 'The three moments of New Labour's health policy discourse', *Policy & Politics*, vol 32, no 3, pp 303–16.

Greener, I. (2005) 'The role of the patient in healthcare reform: customer, consumer or creator?', in S. Dawson and C. Saussman (eds) *Future healthcare organisations and systems*, Basingstoke: Palgrave, pp 227–45.

Greener, I. and Powell, M. (2009, forthcoming) 'The evolution of choice policies in UK housing, education and health policy', *Journal of Social Policy*.

Ham, C. (2000) *The politics of NHS reform 1988–1997*, London: King's Fund.

Hansard (1989) House of Commons, 31 January, Debate on *Working for Patients*.

Herzlinger, R. (2002) 'Let's put consumers in charge of healthcare', *Harvard Business Review*, vol 80, no 7, pp 44–55.

Higgins, J. (1988) *The business of medicine*, Basingstoke: Macmillan.

Hilton, M. (2005) 'Michael Young and the consumer movement', *Contemporary British history*, vol 19, no 3, pp 311–19.

Hilton, M. (2007) 'Social activism in an age of consumption: the organized consumer movement', *Social History*, vol 32, no 2, pp 121–43.

Hogg, C. (1999) *Patients, power and politics: From patients to citizens*, London: Sage.

Hood, C., Peters, G. and Wollmann, H. (1996) 'Sixteen ways to consumerize public services: pick 'n' mix or painful trade-offs', *Public Money and Management*, vol 16, no 4, pp 43–50.

Klein, R. (2003) 'Governance for NHS foundation trusts', *British Medical Journal*, no 326, pp 174–5.

Klein, R. (2006) *The new politics of the NHS*, Oxford: Radcliffe.

Klein, R. and Lewis, J. (1976) *The politics of consumer representation*, London: Centre for Studies in Social Policy.

Klein, R. and Millar, J. (1995) 'Do-it-yourself social policy', *Social Policy and Administration*, vol 29, no 4, pp 303–16.

Kroen, S. (2004) 'A political history of the consumer', *Historical Journal*, vol 47, no 3, pp 709–36.

Le Grand, J. (2007) *The other invisible hand*, Princeton, NJ: Princeton University Press.

Leadbeater, C. (2004) *Personalisation through participation*, London: Demos.

Lees, D.S. (1965) 'Health through choice', in R. Harris (ed) *Freedom or free-for-all?* London, IEA, pp 21–85.

McDonald, R., Mead, N., Cheraghi-Sohi, S., Bower, P., Whalley, D. and Roland, M. (2007) 'Governing the ethical consumer: identity, choice and the primary care medical encounter', *Sociology of Health and Illness*, vol 29, no 3, pp 430–56.

Malpass, A., Barnett, C., Clarke, N. and Cloke, P. (2007) 'Problematizing choice: responsible consumers and sceptical citizens', in M. Bevir and F. Trentmann (eds) *Governance, consumers and citizens*, Basingstoke: Palgrave, pp 231–56.

Merrison, Sir A. (1979) *Royal Commission on the NHS Report*, London: HMSO.

Milburn, A. (2004) 'In public services too, make the consumer king', *Wall Street Journal*, 17 March.

Mohan, J. (2002) *Planning, markets and hospitals*, London: Routledge.

Needham, C. (2007) *The reform of public services under New Labour*, Basingstoke: Palgrave.

NHSME (National Health Service Management Executive) (1992) *Local voices*, London: DH.

Potter, J. (1988) 'Consumerism and the public sector: how well does the coat fit?', *Public Administration*, vol 66, no 2, pp 149–64.

Powell, M. (1997) *Evaluating the NHS*, Buckingham: Open University Press.

Powell, M. (1998) 'In what sense a national health service?', *Public Policy and Administration*, vol 13, no 3, pp 56–69.

Powell, M. (2003) 'Quasi markets in British health policy: a longue duree perspective', *Social Policy and Administration*, vol 37, no 7, pp 725–41.

Prime Minister (1991) *The citizen's charter*, London: HMSO.

Propper, C., Wilson, D. and Burgess, S. (2006) 'Extending choice in English healthcare: the implications of the economic evidence', *Journal of Social Policy*, vol 35, no 4, pp 537–57.

Schwartz, B. (2004) *The paradox of choice: Why more is less*, New York, NY: Harper Collins.

Scott, A. and Vick, S. (1999) 'Patients, doctors and contracts: an application of principal–agent theory to the doctor–patient relationships', *Scottish Journal of Political Economy*, vol 46, no 2, pp 111–34.

Sheaff, M. (2005) *Sociology and healthcare*, Maidenhead: Open University Press.

Smee, C. (2005) *Speaking truth to power*, Oxford: Radcliffe Publishing.

Smith, G. (2005) 'The rise of the "new consumerism" in health and medicine in Britain, c.1948–1989', in J. Burr and P. Nicolson (eds) *Researching healthcare consumers*, Basingstoke: Palgrave Macmillan, pp 13–38.

Spiers, J. (2003) *Patients, power and responsibility: The first principles of consumer-driven reform*, Abingdon: Radcliffe Medical Press.

Stacey, M. (1976) 'The health service consumer: a sociological misconception', in M. Stacey (ed) *The sociology of the National Health Service*, Sociological Review Monograph 22, Keele: University of Keele, pp 194–200.

Stopp, E. (2002) 'Complementary therapies in the NHS', PhD, Bath: Bath University.

Titmuss, R. (1968) *Commitment to welfare*, London: George Allen and Unwin.

TNA BS6/2661 (1979) *The NHS and the consumer*, Paper for the Royal Commission on the NHS.

Toynbee, P. (2008) 'Quackery and superstition: available soon on the NHS', *The Guardian*, 8 January (www.guardian.co.uk/Columnists/Column/0,,2236974,00.html).

Winkler, F. (1987) 'Consumerism in health care: beyond the supermarket model', *Policy & Politics*, vol 15, no 1, pp 1–8.

Witness Seminar (2006) 'Consumerism and choice in the Conservative Internal Market 1987–1992 (draft transcript)', Institute for Health Research, University of London, 27 October.

Wood, B. (2000) *Patient power? The politics of patients' associations in Britain and America*, Buckingham: Open University Press.

SEVEN

The consumer in education

Catherine M. Farrell

Introduction

The consumer role in education is one that has historically existed prior to legislative reform. Parents have always had choices about 'which school' in terms of private or state school, religious or non-religious, and also choices about where they live and, by implication, where their children go to school. It is now almost 30 years since the introduction of legislative reforms promoting additional elements of choice in the UK education service. Following the reforms put in place during the 1980s, parents, pupils and users have been empowered to participate further in the selection of services. In addition to the consumer-oriented reforms, elements of the reform agenda have also stressed the involvement of citizens in education and there are now opportunities for parents and users to have an input into the management and leadership of schools. Using the 'voice', 'choice' and 'exit' framework, the aim of this chapter is to discuss the consumer in education. It is divided into three parts. Part one focuses on the involvement of citizens, consumers and parents in education. In part two, the mechanisms of consumption are reviewed. The use of the market, catchment areas and also the allocation of school places by lottery are each investigated. Part three outlines the different faces of consumerism and citizen participation in education. Conclusions are drawn about the involvement of citizen-consumers in education services.

Citizens, consumers and parents in education

Prior to 1979, the language used in all public services to describe those receiving them was centred around notions of professional autonomy and the dependency of clients (Clarke and Newman, 1997). Words including 'patients', 'parents', 'pupils', 'prisoners', 'tenants' and 'clients' each suggest users who were the recipients of public services. Further, they suggest users who are having services provided to them with little activity or participation on their behalf. Le Grand (2003) argues that these users were considered to be passive. Le Grand (2003, p 6) elaborates further in relation to patients:

> Patients were supposed to live up to their appellation and be patient. They were to wait patiently in queues at general practitioners' surgeries or at outpatient clinics; if they needed further treatment they had to be prepared to wait their turn on hospital waiting lists. When the time arrived for them to actually go to hospital, they were supposed cheerfully to accept being on a public ward, being served horrible food and, most significantly, being treated by doctors too busy or too elevated, to have time to explain what was happening to them.

Similar arguments are advanced by Le Grand (2003, p 9) about parents (pupils), social security recipients and also council tenants. He describes the relationship in many public services as being one 'financed and operated by knights for the benefit of pawns'. Needham (2006, p 848) also highlights that the 'designation of public service users as clients captured the "professional dependency" of their relationship'.

With the election of the Conservative government in 1979 came a range of reforms which aimed to promote choice and consumerism, reduce public welfare, encourage a range of providers in welfare and also break up a dependency on welfare and public services (Powell, 1999). In addition to policies promoting user participation in public services, a new agenda encouraging more collaboration between providers and users has also been put in place (Simmons and Birchall, 2005). Needham (2007) highlights that the reform of public services under New Labour has emphasised both the consumer and a citizen at the centre in terms of driving forward improvement. Within the context of 'New Public Management', Aberbach and Christensen (2005) draw attention to the tension between the needs and requirements of citizens and consumers. This chapter uses the 'voice, choice and exit' analysis to review the status and extent of power of users in education. This framework, developed by Hirschman (1970), is concerned with the review of effective choice strategies, the ability of service users to exit from services and also to use the mechanism of 'voice' within services to make public services more responsive to them.

In education, since the 1980 Education Act, parents have been given a right to be involved in the selection of school places for their children. Before this, local authorities were to have regard for parental choices in the allocation of school places. The 1980 reforms, which introduced the right to be involved, were strengthened significantly by the 1988 Education Reform Act, placing parents in a central position in terms of school selection and choice. To support parents in their choice, new information tables about school performance were to be published and school funding was predominantly based on a per pupil allocation. This aspect put in place a system which made schools dependent on children. While choice was presented to parents as one of the benefits of the changes, it was the lesser benefit of 'preference' which was really put in place (Farrell and Jones, 2000). Parents were entitled to express to local education authorities their preference of school, and this preference was only granted where places in the relevant school existed. All schools, except for religious and selective ones, had to accept pupils up to their physical capacity. Schools which were oversubscribed developed admissions criteria and these generally included geographical proximity, sibling attendance and medical reasons. Schools were also permitted to select a percentage of children on the basis of academic criteria. Le Grand (2003, p 108) argues that this system amounted to a voucher system in education, as 'in theory, parents could choose their child's school and the money would follow their choice. Schools that were successful in attracting pupils would thrive; those that were not would decline.'

The 1988 reforms in education were intended to introduce a market in education. Additional aspects of the reform agenda in terms of this market included the 'Popular Schools Initiative', grant-maintained (GM) status and city technology colleges (CTCs). The Popular Schools Initiative was introduced to support the expansion of those schools which were successful in attracting pupils. Where schools were not successful, the market mechanism of contraction and closure should come into effect. The users' use of 'choice' therefore would eventually lead to the closure of schools which were not in demand. The introduction of new types of schools, both GM and CTCs, was intended to provide consumers with additional choices in the types of education. Another market-oriented policy in the form of nursery vouchers was introduced in 1997. However, this was not implemented, due to a change of the party in government at the time.

In relation to 'voice', policies promoting voice focus on user participation and involvement in services. Voice concerns giving 'users a more effective say in the direction of services, by means of representative bodies, complaints mechanisms and surveys of individual preferences and views' (PASC, 2005, p 5). Over a number of years, mechanisms have been put in place in education which have promoted the mechanism of voice. Farrell and Jones (2000) highlight that 'voice' can be collective or individual. In their collective voice role, parents are participating more in a 'citizen' capacity rather than in a 'consumer' one (Beecham, 2006). It is also the case that parents can act as collective consumers, for example, when groups of parents get together to seek changes to school policies.

In their collective citizen role, parents have a number of opportunities to participate in schools and express their views. First, as members of school governing bodies, they have a forum to present the 'parent view'. The official position is that parent–governors are not representative of parents in the school. In their membership, parents can become involved in a range of activities, including setting strategic policies for schools and the selection of new teachers, for example. The involvement with the governing body means that parents have a strategic corporate role in school management.

Second, parents are invited to an 'Annual Report to Parents' meeting, where the school's governing body presents the annual report. Parents are invited to ask questions and provide comments. The need to hold an annual meeting, which was a legal requirement right from the 1976 Education Act, has in recent years been changed. Following the 2005 Education Act, governing bodies are no longer required to hold an annual meeting for parents or to produce an annual report to parents. Instead, in England, schools are required to produce a 'School Profile' which will present information about the school in terms of progress and performance, for example. In Wales, schools have to produce the annual report and provide this to parents if requested. In the case of the annual meetings, a school must hold these if parents in the school require it. The changes in the legislative requirements around both the annual report and the meeting have undermined this collective forum of parental involvement.

A third arena where parents have a collective voice is in the meeting with the school inspectors prior to the start of a school's inspection. Here, all parents in the school to be inspected are invited to an open forum in which they have an opportunity to feed into the inspection process. This 'voice' arena is also an example of a collective voice in which parents are acting in a citizen rather than a consumer-oriented capacity. Simmons and Birchall's (2005) evidence on participation indicates that citizens are more likely to become involved in public services where they can see benefits for groups of people rather than individuals. Pupils too, in recent years, have been encouraged to participate in school councils, and in these they are participating as citizens. To support pupils in their roles, the government has provided web-based support through the website www.schoolscouncil.org.

As well as these collective forums, clearly, all parents in schools have individual opportunities to be involved in meetings with school representatives about their children's progress. Individual parents can visit schools and discuss their children. In these meetings, parents are there to discuss their own children and are free to complain, compliment and comment on all aspects of school life relating to their children. In these meetings, parents are acting in an individual capacity and are essentially acting as consumers.

It is when groups of parents get together to meet with school representatives to discuss their children, or the curriculum for the year group, or the reading policy of the school, for example, that they have a collective consumer role. Here, parents are acting as consumers and expressing views relating to this role. There is insufficient evidence on whether or not groups of parents expressing their collective consumer voice is effective.

Mechanisms of consumerism

As highlighted in Chapter One of this text, 'choice' has a number of different dimensions (6, 2003; Le Grand, 2007). The term is actually used in different ways within the broad area of education. As highlighted earlier, despite the language of 'choice', parents have only ever been permitted to express a 'preference' over schools. Using Le Grand's (2007) dimensions, the changes to the choice framework in education are summarised in Table 7.1.

As highlighted in Table 7.1, consumer choices are most prominent over the initial choice of school. Even before the Conservative reforms, there were choices about whether to 'go private' or not, or whether to have home teaching. Within the state sector, that is, the public sector, new categories of schools have been introduced by both the Conservative and the New Labour reforms, right from the 1988 Education Reform Act. The Conservative reforms championed the idea of consumer choice and consequently undermined the traditional catchment area allocation of the school place. New Labour's reforms, while retaining an element of choice, have raised the status of catchment areas again. The system put in place in most areas entitles pupils to attend their local catchment area school. Where there are vacancies, parents from outside the catchment area can choose for their children to attend. Choices are therefore dependent on the availability of places once local children have been accommodated. New Labour's reforms in relation to catchment areas have therefore undermined choice. The abolition of the nursery voucher may also have undermined choice. The voucher, intended for use by all parents of nursery-age children in an approved private or public sector setting, was abolished very soon after New Labour's entry into government. After abolition, parental choice was restricted to receiving nursery education from a school within the catchment area or paying for private education.

Table 7.1: Changes in choice in education, using Le Grand's dimensions of choice

Dimension	Classic welfare state	Conservatives (1979–97)	New Labour (1997–)
Choice of provider (where?)	Catchment areas dominant	Choice of school	Catchment areas put back in place alongside choice of school
	Home tuition		
	Private schools (fee paying)	New categories of schools (City Technology Colleges, grant-maintained schools)	New categories of schools incorporating the CTCs and GM schools into public sector (Foundation, Community, Voluntary Aided and Aided), 1998
			City Academies introduced
		Nursery education voucher 1996	Nursery voucher removed 1997
Choice of professional (who?)	No choice of headteachers/teachers	No choice of head teachers/ teachers	No choice of head teachers/teachers
Choice of service (what?)	Limited curriculum choices within schools	Limited curriculum choices within schools	Limited curriculum choices within schools, but new developments around the Baccalaureate
		New choices over types of schools and their specialisms	Continuation of choices around types of schools and their specialisms
Choice of appointment time (when?)	No choice over delivery	No choice over delivery	No choice over delivery
Choice of access channel (how?)	Limited	Limited	Limited
Choice of additional services	Limited	Limited	Limited

In relation to the other dimensions of choice, including choice of professionals, the type of service, the 'when' of service, and access, there are limited choices in education. Children or their parents have no control over who teaches their children in the classroom, what curriculum is delivered and when. In fact, the existence of the national curriculum itself undermines choice, as it has made all schools teach to the same framework. Similar restrictions on choice were put in place when the Literacy and Numeracy Hours were introduced in primary schools. Children do not have a choice over when they receive education, as it is a legal requirement to attend either school or other inspected learning, for example home teaching, from the school year in which they turn five. In other European countries, these restrictions do not exist and children are permitted to start school when parents think it is appropriate. There are more choices at secondary level. Here, pupils have more choice about the orientation of their curriculum in the post-14 stage, in that they can select a more vocational or academic curriculum. Further, some schools have also widened the secondary curriculum to offer the Baccalaureate qualification. In sum, the Conservative reforms focused on the key issue of choice of school. It was only when the New Labour government came to power that the limitations and deficiencies in the choice regime in schools were recognised. As highlighted by David Miliband, MP:

> we need to embrace individual empowerment within as
> well as between schools. This leads straight to the promise
> of personalised learning. It means building the organisation
> of schooling around the needs, interests and aptitudes of
> individual pupils; it means shaping teaching around the
> way different youngsters learn; it means taking the care to
> nurture talents of every pupil. (Miliband, 2004)

In terms of which school children attend, this choice is one which can be made either by parents and children as consumers, by the state through catchment areas or through some form of lottery system. Each of these will now be examined.

Allocation by parental preference

Where parents select schools, some authors, including Burgess (2006), suggest that this has a positive effect on those including children from the poorest families. This is because these consumers can select schools outside their areas and improve their life opportunities overall. His views about the selection of schools being made by the state are that this results in 'some parents moving to good schools by moving house. It therefore produces ghettos of the rich around good schools and poor around bad schools' (Burgess, 2006). These arguments therefore support parental choice of schools. Research by Gorard and Fitz (1998) supports Burgess's (2006) arguments. Gorard and Fitz's (1998) work focused on choices made by middle- and working-class parents in education between 1991 and 1996. The findings of the study indicate that while the middle-class parents participated in the choice of schools first, once working-class parents also started to become familiar with their rights to choose, they fully engaged with them to select schools for their children. Evidence from the US, where the opportunities for school choice have expanded since the 1990s, suggests that more parents are becoming involved in using their choices and are happier that these options are available to them (Tice et al, 2006).

The right to express their preference over choice of school is found by most researchers to be regarded favourably by parents. 6 (2003), for example, finds that choice is liked by parents and has an impact on their voting behaviour and preferences. Choice is clearly an important component of the 'voice, choice and exit' framework put forward by Hirschman (1970).

Allocation by catchment areas

In contrast to the work of Burgess (2006), Ball (2006) argues that the allocation of school places on the basis of catchment areas is the most appropriate form of allocation. Ball (2006) makes five key points about choice in education. These are:

- Choice is made use of by middle-class families to achieve their educational outcomes.
- Making and getting a choice involves resources, social skills, persistence and energy. These skills are unevenly spread across people.
- Choice is relational – who do you want your child to go to school with? It is about exclusivity and avoidance of some schools.
- Choice produces opportunistic behaviour. Choice can bring out the worst in people and in schools.
- Choice systems are very difficult to manage. Choice seems like the solution to the problems but it creates administrative and admission difficulties.

Ball's (2006) arguments are supported by the work of Noden (2000, 2002). This author's work presents many negative effects of choice on social segregation. The National Commission on Education's (1996, p 6) report on schools in disadvantaged areas reports that parental choice and consumer power can 'easily discriminate against schools serving disadvantaged communities'. Schools in these areas are populated by children who cannot exercise their choices, due to limited financial resources. Similar findings are presented in Jordan (2006), where there is evidence that parents who can afford to do so move house so as to be located in catchment areas with good schools. Estate agents also report a school factor in the selling price of many properties. Recent evidence presented about choice in East London (Butler et al, 2007) suggests that the schools with the best-performing pupils recruit from the 'better' postcode areas. Similar findings have been presented by Gewirtz et al (1995) over a decade ago. A US study (Goldring and Phillips, 2008) finds that 'active choosers' are most likely to be middle-class parents who are very involved in their children's schooling.

In support of catchment area allocative systems, West's (2006) work argues that the allocation of school places should not rest with schools themselves. Her arguments against parental choice allocation centre on social justice and equity for all pupils. She argues that local authority allocation of school places allows choices to be 'controlled' so as to allow for factors such as social groups, ability and attainment groupings to be more equally distributed across schools. A recent review of school admissions by Tough and Brooks (2007) is supportive of local authority allocated places.

The 'Schools Admissions Code' promotes greater openness in the allocation of school places (DfES, 2007, p 7). This code, which admissions authorities are supposed to 'act in accordance with', is intended to promote fairness in the allocation of school places and rule out any practices such as interviewing children, taking account of parental occupation, financial or marital status, and also ruling out the first preference first system.

The regulations apply to all maintained schools, including faith schools, with the exception of designated grammar schools. They relate to England only, as education has been devolved in Scotland, Wales and N. Ireland. Under the new code, parents choose schools in the normal way. All children who have applied for a place should receive one. Where there are more children applying than there are places, then the new regulations come into play. These 'admissions oversubscription criteria' need to be objective, clearly understood, transparent and fairly used. The code provides guidance on what criteria admissions authorities should adopt but does not prescribe a list. The code suggests that authorities may use some of the following criteria:

- siblings of children who are still at school
- siblings at primary school
- social and medical need
- distance between home and school
- ease of access by public transport
- random allocation (examined below).

The code reinforces the continued use of catchment areas in the allocation of school places and suggests that 'giving priority to local children whose parents have expressed a preference for the school' is acceptable (DfES, 2007, p 52).

Random allocation

The random allocation of school places is a relatively new form of allocation in the UK public services. This is a mechanism which has its origins in the US. Here, schools must accept pupils with vouchers on the basis of a lottery allocation (Hoxby, 2003). In Britain, the allocation of places randomly or by a lottery system has been used in the 2008/09 academic year by some local authorities in England.

The random allocation system, it is suggested, 'can be good practice particularly for urban areas and secondary schools. However, it may not be suitable in rural areas' (DfES, 2007, p 51). Further, it is argued that 'random allocation can widen access to schools for those unable to afford to buy houses near to favoured schools and can create greater social equity'. Allocating school places randomly therefore means that places get allocated to those parents (pupils) who have applied. Under the system, parents choose their favoured school in order of preference. The system means that children living in close proximity to a school may not get selected, and also undermines historical catchment areas. One source reported that the 'homes surrounding some of the best state secondary schools were up to £250,000 more expensive than those outside the catchment area' (*Daily Telegraph*, 2007). The lottery allocation 'may loosen the grip of middle-class parents on the best state schools' (*Independent*, 2007).

Some secondary schools under Brighton and Hove City Council have allocated places in oversubscribed schools using the random electronic system. The Labour-run authority claims that the system gives more children a better chance to get into popular schools (BBC,

2007). The system operates by dividing the city into six areas and pupils are expected to attend the schools in their areas. Where there are two schools in one catchment area, the places are allocated by electronic lottery. Another authority, Hertfordshire County Council, is also planning to use a 'lucky draw' system in its seven oversubscribed single-sex schools in the allocation of places.

The allocation of school places by individual parental preferences involves parents acting as consumers in the education market. This model can work effectively for all parents, as everyone has the same choices. However, there are arguments that those with fewer resources have a lower ability to secure places in the best schools and therefore have to accept the schools that are left. These arguments therefore put forward the use both of catchment areas and of random allocation. Both of these undermine individual consumer participation and choice, as the school places are given either to geographically local children or those who receive them randomly.

Aside from the choice of school, which is actually a preference rather than a choice, there are few choices in education about when services are delivered, how they are accessed and which teachers deliver in classrooms. There are few choices in the primary school curriculum, with the national curriculum and literacy and numeracy frameworks to be implemented, and some choices about the curriculum in secondary schools. In some schools pupils can choose a more vocational or a more academic subject base, or the Baccalaureate where it is available. It is clear that in terms of the allocation of school place, allowing parents this choice, or allocating by either catchment areas or the lottery, raises many new issues for choice in education.

Faces of the citizen-consumer in education

As highlighted above, it is the parent as 'chooser', making choices about schools, which has commanded a great deal of attention in education. Less attention has focused on other 'faces' of the consumer in education. These faces include 'clients' (more often applied to adult learners), 'pupils/students/participants' (all of these are used and apply to individuals within the primary, secondary and further/higher education sectors) and 'citizens', which is a consumer 'face' that also has some prominence in education. The 'citizen-consumer' face is examined further below.

At the three levels of participation, choice, voice and exit, it can be argued that in terms of choice, once the initial choice of school place is decided, there is little role for consumers. In most cases, the choice lasts for five or seven years (the periods of primary and secondary schooling), as children rarely move from one school to another. Parents are not likely to take the decision to move children from one school to another lightly, as the movement is difficult after children have developed their friendships. As highlighted in Table 7.1, there are few choices within schools beyond the initial choice of school. For example, there are limited choices about learning styles, when material is delivered, teachers and books. Lewis (2006) has argued that in Wales there are choices about whether children go to independent/mantained, Welsh/English, religious/non-religious schools, but that there are no real choices beyond this. In England, where there are different types of schools, including CTCs and city academies, there are more choices. However, the choices for individual parents must be influenced by the schools in the locality, and this therefore makes choice a geographical issue. There are further limitations on the market in education to respond to parental choice. First, schools have limited capacity to expand and contract in response to market choices, as buildings cannot open and close easily. Second, and this issue was highlighted by research undertaken by the *Times Educational Supplement*, successful schools are unwilling to expand to meet increased demand (TES, 2005). This may be because they feel that their success would be undermined by increases in size.

In relation to exit, it can be argued that this is a one-off activity. It involves removing, or threatening to remove, pupils from school. The use of the 'exit' mechanism in schools may be considered weak, as, in reality, children cannot be easily removed. They have made their friends, parents also have friendship networks through school, and also the removal of a child from any school is clearly dependent on the availability of places in other schools in the locality. Having a number of schools locally may not be something found in every area, and this therefore undermines the effectiveness of the consumer as chooser. Schools cannot easily expand and contract in response to market demand. These arguments about the limitations of the consumer as chooser are highlighted in a Public Administration Select Committee report (PASC, 2005). Here it is argued that 'for choice to be effective, we found it was necessary to ensure additional capacity in the appropriate places. This not only comes at a cost, but expanding a successful school or closing a hospital cannot be an immediate, or even a practical, response to user choice' (PASC, 2005, p 3). Further, it may be that threatening to withdraw children from school will be used instead of actually withdrawal. However, if this option is used too frequently, schools will not take it seriously.

Thus, the use of both choice and exit are limited in education. Simmons (2006) argues that this is true of public services more generally. This is because choice is dependent on users exercising their exit opportunities, which are limited in public services. Focusing on healthcare choices, Exworthy and Peckham (2006, p 268) highlight that 'the exercise of choice by patients is mediated by knowledge, resources, family circumstances, residential location and the accessibility of alternative providers'.

Moving on to voice, there are individual and collective voices. The individual voice has been likened to the consumer role and the collective voice to the citizen role (Beecham, 2006). Schools may or may not be responsive to parents as individual consumers. It is the case that some parents are more able to express themselves than others and therefore have a greater chance of being heard. There may also be arguments around whether problems are created for children whose parents complain a great deal. This therefore could undermine parents' involvement in schools as consumers. As highlighted in a recent review of choice and voice, current voice mechanisms 'require energy and commitment to be active; they take a good deal of time to operate; and they create defensiveness and distress among those complained against. They favour the educated and articulate' (cited in PASC, 2005, p 51). In relation to collective voice, this remains an under-researched field and the extent to which schools are responsive to groups of parents as consumers needs investigation.

To what extent are schools responsive to the citizen role? There is not much evidence that they are. While the opportunities exist for citizen involvement, these are not always as effective as they might be. Schools governing bodies are dominated by head teachers in schools (Ranson et al, 2005). Despite having responsibility for strategy, there is evidence that governors are rarely involved in strategy and decision making in schools (Farrell, 2005). There are no mechanisms for the community to be involved in schools.

The involvement of citizens more fully in education, to improve citizen voice, is central to the success of current government policies. As highlighted above, citizen involvement is central in education, where exit, choice and individual consumer participation are not very strong. Recent evidence from the US about citizen participation suggests that the use of the internet is another mechanism of promoting citizen voice and participation that can be effective in some areas. Robbins et al (2008) find that the use of a web survey offering citizens different policy options about taxes raised and services provided is a mechanism that could be adopted in other services. Using surveys in education may be one mechanism of providing citizens with key choices on aspects including curriculum, access and when services are received. A further approach in which citizen voice may be enhanced within services may be by the 'co-production' initiative. Bovaird's (2007) paper in this area highlights that through involving users in the planning and delivery of services, they become more powerful. This issue is examined further in other chapters of this book. Farrington-Douglas and Brooks (2007) suggest that another possibility is to bring the relationship between choice and voice closer together – while permitting choice for consumers, there should be an obligation on providers to collect information relating to users' views on services.

Conclusion

This chapter has focused on consumers in education and reviewed the 'voice, choice and exit' framework to identify more about the role of users in education. The findings suggest that the government's drive to continue to promote the consumer choice agenda in education services is not empowering users in education. Parents and pupils in some areas have a choice about 'which school', and express their preferences. These can only be matched where places exist in schools. Where the choice of school is removed, and allocation is by catchment areas, parents have a low level of participation. This is also the case where the school place is randomly allocated through the lottery system.

In education, there are no choices about professionals delivering the service, when it is received, how it is accessed and so on. The power of 'exit' is weak in education, as the capacity to move from school to school is undermined by children's and parents' friendships and belonging in schools. Choices, for the most part, last for the length of stay in school – seven years. Individual consumer voice may be limited by parental effort, time to become involved and so on. Parents may not wish to complain, as they fear their children may be adversely affected. Consumers also have the opportunity to come together with other parents to have their voices heard. It is not clear whether parental voice as collective consumers is effective or not. In contrast, it is in the citizen role, where individuals have opportunities to express their 'voices', that individuals are likely to be more empowered. Improving these mechanisms for collective voice is an area which needs further work if the 'citizen–consumer' in education is to be empowered.

References

6, P. (2003) 'Giving consumers of British public services more choice', *Journal of Social Policy*, vol 32, no 2, pp 239–70.

Aberbach, J.D. and Christensen, T. (2005) 'Citizens and consumers – A NPM dilemma', *Public Management Review*, vol 7, no 2, pp 225–45.

Ball, S. (2006) ESRC Debates: 'Your voice, whose choice? Choice in education – do parents and pupils have a meaningful choice in education? How much choice is there in education and who gets to exercise it?', Cardiff, St David's Hotel, 15 November.

BBC (2007) 'Schools to give places by Lottery', *BBC News*, 7 March.

Beecham, J. (2006) *Beyond boundaries: Citizen-centred local services for Wales*, Review of Local Service Delivery, Report to the Welsh Assembly Government, Cardiff: HMSO.

Bovaird, T. (2007) 'Beyond engagement and participation: user and community coproduction of public services', *Public Administration Review*, vol 67, no 5, pp 846–60.

Burgess, S. (2006) ESRC Debates: 'Your voice, whose choice? Choice in education – do parents and pupils have a meaningful choice in education? How much choice is there in education and who gets to exercise it?', Cardiff, St David's Hotel, 15 November.

Butler, T., Hamnett, C., Ramsden, M. and Webber, R. (2007) 'The best, the worst and the average: secondary school choice and education performance in East London', *Journal of Education Policy*, vol 22, no 1, pp 7–29.

Clarke, J. and Newman, J. (1997) *The managerial state*, London: Sage.

Daily Telegraph (2007) 'School catchment areas to be scrapped', 7 March.

DfES (Department for Education and Skills) (2007) *School admissions code*, London: HMSO.

Exworthy, M. and Peckham, S. (2006) 'Access, choice and travel: implications for health policy', *Social Policy and Administration*, vol 40, no 3, pp 267–87.

Farrell, C.M. (2005) 'Governance in the public sector – the involvement of the board', *Public Administration*, vol 83, no 1, pp 89–110.

Farrell C.M. and Jones, J. (2000) 'Evaluating stakeholder participation in public services – parents and schools', *Policy & Politics*, vol 28, no 2, pp 251–62.

Farrington-Douglas, J. and Brooks, R. (2007) *The future hospital: The politics of change*, London: IPPR.

Gewirtz, S., Ball, S.J. and Bowe, R. (1995) *Markets, choice and equity in education*, Buckingham: Open University Press.

Goldring, E.B. and Phillips, K.J.R. (2008) 'Parent preferences and parent choices: the public–private decision about school choice', *Journal of Education Policy*, vol 23, no 3, pp 209–30.

Gorard, S. and Fitz, J. (1998) 'Under starters orders: the established market, the Cardiff Study and the Smithfield Project', *International Studies in Sociology of Education*, vol 8, no 3, pp 365–76.

Hirschman, A. (1970) *Exit, voice and loyalty: Responses to decline in firms, organizations and states*, Cambridge, MA: Harvard University Press.

Hoxby, C. (2003) 'School choice and school competition: evidence from the United States', *Swedish Economic Policy Review*, 10.

Independent, The (2007) 'Parents face lottery for school places', 7 March.

Jordan, B. (2006) 'Public services and the service economy: individualism and the choice agenda', *Journal of Social Policy*, vol 35, no 1, pp 143–63.

Le Grand, J. (2003) *Motivation, agency and public policy: Of knights and knaves, pawns and queens*, Oxford: Oxford University Press.

Le Grand, J. (2007) *The other invisible hand*, Princeton, NJ: Princeton University Press.

Lewis, S. (2006) ESRC Debates: 'Your voice, whose choice? Choice in education – do parents and pupils have a meaningful choice in education? How much choice is there in education and who gets to exercise it?, Chief inspector of schools in Wales', Cardiff, St David's Hotel, 15 November.

Miliband, D. (2004) 'Choice and voice in personalised learning', DfES Innovation Unit/Demos/OECD Conference, 24 May. (Speech cited in the House of Commons Public Administration Select Committee Report, 'Choice, voice and public services', vol 1, Fourth Report of Session 2004–05, London: The Stationery Office).

National Commission on Education (1996) *Success against the odds: Effective schools in disadvantaged areas*, London Routledge.

Needham, C.E. (2006) 'Customer care and the public service ethos', *Public Administration*, vol 84, no 4, pp 845–60.

Needham, C. (2007) *The reform of public services under New Labour: Narratives of consumerism*, Basingstoke: Palgrave.

Noden, P. (2000) 'Rediscovering the impact of marketisation: dimensions of social segregation in England's secondary schools 1994–1999', *British Journal of Sociology of Education*, no 21, pp 371–90.

Noden, P. (2002) 'Education markets and social polarisation: back to square one?', *Research Papers in Education*, vol 17, no 4, pp 409–12.

PASC (Public Administration Select Committee) Report (2005) 'Choice, voice and public services', vol 1, Fourth Report of Session 2004–05, London: The Stationery Office.

Powell, M. (1999) *New Labour, new welfare state: The 'third way' in British social policy*, Bristol: The Policy Press.

Ranson, S., Arnott, M., McKeown, P., Martin, J. and Smith, P. (2005) 'The participation of volunteer citizens in school governance', *Educational Review*, vol 57, no 3, pp 357–71.

Robbins, M.D., Simonsen, B. and Feldman, B. (2008) 'Citizens and resource allocation: improving decision making with interactive web-based citizen participation', *Public Administration Review*, May/June, pp 564–74.

Simmons, R. (2006) 'Understanding the "differentiated consumer" in public services: implication for choice and voice', Paper for seminar, *The Differentiated Consumer in Public Services*, Henley Upon Thames, 14–15 December.

Simmons, R. and Birchall, J. (2005) 'A joined-up approach to user participation in public services: strengthening the "participation chain"', *Social Policy and Administration*, vol 39, no 3, pp 260–83.

TES (*Times Educational Supplement*) (2005) Survey reported in Public Administration Select Committee Report, 'Choice, voice and public services', vol 1, Fourth Report of Session 2004–05, London: The Stationery Office, 14 January.

Tice, P., Princiotta, D., Chapman, C. and Bielick, S. (2006) *Trends in the use of school choice: 1993 to 2003* (NCES 2007–045), Washington, DC: US Department of Education, National Center for Education Statistics.

Tough, S. and Brooks, R. (2007) *School admissions: Fair choice for parents and pupils*, London: Institute for Public Policy Research.

West, A. (2006) 'School choice, equity and social justice: the case for more control', *British Journal of Educational Studies*, vol 54, no 1, pp 15–33.

EIGHT

The consumer and social housing

Nick Mills

Introduction

The position of social housing as a service that is slightly removed from other public services, the 'wobbly pillar' of the welfare state, is well known (Malpass, 2005).[1] As Kemeny (2006) notes, housing is different because vested market interests have a stronger historical stake than they do in areas such as health and education. The role of the private consumer is not as strange to housing as it is to the worlds of education or health: most people in the UK choose their own housing in the market.

The relationship is further complicated by the nature of housing choices. Jordan (2006) states that welfare services have a temporal nature, as they are dependent on human relationships, while goods have a more permanent character. What is notable about housing as opposed to basic healthcare and education is that the service user is effectively choosing capital goods rather than services. Social landlords do provide many services for their tenants, but applicants have no definite way of knowing what level of service to expect. In this respect it is possible to claim that housing is the area that is most suited to choice-based mechanisms. Choosing a property is a decision based on tangible factors, whereas individuals choosing a service are reliant on information that they may not believe and opinion that they may not trust. While housing applicants are also reliant on experts and there is still a temporal aspect in that faults in a house become apparent over time, it is nevertheless the case that houses themselves provide grounding on which to base a decision. The extent to which that decision can be considered to be a genuinely empowered one is at the centre of issues of consumerism in social housing.

To be genuinely offered meaningful choices, tenants also have to be able to influence the services they are offered. Choices such as decoration, or appointment times, are likely to be dependent on individual circumstances and taste, and in recent times housing policy has emphasised the importance of responsive landlords. However, choices in social housing also vary between landlords, and the Cave Review (2007) has highlighted that more needs to be done to ensure that there is effective regulation. Moreover, social housing has a rich history of tenant activism influencing local authority decision making and, in some cases, national policy.

In the post-war era most governments have encouraged tenants to 'exit' the social housing sector and have supported individuals in the market through a variety of mechanisms (mortgage tax relief, discounted council house sales) that use public money to subsidise the ownership of private citizens. Housing policy from the 1950s onwards has sought to encourage individuals to become consumers, and maintained that owner occupation is a beneficial tenure both financially and socially. The encouragement of owner occupation has frequently come at the expense of other tenures, and this has meant that in some areas the state only houses the poorest families and individuals.

Equally, the prevailing image of social housing in the post-war era has been one in which tenants have limited choices. This has been offset by subsidised rent, but perhaps the most dominant image in social housing is that of the tenant as a client, dictated to by bureaucratic local authorities:

> Council tenants are becoming the serfs of the 1970s and are constantly under the wing of their landlords, the local authorities, who run council estates from their plush council offices and often know nothing about individual problems. (Durand, quoted in *Hansard*, 21 April 1977, vol 930, col 424)

As a result, many of the reforms of the past 30 years have aimed to provide more reflexive landlords and providers. However, the recent emphasis on choice has led to some tension between the 'residual' role of social housing, as a tenure for those who cannot support themselves in the housing market, and a desire to expand choice to users of housing services.

In this chapter I will examine the role ascribed to social housing tenants and consider the various roles ascribed in policy. Initially this discussion will define three labels: clients, citizens and consumers, and this will be developed through the chapter to consider what these roles mean in relation to social housing. The appearance of consumers in post-war housing policy will be examined, and finally the mechanisms of consumerism applied to housing will be discussed.

Citizens, clients and consumers

A number of studies have categorised social housing tenants according to various typologies, several considering whether these tenants can be classed as clients, consumers or citizens. The definitions of these labels and the differences between them are important in assessing the extent to which occupants of social housing can make their own decisions regarding their choice and use of their housing.

Symon and Walker (1995) have distinguished between clients, customers, consumers and citizens, but in this account the consumer is characterised as a relatively passive figure in relation to the citizen. Citizenship is expressed through 'voice' (Hirschman, 1970), while consumers impact on the quality of provision through 'exiting' unsatisfactory services. Clients and customers are relatively similar in this typology, as both imply a passive role for the service user in relation to the provider or the bureaucrat. Cairncross et al (1996) are less explicit about any division between citizens and consumers, but note that the former are generally seen as collective, the latter as individual. However, much of the sociological material on consumerism questions this individualistic bias and this material will be discussed later in the chapter.

There is no clear consensus on terminology in housing policy documents. For example, the evaluation of English housing policy by the Office of the Deputy Prime Minister (ODPM) questions whether 'customer' or 'consumer' is an appropriate label for tenants in social housing, particularly as many do not have the means to exit the sector (ODPM, 2005).

Clients

The role of a client is seen as a relatively passive one in which an individual has limited power in relation to the expert professional. This hierarchical relationship has often been identified in studies of housing in the post-war period, where housing officers act as 'gatekeepers' to control access to social housing and subsequently offer limited choice to the client–tenant.

Dunleavy (1981) has extensively discussed clientism in the period 1945–75, particularly in relation to the resettlement of tenants following slum clearances in the 1950s. He illustrates the relationship by listing the relative power resources open to tenants and officers, showing how tenants effectively only had recourse to local democratic channels or direct action, while local authority officers held a monopoly on decision making as well as the power to enact punitive measures on troublesome tenants.

One sense in which the term 'client' is still frequently used is in relation to homelessness. Significantly, it is generally used by professionals in relation to groups that have particular difficulties that may hinder their ability to live independent lives, for example addiction problems or mental health issues (for example, see Anderson, 2007).

Citizens

In what sense are citizens different from clients or consumers? Citizenship is a broad concept, but perhaps the defining difference is that it is essentially a legal concept. Citizenship sets out the boundaries of who is and is not included within a polity and sets out the content of individuals' rights and responsibilities (Isin and Wood, 1999). This has some relevance for social housing, as, while the service is funded by the state, it is only used by a relatively small proportion of citizens.[2] This was not the original design for local authority housing, indeed Bevan explicitly warned against the 'segregation of different income groups' (quoted in Forrest and Murie, 1988, p 23).

The main difference with clients is the level of autonomy granted to the individual, but this is not just the straightforward choice from a menu that is implied by some versions of consumerism. Citizens are imagined to actively influence the service they consume, provide feedback to the providers and assist in designing new provision. This implies some access to decision-making channels beyond the normal democratic input of voting for political representatives: it implies that tenants should interact with the officer who shapes and delivers the service. In the post-war era social housing landlords have been poor at allowing this type of participation, and tenant groups have frequently had to resort to unconventional channels in order to present their case (Shapely, 2006). Equally, Birchall (1992) notes that more formal tenants' groups have traditionally been unsupported and this has hindered their influence over decision making.

Since the *National framework for tenant participation compacts* (DETR, 1999) was published, tenants have had a more formal mechanism for involvement in housing delivery. However, concerns remain about the extent to which tenants' representatives reflect the views of those they are speaking for, as well as their ability to influence decisions in real terms (Mayo, 2002).

Consumers

Just as the term 'citizen' can conjure a variety of different meanings, so the 'consumer' of social policy is equally contested and, according to which definitions are adopted, there are often significant areas of overlap between the two. Much of the academic literature on choice in social policy has been critical of the government's vision of consumer choice. Commentators have questioned whether the government is simply trying to shift responsibility from providers to users (Gilliat et al, 2000) and there remains a concern that choice will exacerbate inequalities in service provision, while Jordan (2005) notes that there are unresolved issues regarding the future of services and institutions that prove to be unpopular with consumers.

As Needham (2003) notes, consumers can frequently be seen as passive, simply choosing from set options. However, in private housing this is not the case – few buyers will offer the seller's asking price, at least not straight away. Consumption is in this sense a two-way process, with consumers effectively altering the package they are being offered.

This is not to imply that choices are unrestrained in the private market. Clearly, buyers are limited by factors such as cost and location. Equally, it is inaccurate to suggest that consumers in the housing market operate without financial subsidy from government. In the post-war period owner occupation has been supported through a variety of subsidies and at-source tax relief. To some extent this has been considered to distort the operation of the market: for example, Nigel Lawson wished to abolish mortgage interest tax relief during his tenure as chancellor (King, 2001). Further, the method of subsidisation for tenants has had some influence in promoting consumerism, as successive governments have moved from direct subsidy (through rent controls, or heavily subsidised rents in local authority housing) to targeted personal subsidies through housing benefit. This has culminated in the consideration of a local housing allowance rather than direct payments to landlords, although this is only effective in the private rented sector (DWP, 2002).

Choice-based allocations in social housing aspire to offer market conditions, but a number of writers have questioned the extent to which this can be achieved. Choice and bargaining in a private market involves a degree of risk, with the possibility that the purchaser may lose the property. As Brown and King (2005) have noted, this cannot be replicated in social housing, as it would contravene the local authorities' legal responsibility to accommodate those in housing need in their area.

History

In this section I will highlight the changing government conception of tenants, specifically with reference to consumerism. Key instances of government encouraging consumerism were initially limited to the support of owner occupation from the 1950s, opportunities to change landlords from the 1980s, and choice of property from 2000 onwards. However, it is important to note that the practical demands of ensuring a national housing stock have often taken precedence over ideology.

When considering the emergence of consumerism and choice in housing there are two major factors to bear in mind. First, in the immediate post-war period there was a need to rebuild following damage caused by bombing. In this climate the state was to take a lead in building and there was a strong commitment by the government to local authority ownership of housing. Significantly, references to choice in the 1945 White Paper (MoR, 1945) refer to the Ministry of Town and Country Planning, rather than to individual tenants.

Second, it is important to consider for whom social housing is intended. In the immediate post-war period Bevan referred to the role of local authorities as one in which the housing needs of lower-income groups were given priority, but by 1949 the government was committed to a social mix in local authority housing. However, since this time it has been frequently noted that social housing is intended for those who cannot enter the private market (Malpass, 2005).

The initial period of rebuilding was characterised by a focus on government planning and a social mix in state housing; however, Jones and Murie (2006) note that while Conservative housing policy continued to expand housing building targets, there was also a general shift in emphasis towards the encouragement of private provision. The 1953 White Paper contains considerable evidence of the support for owner occupation, for example:

> Of all forms of ownership this is one of the most satisfying to the individual and the most beneficial to the nation. (MoHLG, 1953, p 2)

However, the Conservative government did not simply imagine that the spread of affluence would lead to the eventual eclipse of local authority housing by private ownership and renting. Malpass (2005) draws attention to Macmillan's personal contention that there were limits to the spread of owner occupation, as 'not everyone can afford to buy or ought to be his own landlord' (Macmillan, quoted in Malpass,

2005, p 80). This was acknowledged in the White Paper of 1961, as, while much of the housing need of the 'prosperous society' was to be met by private development, there was a continued role for local authorities in providing housing for those who could not afford non-subsidised rents or mortgages (MoHLG, 1961, p 3).

Choice for social housing tenants in this era was enabled through early council house sales. Initially, the government allowed the sale of council housing where the local authority and the tenant wished this to happen. In this way the Conservatives of the 1950s encouraged consumerism in the sense that they enabled increased private provision of homes both for rent and sale, and encouraged tenants to exit the sector.

In the early post-war period housing shortages were therefore the central concern of government, with little choice for social housing tenants. By the 1960s these shortages had not been completely eradicated, but the increasing prosperity of the country meant that the government was able to plan beyond the immediate completion of building programmes. The fundamental change in the first Wilson government's approach to housing, as compared to the Attlee government, was in the area of owner occupation. The housing White Paper of 1965 announced a considerable increase in subsidised building, but noted that this should be seen as an exceptional measure to ease remaining shortages, and that owner occupation should be viewed as the 'normal' tenure subsequently (MoHLG, 1965, p 3). The proposed building targets were never reached and by 1968 the government shifted its focus to the rehabilitation of older properties, partly because of wider economic conditions by the late 1960s and partly because of the declining reputation of local council housing. By the time that Labour left office in 1970, owner occupation had become the majority tenure in Britain.

However, Labour remained opposed, in principle, to encouraging council house sales, and in 1968 it introduced restrictions to ensure local authority housing stock was retained. Likewise, Morgan's (1997) biography of James Callaghan notes that the Labour leader considered allowing a right to buy scheme in the late 1970s, but felt that it would be unpopular with the core Labour vote.

The 1968 housing White Paper also imagined an enhanced role for housing associations in the rehabilitation of older properties. The development of this sector continued in 1974 as capital grants were introduced. Potentially, this offered a second option in social housing: an opportunity for choice without exit from the social housing sector, which had not previously existed. As the 1977 Green Paper stated:

> Housing associations, in co-operation with local authorities, can offer an important element of choice in socially owned rented housing, and are able to specialise in dealing with groups such as mobile key workers, the elderly and the disabled. (DoE, 1977, p 47)

However, with the arrival of the Conservative government, the focus returned to encouraging exit from social housing. Chiefly this was enabled through the Right to Buy, which developed previous policy on council house sales by allowing a statutory right to buy for sitting tenants and provided much higher discounts of up to 50% than the previous discretionary sales. This policy and its effects have been well documented elsewhere (Malpass and Murie, 1999; Balchin and Rhoden, 2002; ODPM, 2005). However, it is important to note that, while the effects on the stock of social housing are still being felt today (Murie, 2007), Mort (1996) claims that the lasting legacy of this period was the cultural change brought about by the policy of privatisation in the 1980s. He notes that the popularity of Thatcherism drew attention to the language of consumption from beyond the private sector and into politics.

In this context, the 1987 White Paper is notable on two counts. First, it highlighted a desire to introduce choice in social housing and imagined that social housing could be provided by semi-privatised housing associations. Second, it contained the first mention of consumerism in post-war housing policy:

> In the public sector the emphasis must be on greater consumer choice and more say for tenants. This can be achieved by offering a variety of forms of ownership and management; this will help to break down the monolithic nature of large estates. (DoE, 1987, p 3)

The government was seeking to introduce a number of measures aimed at empowering social housing tenants through giving them a choice of landlords. Famously, the so-called 'tenants' choice' was ignored by tenants, who saw no reason to change landlord, and by private developers, who were deterred by potential repair costs and a complicated regulatory system (ODPM, 2005). It is perhaps interesting to briefly consider Jordan's (2006) earlier point about the nature of services and goods in this instance, as, effectively, tenants were asked to change landlord in order to receive a better service and levels of repair, this balanced against a potential rise in rent (King, 2001). Thus, decisions had to be made according to a judgement about a service which tenants had no way of judging.

Ironically, the early attempts to introduce housing action trusts, private bodies that would oversee the repair and upgrade of deprived estates, were hampered by a lack of choice for tenants. The failure to include a tenants' ballot in the original proposals led to mistrust of the government's motivations and local authorities lobbied to ensure that the scheme was not heavily used (Karn, 1993). Equally, large-scale voluntary transfer of estates to semi-private housing associations arose as an unforeseen consequence of the tighter financial regime imposed on local authorities, although the Major government later tightened up regulation in this area.

While the Conservatives of the 1980s encouraged exit from social housing, the recession in the housing market of the early 1990s provoked some reappraisal of the value of this sector (DoE, 1995). This trend was initially continued by the incoming Labour government, which invested in a declining social housing stock through making capital receipts available.

The first major housing document of the New Labour government, *Quality and choice: A decent home for all* (DETR, 2000), set out many mechanisms that are still being implemented. Three specific objectives for using choice are considered:

- empower people to make decisions over where they live, and exercise choice;
- help create sustainable communities; and
- encourage the effective use of the nation's housing stock. (DETR, 2000, p 78)

One of the central proposals is that 'choice should be as wide as possible' and should be extended beyond the decision of which landlord to select and move to a choice between property through choice-based lettings (DETR, 2000, p 82). As noted in the Green Paper, this can be seen as an attempt to model allocation mechanisms on the private housing market (DETR, 2000, p 84). As such, a degree of individual freedom is imagined, although the Green Paper notes that choices are always bound by circumstance to some extent; even in the private sector, 'choice implies a trade-off between people's needs and aspirations on the one hand, and the availability of housing they can afford on the other' (DETR, 2000, p 79). This issue highlights a central paradox for government, which is especially apparent in the section of the Green Paper that deals with choice in social housing. Every point that promises a positive right to choose is counterbalanced by a qualifying statement that notes the structural constraints that may prevent this opportunity arising. The opportunities for 'empowered' users are constrained by the need-based priorities of social housing for those who would struggle to meet housing costs in the open market, which means that consumer choices can never be properly free.

Choice in this instance therefore emerges as a limited entity, a position that has been supported by the subsequent assessment of choice-based letting pilot schemes (Marsh et al, 2004). Despite this, the Hills Report (2007) notes that the extra choice has been welcomed by tenants, and that worries over the scheme exacerbating housing inequalities or ethnic segregation appear to have been unfounded. However, Hills does note that one area that could be improved is the opportunity for cross-regional choices: at present choices are frequently constrained by local authority area.

Labour's moves to introduce a user-centred approach to social housing have in part been driven by the realisation that inflexible systems of allocation can lead to a miscalculation of tenants' needs, which subsequently become costly to rectify. One example of this is the reforms to the housing benefit system (DWP, 2002), which backtrack on the 2000 Green Paper's scepticism and offer a flat-rate allowance which claimants in the private sector may use as they see fit. It is hoped that the rational, instrumental behaviour of consumers will lead to a more effective use of social housing; claimants have the opportunity to gain financially by cutting their housing costs, this in turn helping to reduce the over-consumption of housing that has been identified as a deficiency of the old housing benefit system (Stephens, 2005). However, disparity between rent levels means that this scheme has only been adopted for private sector renting, and interim research for Shelter suggests a mixed picture in terms of improving choice and increasing availability in this sector (Neuburger and Long, 2005).

With the difficulties surrounding the issue of supply that were identified by Barker (2004), and in the wake of the Hills Report into social housing, it is unsurprising that the Green Paper *Homes for the future: More affordable, more sustainable* (CLG, 2007) focuses heavily on providing new housing through a variety of different channels. Choice in social housing is a feature of the Green Paper, but references are generally focused on ensuring that there is a sufficient supply of homes to enable a genuine choice and to ensure affordability. Perhaps significantly, consumers are only mentioned in reference to the private sector and these occurrences are frequently preceded by the word 'informed'. As was the case with the 2000 Green Paper, social housing tenants are again referred to as customers rather than consumers – a split that may be considered insignificant, but nevertheless carries an implication of passivity, particularly in reference to Symon and Walker's (1995) typology.

This chronology of housing policy reveals that policy has encouraged 'exit' from the social housing sector as far back as the 1950s. Equally, choice for tenants within the social housing sector was extremely limited up until the Conservative government of the 1980s, and even then reforms were focused on exit from the sector rather than choice with it. New Labour embraced choice within social housing from an early point in its term, but these changes are still being implemented to a large extent. Moreover, evidence from the recent Cave Review and Hills Report suggests that choice is still limited by scarcity of social housing in many areas, rigid divisions between local authorities and variable landlords. The Barker Report (2004) has suggested that, to meet demand, it is necessary to loosen planning restrictions in some areas, while ensuring that developer contributions provide for a supply of affordable housing. Some of these factors will be considered in the next section.

Mechanisms of consumerism

Summarising social housing tenants' opportunities for choice is difficult, as different landlords are likely to offer different services. Therefore Table 8.1, using Le Grand's (2007) dimensions, identifies some service choices that may be available in some areas and not others. Equally, some schemes, such as choice-based letting, are widespread, but not yet universal. However, larger structural schemes such as the Right to Buy apply nationally.

As the table shows, choices in social housing during the 'classic' welfare period were extremely limited and generally restricted to opportunities to exit the sector for those with sufficient means. Allocations were governed by a points-based system, although it could be argued that tenants had the 'choice' of whether to accept the offer or not. Housing associations represented a state-funded alternative landlord after 1974, but comprised a small share of the social rented sector.

In the 1980s the Conservatives fundamentally wished tenants to exit social housing and provide their own accommodation through private means. Clearly, the Right to Buy is the prime example of this, but equally relevant was the reduction in funding to local authorities (Balchin, 2005) and the eventual reorganisation envisaged by the 1987 White Paper, which encouraged tenants to exit the social sector in favour of semi-private housing associations. What is notable about these changes is that the Conservatives did not aim to provide choices for the majority of social housing tenants who were housed by local authorities, beyond the ability to choose an alternative landlord.

New Labour has undoubtedly increased the choices available to social housing tenants, particularly through choice-based letting, discussed earlier. However, a limited choice between houses does not necessarily result in empowered consumers: for this to occur there

Table 8.1: Le Grand's dimensions of choice applied to housing

Dimension	Classic welfare state	Conservatives (1979–97)	New Labour (1997–)
Choice of provider (where?)	Right to buy in agreed circumstances	Right to Buy	Right to Buy
	Choice of housing associations as a social provider after 1974	Choice of landlords under 'tenants' choice'	Choice of landlord through tenant ballots
			Shared equity
Choice of professional (who?)	Limited	Choice of landlords under 'tenants' choice'	Choice of landlord through tenant ballots
Choice of services (what?)	Limited	Choice of landlords under 'tenants' choice'	Board representation through tenant participation
		Choices through incentives for tenants to vote for Housing Action Trusts	Choice of houses through choice-based lettings
			Choice of decorative schemes in some cases (individual)
			Choice of estate services (collective)
			'Gold Standard' services
Choice of appointment time (when?)	Allocation governed by waiting list	Allocation governed by waiting list	Allocation governed by waiting list
			Choice of access times for tradesmen in some cases
			Choice of payment methods in some cases
Choice of access channel (how?)	Limited	Limited	Choice-based letting advertised online and in local newspapers
Choice of additional services	Limited	Limited	Some landlords offering priced additional services

needs to be both reasonable alternatives to choose from and, crucially, an opportunity to influence the goods and services offered. In some respects the formalised arrangements for Tenant Participation Compacts could be seen to enable this, but concerns remain about the real effect that official groups can have (see, for example, Millward, 2005).

The Cave Review (2007) of regulation in social housing is relatively critical of the extent of existing choices for most tenants:

> Tenants are largely captive consumers, with few choices and the extent to which they have a say is variable. (Cave, 2007, p 48)

However, considering choice of services is problematic, as some landlords are likely to offer more choice than others. Thus, Cave notes that better landlords may offer enhanced choices in decoration or incentivised service schemes, such as the Irwell Valley Gold Standard scheme – but regulation should ensure that more of these opportunities are open to all tenants. Flint (2004) has claimed that such measures constitute a deepening of tenant responsibilities, in that services can be dependent on both financial contribution and behaviour.

Consequently choice of homes and services is uneven across the social housing sector, and this is exacerbated by the implementation times for schemes such as choice-based letting, which is supposed to be available nationwide by 2010. However, in the main, choice has been heavily concentrated on encouraging exit from the social housing sector.

Faces of consumerism

As Marsh (2004) has noted, New Labour's focus on choice, particularly in reference to choice-based letting, has been generally focused on rational decision making. Equally, much of the housing literature on choice has focused on consumers as 'victims' (Schwartz, 2004), being offered illusory or confusing choices. However, sociological material on consumers has developed other 'faces' in order to consider different perspectives and behaviour.

In their seminal study of consumerism, Gabriel and Lang (2006) developed a typology to classify different motivations for consumer behaviour. This has proved to be influential on subsequent work, with both Edwards (2000) and Aldridge (2003) considering Gabriel and Lang's 'faces' of consumerism before attempting to modify the classification. All three texts note that each consumer 'face' is an incomplete representation of individual action: one consumer may assume any number of the 'faces' at different times and in different contexts. In this sense, all three follow Miller (1989), as goods and services should be considered in their proper context, this including the effect that people have on them. All three are notable for the breadth of factors that they consider in relation to individual motivation, and which take the debate beyond the narrow confines of choice in social housing literature. Likewise, all three note that consumers do not always act in an individualistic and self-interested manner, and there are numerous examples of collective consumer action. In the context of this chapter there are three key points the consideration of which should add to the understanding of a consumer in social housing.

First, sociological material has developed theoretical motivations for choices, and in particular has considered the extent to which choices are expressive or formative of identity. Aldridge (2003) states that choices should be evaluated to consider whether they are expressive or instrumental, dominant or dominated. Gabriel and Lang's (2006) 'faces' provide even more options in this area, but this branch of theory is underused in housing research. One exception is the attempt to apply Bourdieu's (1984) ideas on (dominated) taste and distinction to housing, which has been made by Gram-Hanssen and Bech-Danielsen (2004), who present a series of interviews with Danish householders. They examine the attitudes of householders to their homes and their practices in relation to the dominant norms of their particular neighbourhoods, and assess whether a model of consumption based around entrenched class identities or the self-creation of identity is more important.

Second, sociological literature on consumption has noted that consumers do not simply pick between available options, but can be instrumental in affecting the character of the service offered. For example, Shapely (2006) refers to particular council tenant groups in the post-war era as 'consumer groups', holding their landlord accountable for the service they received. He notes how the attempts by Conservative governments to empower consumers through tenant participation had unintended consequences, as the groups became politically active, but also contends that such groups were not party political and were driven by a consumerist ethos. The producer (the council) would be held to account for the service it provided, by groups representing myriad opinions and viewpoints. The net result of this action was increased recognition of tenants' voices in the rebuilding of Hulme in Manchester, the area that Shapely focuses on in the latter half of the paper. This type of activism has been documented frequently in housing research, but rarely with reference to consumerism.

Third, consumers are not as individualistic as is often presupposed in the housing literature, nor do they always act in isolation. Hilton (2005) has pointed to the social democratic agenda of the Consumers' Association, while Shapely (2006) claims that tenant groups took their influence from the direct action of consumer groups in the US.

Finally, Gabriel and Lang (2006) and Edwards (2000) have also noted the potential of 'rebel' consumers to act outside the law to satisfy their own needs, and how this behaviour can lead to the re-imagining of the parameters of a service. Ward (2002) has documented the historical instances of this very phenomenon: of particular relevance to this chapter is the case of post-war 'squatters' occupying army accommodation, due to housing shortages. Ward documents how squatters formed communities in the camps, but also how the government reacted to claims that they were 'jumping the queue' for housing.[3] He draws attention to one community in Oxfordshire that was eventually rehoused on the site of army accommodation that it had occupied for 10 years.

Conclusion

Although a high proportion of private users consume housing through a market, actual attempts to introduce choice into the social housing sector, as opposed to simply encouraging tenants to leave the sector, have only occurred relatively recently. Even though the Conservative governments of the 1980s and 1990s used the language of consumerism and introduced choice-based mechanisms, these were really aimed at encouraging exit from local authority housing. In this sense, Bauman's (2005) thesis that the poor are denied choice in a consumer society has some relevance to social housing, particularly as social housing has become a residualised tenure.

New Labour's choice-based mechanisms have increased opportunities for the poorest tenants, but have also been hampered by a lack of availability of social housing in some areas. Moreover, there is a problem with offering choice to tenants who can then find themselves 'trumped' by an applicant with priority status: the role of social housing as a tenure for those unable to afford private housing would appear to severely limit the opportunities for a meaningful choice.

Hills (2007) notes that even a small increase in the degree of choice is appreciated by tenants, and has proposed that a wider variety of options should be available. Equally, Cave (2007) has noted the diverse services already offered by some landlords and proposed that part of the role of the new regulator of social housing should be to ensure that tenants are empowered consumers. However, both note that the main concern for tenants is a sound basic level of service.

It is perhaps surprising that there has been so little choice in social housing and that 'consumers' have often had to battle against inflexible landlords, or leave the sector entirely in order to gain a useful voice. New Labour's reforms appear to have helped this situation very slightly, although it remains to be seen whether more time and further regulation will enable more empowered consumers.

Notes

[1] Malpass (2008) has subsequently qualified this analogy, noting that housing's relationship with the welfare state should be considered in more holistic terms than the consideration of social housing in isolation from other tenures.

[2] Of course, this has been one of the main arguments used by the Right against council housing. In recent years the Defend Council Housing group has countered these claims by pointing out that social housing rents have been used to subsidise the Treasury (Defend Council Housing, 2006).

[3] Ward disputes this on the grounds that the accommodation occupied by squatters was not intended for use as domestic housing.

References

Aldridge, A. (2003) *Consumption*, Cambridge: Polity.

Anderson, I. (2007) 'Tackling street homelessness in Scotland: the evolution and impact of the Rough Sleepers Initiative', *Journal of Social Issues*, vol 63, no 3, pp 623–40.

Balchin, P. (2005) *Housing policy: An introduction*, London: Routledge.

Balchin, P. and Rhoden, M. (2002) *Housing policy: An introduction* (4th edn), London: Taylor and Francis.

Barker, K. (2004) *Delivering sustainability: Securing our future housing needs*, London: HM Treasury.

Bauman, Z. (2005) *Work, consumerism and the new poor*, Maidenhead: Open University Press.

Birchall, J. (ed) (1992) *Housing policy in the 1990s*, New York, NY: Routledge.

Bourdieu, P. (1984) *Distinction: A social critique of the judgment of taste*, London: Routledge.

Brown, T. and King, P. (2005) 'The power to choose: effective choice and housing policy', *European Journal of Housing Policy*, vol 5, no 1, pp 59–75.

Cave, M. (2007) *Every tenant matters: A review of social housing regulation*, London: Department of Communities and Local Government.

Cairncross, L., Clapham, D. and Goodlad, R. (1996) *Housing management: Consumers and citizens*, London: Routledge.

CLG (Department of Communities and Local Government) (2007) *Homes for the future: More affordable, more sustainable*, London: HMSO.

Defend Council Housing (2006) *The case for council housing in 21st century Britain*, Nottingham: The Russell Press.

DETR (Department for the Environment, Transport and the Regions) (1999) *National framework for tenant participation compacts*, London: HMSO.

DETR (2000) *Quality and choice: A decent home for all*, London: HMSO.

DoE (Department of the Environment) (1977) *Housing Green Paper*, London: HMSO.

DoE (1987) *Housing: The government's proposals*, London: HMSO.

DoE (1995) *Our future homes: Opportunity, choice, responsibility*, London: HMSO.

Dunleavy, P. (1981) *The politics of mass housing in Britain 1945–1975*, Oxford: Oxford University Press.

DWP (Department for Work and Pensions) (2002) *Building choice and responsibility: A radical agenda for Housing Benefit*, London: HMSO.

Edwards, T. (2000) *Contradictions of consumption: Concepts, practices and politics in consumer society*, Milton Keynes: Open University Press.

Flint, J. (2004) 'The responsible tenant: housing governance and the politics of behaviour', *Housing Studies*, vol 19, no 6, pp 893–910.

Forrest, R. and Murie, A. (1988) *Selling the welfare state: The privatisation of public housing*, London: Routledge.

Gabriel, Y. and Lang, T. (2006) *The unmanageable consumer* (2nd edn), London: Sage.

Gilliat, S., Fenwick, J. and Alford, D. (2000) 'Public services and the consumer: empowerment or control?', *Social Policy and Administration*, vol 34, no 3, pp 333–49.

Gram-Hanssen, K. and Bech-Danielsen, C. (2004) 'House, home and identity from a consumption perspective', *Housing, Theory and Society*, no 21, pp 17–26.

Hills, J. (2007) *Ends and means: The future role of social housing in England*, London: CASE.

Hilton, M. (2005) 'Michael Young and the consumer movement', *Contemporary British History*, vol 19, no 3, pp 311–19.

Hirschman, A. (1970) *Exit, voice and loyalty: Responses to decline in firms, organizations and states*, Cambridge, MA: Harvard University Press.

Isin, E. and Wood, P. (1999) *Citizenship and identity*, London: Sage.

Jones, C. and Murie, A. (2006) *The right to buy*, Oxford: Blackwells.

Jordan, B. (2005) 'New Labour: choice and values', *Critical Social Policy*, vol 25, no 4, pp 427–46.

Jordan, B. (2006) 'Public services and the service economy: individualism and the choice agenda', *Journal of Social Policy*, vol 35, no 1, pp 143–62.

Karn, V. (1993) 'Remodelling a HAT: the implementation of the Housing Action Trust legislation, 1987–92', in P. Malpass and R. Means (eds) *Implementing housing policy*, Milton Keynes: Open University Press, pp 74–90.

Kemeny, J. (2006) 'Corporatism and housing regimes', *Housing, Theory and Society*, vol 23, no 1, pp 1–18.

King, P. (2001) *Understanding housing finance*, London: Routledge

Le Grand, J. (2007) *The other invisible hand: Delivering public services through choice and competition*, Princeton, NJ: Princeton University Press.

Malpass, P. (2005) *Housing and the welfare state: The development of housing policy in Britain*, London: Palgrave Macmillan.

Malpass, P. (2008) 'Housing and the new welfare state: wobbly pillar or cornerstone?', *Housing Studies*, vol 23, no 1, pp 1–19.

Malpass, P. and Murie, A. (1999) *Housing policy and practice* (5th edn), London: Palgrave Macmillan.

Marsh, A. (2004) 'The inexorable rise of the rational consumer? The Blair government and the reshaping of social housing', *European Journal of Housing Policy*, vol 4, no 2, pp 185–207.

Marsh, A., Cowan, D., Cameron, A., Jones, M., Kiddle, C. and Whitehead, C. (2004) *Piloting choice-based lettings: An evaluation*, London: The Stationery Office.

Mayo, M. (2002) 'Learning for active citizenship: training for and learning from participation in area regeneration', *Studies in the Education of Adults*, vol 32, no 1, pp 22–35.

Miller, D. (1987) *Material culture and mass consumption*, Oxford: Blackwell.

Millward, L. (2005) '"Just because we are amateurs doesn't mean we aren't professional": the importance of expert activists in tenant participation', *Public Administration*, vol 83, no 3, pp 735–51.

MoHLG (Ministry of Housing and Local Government) (1953) *Houses: The next step*, London: HMSO.

MoHLG (1961) *Homes for today and tomorrow*, London: HMSO.

MoHLG (1965) *The housing programme 1965–70*, London: HMSO.

MoR (Ministry of Reconstruction) (1945) *Housing*, London: HMSO.

Morgan, K. (1997) *Callaghan: A life*, Oxford: Oxford University Press.

Mort, F. (1996) *Cultures of consumption*, London: Routledge.

Murie, A. (2007) 'Housing policy, housing tenure and the housing market', *Social Policy Review 19*, pp 49–67.

Needham, C. (2003) *Citizen-consumers: New Labour's marketplace democracy*, London: Catalyst Working Paper.

Neuberger, J. and Long, G. (2005) *Policy briefing: Housing Benefit*, London: Shelter.

ODPM (Office of the Deputy Prime Minister) (2005) *An evaluation of English housing policy*, London: HMSO.

Schwartz, B. (2004) *The paradox of choice: Why more is less*, New York, NY: Harper Collins.

Shapely, P. (2006) 'Tenants arise! Consumerism, tenants and the challenge to council authority in Manchester, 1968–92', *Social History*, vol 31, no 1, pp 60–78.

Stephens, M. (2005) 'An assessment of the British Housing Benefit system', *European Journal of Housing Policy*, vol 5, no 2, pp 111–29.

Symon, P. and Walker, R. (1995) 'A consumer perspective on performance indicators: the local authority reports to tenants' regimes in England and Wales', *Environment and Planning C: Government and Policy*, vol 13, pp 195–216.

Ward, C. (2002) *Cotters and squatters: The hidden history of housing*, Nottingham: Five Leaves Publications.

NINE

The people's police? Citizens, consumers and communities

John Clarke

Introduction

Policing has an uncomfortable relationship to the dominant model of public service reform because of its relationship to law and the exercise of legal authority by police officers. The chapter draws on empirical work in two English urban settings to consider how both police and public view the usefulness of the ideas of consumers and customers. The idea of communities as a collective customer or user is then considered, raising some questions about how communities are to be discovered and engaged in the business of policing, with links to anxieties about local accountability in the recent Flanagan Report on the future of policing in England and Wales (2008). The chapter concludes by reflecting on the problematic relationship between publics, politics and power in policing.

Ideas of the consumer or customer emerged in debates about the future of policing during the late 1980s, reflecting pressures to modernise and managerialise the organisational structures and cultures of policing, culminating in the Sheehy Report of 1993. Sheehy attempted to install core principles of the New Public Management at the core of what proved to be a much-resisted and relatively unsuccessful programme of reform (Leishman et al, 1995). Police forces, notably the Metropolitan Police, were also seeking to improve their relationships with the public as various indicators suggested deepening levels of mistrust and antagonism between the police and at least some sections of the public (Heward, 1994). Especially in the case of the Met, this involved worsening relations with Afro-Caribbean sections of the London public, especially young black men. Questions of both canteen culture racism and what the Macpherson Inquiry (Secretary of State, 1999) into the Met's investigation of the murder of Stephen Lawrence was later to call institutional racism were issues of continuing concern.

In this period, the question of consumers and customers tended to focus on what might be described as front-line handling of citizen encounters, such that a greater focus was placed on customer care and customer satisfaction (Heward, 1994, pp 246–7). This immediately raises – in a sharper form than most other public services – questions about who is the consumer/customer of policing. It will be evident that embodying the rule of law (and the power of the state) in the 'office of the constable' establishes the possibility of uncomfortable or even antagonistic relations between the police and citizens. The institutional and occupational predisposition of the police has been to distinguish between the law-abiding and the villains, or the respectable and the rough (Westmarland, 2001). In such framings, are customers merely the 'law-abiding' or 'respectable' citizens who have complaints or wish to report becoming victims, or does the customer identity extend to those who consume police services unwillingly? For example, in 1992 Sir John Woodcock, Her Majesty's Chief Inspector of Constabulary, argued that 'The abusing husband, the foul drunk, the lager lout and the belligerent squatter are customers. … Different but equally as much customers as the victims of crime, the frightened child, the tourist asking the time' (Campbell, 1992, p 1, quoted in Heward, 1994, p 250).

The focus on the consumer or customer as an individual engaged in encounters with public services tends to conceal questions about the relationship between the service and publics in a more collective sense. The police are, after all, intimately concerned with matters of public order (maintaining the Queen's peace and so on) in ways that presume a collective consumption of their work. Often this collective consumer is local – in the UK policing has never been unified as a national system. The street, the neighbourhood, the community remain as critical locations in public, political and professional debates about policing (Flanagan, 2008) and are recurrently summoned up in two powerful linked images – the popular enthusiasm for local foot patrols ('the bobby on the beat') and the film/TV figure of Sergeant Dixon (Dixon of Dock Green) – as the high-water mark of English policing.

New Labour, consumerism and public service reform

In New Labour's eyes, public services needed reform to bring them into line with defining characteristics of the modern world. This conception of modernity was a powerful organising theme in New Labour discourse: it defined a sense of time, constructed New Labour's 'newness', disarmed criticism ('old thinking') and linked questions of the nation's future to its place in a modern world (Finlayson, 2003; Clarke and Newman, 2004). In New Labour's discourse of modernity, globalisation had changed the economy and the forms and habits of work that were appropriate, having an impact on gender roles and patterns of family or household formation. Importantly for public services, Britain was seen as having become a 'consumer society' in which a proliferation of goods and services enabled a wide variety of wants and needs to be satisfied. This everyday experience of 'changing expectations and aspirations' was a crucial theme in many calls for public service reform, including policing:

> No institution, be it a private business, voluntary association or public service, can be immune to the changes in British society. The pace and scope of change – to the way we work, to our family life, and to how we live – present a huge range of challenges to all public services. Added to these demographic and technological changes is a rise in people's expectations and aspirations for their services. So the police service, as with all public agencies, has been and must carry on addressing the need for continuing modernisation and reform. (Home Office, 2003, foreword by David Blunkett)

This narrative of social change was a regular feature of New Labour policy documents about public services (eg OPSR, 2002). They typically treated public services in a generic way, even though the specific dynamics of reform varied between services (Clarke et al, 2007; Needham, 2007). Most of the headline examples celebrated by New Labour were drawn from education (especially the policy of parental choice of school inherited from the Conservatives); but also from 'patient choice' in healthcare, and, increasingly, the combination of independence and choice in adult social care (Clarke et al, 2006). Policing was more closely articulated to a rather different set of concerns – around antisocial behaviour, community safety and reducing crime and the fear of crime (see, inter alia, Burney, 2005; Crawford, 2006; Hughes, 2006). Nevertheless, the separation was not complete: for example, in a speech defending the policy of choice in public services in 2004, the then prime minister added the 'law-abiding citizen' to a list of more familiar users of public services:

> In reality, I believe people do want choice, in public services as in other services.... We are proposing to put an entirely

different dynamic in place to drive our public services; one where the service will be driven not by the government or by the manager but by the user – the patient, the parent, the pupil and the law-abiding citizen. (T. Blair, quoted in *The Guardian*, 24 June 2004).

As we will see, identifying the user/consumer/customer of policing is a little problematic. The focus above on the 'law-abiding citizen' is thoroughly in keeping with New Labour's enthusiasm for hard-working, decent people and the need to put their interests closer to the heart of the criminal justice system. This view elaborated a series of distinctions – between the law-abiding and the criminal; between 'decent people and the perpetrator' of antisocial behaviour (Burney, 2005, p 36). From the late 1980s the police were subjected to numerous managerialist pressures 'to make them more business-like', and were discursively represented as 'deliverers of a professional service (rather than a force)' (Loader, 1999, pp 375–6). New Labour connected this orientation to demands for a more responsive and 'customer friendly' service to those who might have once been referred to as 'scumbags' or 'scroates' (Westmarland, 2001):

> response officers have an important ambassadorial role. They are often the first and only point of contact with members of the public, and the impression they leave is crucial … this report advocates better internal communication and customer care training to help soften the impact of poor quality contacts with the police's 'customers'. (Her Majesty's Chief Inspector of Constabulary, 2001a, paras 4.7–4.9)

Alongside the push for consumerist approaches to victims and perpetrators has been a continued pressure towards greater internal efficiency and organisational modernisation. Police services were now also expected to engage in new forms of partnership working around the theme of community safety, and subjected to new systems of performance management and modernisation. But such customer-focused orientations coexisted uncomfortably with a more general orientation towards communities as collective customers, linking older practices of local policing to the contemporary theme of community safety (Hughes and Edwards, 2002):

> Firstly, we want to revive the idea of community policing, but for a modern world. That means a big increase in

uniformed patrol on our streets but linked to 21st century technology – to make sure they have the biggest possible impact on crime and the public's fear of crime. ... And we'll give local communities a real say in deciding the priorities for the new neighbourhood policing teams. (T. Blair, Prime Minister's Foreword in Home Office, 2004).

This has remained a strong commitment, but often compounded with other modernising imperatives. So, for example, the recent Flanagan Report argued that:

> Embedding a customer service and citizen focused approach to policing, including embedding neighbourhood policing and community engagement, is therefore crucial, and should lead to greater public involvement (including information about crimes etc) and fewer complaints and calls for redress or change, including to and from national government. In turn, this should then allow the police more freedom to adopt 'a risk aware' approach so as to be able to take more sensible and thought through risks without losing the confidence of the communities they serve. (Flanagan, 2008, p 84)

In this extract we can trace an elision of citizens, consumers, customers and communities in the discursive repertoire used to construct the 'modernisation' of policing. The Flanagan Report constantly makes use of the multiplying strategy in which customers, citizens, neighbourhoods and communities can all be aggregated without disjuncture. In practice, customers, citizens, neighbourhoods and communities may exist in more troubled and antagonistic relationships (see also Hughes, 1998).

'It's not like shopping': consumerism, choice and policing

Other chapters in this book have used a table derived from Le Grand (2007) to explore the changing mechanisms and dynamics of choice in public services. This works less well in the context of policing (possibly revealing its social policy/welfare derivation), as shown in Table 9.1.

In our study of citizen-consumers, fieldwork conducted in 2003–04 revealed both police officers and users of police services to be deeply uncomfortable about the imagery of consumer choice. This was true for all the services we studied and centred on a view that using

Table 9.1: Le Grand's dimensions of choice in policing

Dimension	Classic welfare state	Conservatives (1979–97)	New Labour (1997–)
Choice of provider (where?)	None	None, but note the expansion of private security services	None, but note the continued growth of private security services
Choice of professional (who?)	None	None	None, but note the personalisation of local beat officers
Choice of service (what?)	None	None (except for contracted policing and public order services – sports events, retail malls etc)	None (except for contracted, including residential areas). But much emphasis on neighbourhood, community and local partnerships discussing services
Choice of appointment time (when?)	None	None, although managerial pressure on improving response times	None, although managerial pressure on response times and reassurance policing
Choice of access channel (how?)	Limited	Limited	Limited, but addition of non-emergency telephone numbers to supplement – and divert from – 999

public services is 'not like shopping' (Clarke, 2007). But it took on a particular weight in relation to policing, as the following interview extracts indicate:

> 'We think the thing is ... that the public actually as a rule have to take the service that they get, they can't actually go out and say, we don't actually like the way [Local Force] Police do this so I'm going to see if we can phone through and get [Neighbouring] Police to come and do it, because on such and such scales they deal with my type of incident in a far better way.'
>
> *(New Town Police senior 02)*

> '[S]ome of the actual business around consumerism, there's difficulty in transferring it from one arena to another ... you know, squaring up to somebody in a situation where they don't want to talk to you as opposed to somebody selling them a tin of beans or trying to sell even double glazing.'
>
> *(New Town Police senior 01)*

Large-scale commercial enterprises provided models from which police officers could distinguish the 'business of policing'. In different ways, both Marks and Spencer and Tesco were used as key points of reference for establishing the problem of a consumer/customer orientation for the police:

'I think we've got a far bigger duty to our customers than that, I mean ... it is difficult in our job because ... if someone wants to make a complaint, but if I was in Marks and Spencer's it is easier to give them vouchers, £60 worth of vouchers and then they go away and say "Thank you very much" and are happy, you know, whereas sometimes I have to say "OK, I appreciate how upset you are about the way the officers dealt with that, but actually they are actually complying with the law, but we are sorry if it causes distress".'

(Old Town Police 2/3)

'I think too, that the difference for us in some ways with Tesco's is, you know, is that we have some people who are not customers by choice.'

(New Town Police 1/2)

However, other officers tried to work with the idea of the customer, in the process revealing some of the problems of identifying the customer (and the problems of limiting it to 'law-abiding citizens'):

'We don't use the term consumer or consumerism but we all have our own ideas of what it means and to me, as a senior police officer, as the Divisional Commander, I do see our key partners, and the community, as people who consume the services that we can provide.'

(Old Town Police 1/3)

'But the community, most definitely, they demand things of me, essentially to reduce crime and disorder, so they are my customer, and I need to deliver that. But in a different way, the offender who comes in through the door to the custody office, even though they have lost their liberty, they are still a customer.'

(Old Town Police 1/3)

Here we see the elusive character of the customer: the interviewee moves from 'key partners' with whom the police are engaged (other local institutions, the business community?), to the (local) community, to individuals consuming the services of the police, not as victims or complainants, but as offenders, those deprived of their liberty by the force of law.

Community policing/policing the community

Even though community has a long history as an object of government, governing *through* community is a distinctive development in recent strategies for 'governing the social' (Rose, 1999; Clarke, 2009; Cochrane and Newman, 2009). It is simultaneously the object, the site and the desired outcome of governance strategies. Such strategies aim to work on communities, to work through communities and to produce communities. The idea of community links conceptions of the nation (as a 'community of communities') with local spaces (as sites of community development, community safety and so on). It also evokes more explicitly cultural conceptions of ways of life: a nation that contains 'diverse' communities in a multicultural society.

In our study of citizen-consumers, when we asked people who they thought they were when they used public services, being a member of the local community was one of the strongly preferred options. Across the three services studied, 24% of responses selected this. But in policing, this identification accounted for 40% (Table 9.2).

Table 9.2: Who are you when you use public services?

	Health	Police	Social care	Totals
Consumer	3 (3.1%)	1 (1.6%)	0	4 (2.2%)
Customer	3 (3.1%)	1 (1.6%)	4 (22.2%)	8 (4.4%)
Patient	30 (30.9%)	0	4 (22.2%)	34 (18.9%)
Service user	23 (23.7%)	6 (9.4%)	6 (33.3%)	35 (19.6%)
Citizen	5 (5.2%)	11 (17.2%)	1 (5.6%)	17 (9.5%)
Member of the public	20 (20.6%)	19 (29.7%)	0	39 (21.8%)
Member of the local community	13 (13.4%)	26 (40.6%)	3 (16.7%)	42 (23.5%)
Totals	97	64	18	179

This identification with the local community is also reflected in the Flanagan Report's view of the public's relationship to policing:

> people are most interested in issues at the very local (their own street) level and in how they are treated. They are

not actually so concerned to participate in more formal accountability mechanisms and structures, although they feel that they should have the opportunity to do so. (Flanagan, 2008, p 83)

But as a locus of governance, community often proves both elusive and difficult to manage in practice (Clarke, 2009). First, you have to find your communities, which means facing the problem of defining the inside and outside:

> 'Wherever you live, that is your community. Wherever I live is my community and that is how they should be termed.... I think it's the most appropriate as well.... I think it's a humanistic word: "community".'
>
> *(Old Town Police staff 1)*

> 'My view is that members of the local community are those people who live and work in the community. Citizens are people from other communities who visit a local community. Everyone is a citizen and everyone is a member of a local community.'
>
> *(Old Town Police staff 3)*

Here we can see how community is elided with the local or the neighbourhood (as in neighbourhood policing), and this locality includes people who live and work there. Other people live in other communities – and may visit this one. This is a strongly *territorialised* version of community (see also Neveu, 2007) and maps, more or less conveniently, onto the territorialised organisational structure of policing. Such a territorial focus is a point of conjunction between ideas of community and the rise of two related varieties of privatisation – on the one hand, the growth of private security (from patrols to DIY security devices), and, on the other, the growth of private/gated communities (see, for example, Wakefield, 2003; Crawford and Lister, 2004 on private policing; and Low, 2003; Atkinson and Flint, 2004; and Macleod, 2004 on gated communities).

But other distinctions run across this territorial conception of community – communities are composed in complex ways:

'Policing has progressed and officers are now responsible for serving all persons from different ethnic and cultural backgrounds who have to integrate. These are all citizens and as such are members of the local community.'

(Old Town Police staff 45)

'Clearly there are limited resources which may have to cover issues in several communities at the same time, one community is unlikely to be aware of the needs or priorities of another community – yet obviously each are equally important to the individuals concerned. It is particularly difficult to ensure that the less vociferous communities get the attention that they deserve.'

(Old Town Police staff 29)

While the first extract here takes the community as a capacious spatial container in which people with different ethnic and cultural backgrounds coexist, the second one is more troubled by the multiple meanings of community in contemporary Britain (Mooney and Neal, 2009). So we can detect several communities (rather than one), which may have different needs or priorities. Communities may also be more or less 'vociferous' – with consequences for the attention they get. This points to a more troubled – and potentially antagonistic – field of relationships between communities and policing. Finally, there is a reminder – to which we will return – that other scales or levels of governing also shape the conditions and possibilities of local policing.

Talking community: the problem of voice

One problem of communities for police services is that they sometimes do know what they want – and that may differ from the professional judgement of the police, or from national priorities, or from what is possible with existing resources. One senior officer explained the problem of expectations and delivery:

'And trying if … what they actually need isn't quite what you want to deliver, try and influence either the way that you deliver or the way that they perceive their needs to match up. But most people don't actually talk about the needs, they talk about a solution…. But they come up with this solution that we want more police officers on foot and in uniform, particularly during the

> evenings, that's what I want, that's the solution. Yet we know that that won't
> actually deliver the reductions in crime that the public think it will do.'
>
> *(Old Town Police senior 03)*

This is a recurrent source of tension for the police, as public desires often conflict with professional or managerial judgements – especially around the issue of foot patrols ('the bobby on the beat'). The greater emphasis under New Labour on what became known as 'reassurance policing' (in which policing was expected to reduce the fear of crime as much as the incidence of crime) intensified this tension by giving a new legitimacy to public demands:

> The visibility of uniformed police officers on the street is a
> source of reassurance to the public – a fact that is sometimes
> understandably difficult for officers locked into a spiral of
> reactive policing to grasp. A customer-focussed Service must
> offer the services those customers demand. (Her Majesty's
> Chief Inspector of Constabulary, 2001, p 7)

In various settings, residential areas, estates or neighbourhoods have developed specific relationships with their local police – through neighbourhood forums, community safety partnerships or paying for 'supplementary services such as extra patrols' (Crawford and Lister, 2004, p 23). In one of our case study sites, the residents' group had paid for mountain bikes for the patrol officers. Some communities – or (more accurately) some people in communities – feel they have constructed excellent relationships with their local police:

> Resident 1: 'This new system they are looking at in the newspaper, where
> you can phone your local police officer, on his mobile, we've been doing it
> for 11 years.'
>
> Resident 2: '... and if we don't get a response and residents tell me I will go
> into the police station and speak to the community sergeant and he will find
> out why there is no attendance.... All I've got to do is ring the sergeant up
> and I get him, unless he is at a meeting, he'll see me immediately and ... we
> will discuss what went on and he'll "go on the swim", that's what they call it,
> and he will find out what went on.'
>
> *(Old Town Residents' focus group 1)*

Such strong relationships contrasted sharply with one of the other residents' focus groups with whom we discussed the police:

> Resident 1: 'I wanted to say that, the police surgeries they are a joke because for those few hours, they are all standing there and they talk to you like they've got this service that they are providing you with and a couple of times I've challenged them on a political front, you know you're an organisation.... They keep pushing it back on us.... They talk as if they are there but they are not. Even if you get through to them on the phone they don't provide the service people in this country need.'
>
> *(New Town Residents' focus group 1)*

This group of residents felt relatively alienated from their local police service and framed this in a larger discourse about questions of power and authority:

> Resident 4: 'That's it: there are so few bobbies on the beat and they don't have the powers. When you were young, you were afraid of the police. He'd clip you round the ear and tell your mum. Now they'll be had up for assaulting you! They have so little power.'
>
> Resident 1: 'What I don't understand ... we don't have enough money to fund the police properly but we do have armies. I don't see why they should be abroad protecting communities out there when we don't have any protection. It would take six months to clean this country up if we had a couple of army guys on the corner of each street.'
>
> *(New Town Residents' focus group 1)*

I have argued elsewhere that desires for community take place around four core themes – restoration, security, sociality and solidarity (Clarke, 2009). The above exchange takes place on the terrain of restoration and security. The first speaker recalls community dominated and disciplined by the fear of the police and laments the loss of power in contemporary policing. Community is a recurrent focus for such nostalgic/restorationist fantasies. But the articulation of questions of security is also crucial – the second comment above does interesting things with the word 'community', contrasting the perceived insecurity 'at home' with the capacity to sustain overseas 'peacekeeping' military interventions. Power and authority are reasserted in the potent image of 'a couple of army guys on each street corner'. Community is a critical element in vernacular – as well as governmental – discourse. 'Community talk' is one of the ways in which issues of social change and social order can be discussed and debated. As the next extract indicates, community also mobilises powerful images of the proper relationships between people and place:

> Resident 2: 'It is the same few families, who have no intention of fitting in and although it is not flavour of the month to bring in the racial element, small 'r', it is a fact that we have had major problems here as a group will come here and try their damnedest to turn this place into the place they have come from.'
>
> *(New Town Residents' focus group 2)*

Community is one of the ways in which relationships between people, race and place are framed (Clarke, 2009). Communities are typically imagined as composed of 'people like us': the place-based conception of community provides a strong spatial basis for talking about racialised difference. Other people come from and belong to elsewhere – the foundation for the nationalist fantasy that they 'should go back where they came from'. It is important to recognise that ideas of community have questions of belonging at their centre (on competing discourses of belonging, see Cooper, 1998). Who belongs to a community is one aspect of this. People often talk about belonging to a place or to a social/cultural grouping. Community works on a dynamic of inclusion and exclusion: 'We belong here; they belong elsewhere'. But this view of who belongs is intimately linked with ideas of *what belongs to people* because they are part of a community: access to common resources such as welfare benefits and public services, for example. This double dynamic of belonging currently brings ideas of community as place and community as 'race' together in difficult and contested ways.

Conclusion: policing, politics and power

Community provides a less-than-solid foundation for thinking about the local control or direction of policing. This chapter began by pointing to the enthusiasm for citizen-centred, customer-focused models of community or neighbourhood policing. But the community proves a rather elusive and even unreliable reference point. Communities present a number of distinctive problems as sites and modes of governance. They are frequently reluctant to appear when summoned, leaving the apparatuses and agents of government scanning the locality anxiously in search of the community – and its usable representatives. When communities do materialise, they often do so as plural, contradictory and contentious entities. Communities are also 'weakly bounded' systems: permeable and leaky. People, ideas and resources move in and out (either spatially, or in terms of affinity and attachment). One version of this is the membership question: who counts as a 'member of the community' and, indeed, who count themselves as members of the community? Governance regimes require a degree of calculability and predictability – but communities threaten to spill over the categories of calculation.

Some aspects of these problems can be seen in the Flanagan Report's anxious discussion of forms of local accountability and/or control of policing (the report was written by the former Chief Constable of the Royal Ulster Constabulary, who might be expected to have views on the relationship between locality, community and politics). The report argues that existing structures of local accountability are failing to deliver either effective public engagement (at the very local level) or transparent processes of accountability. The relationship between the public and the police encounters two difficulties as a result: one involves establishing the right level(s) of engagement and the other concerns the relationship between policing and politics. The report examines several proposals, identifying possible benefits and drawbacks. For example, the idea of directly elected commissioners evokes anxiety about dangers to the autonomy of operational/professional judgement:

> Historically we have, in the United Kingdom, generally shied away from anything that might issue even a remote threat of *politicisation* of policing. This may seem to some as too risk averse, but there must be real concerns about a single person with a *political mandate* exerting pressure that too readily conflicts with operational judgement. (Flanagan, 2008, p 89; emphasis added)

However, making local authorities responsible for policing would encounter the problem of non-matching boundaries between local authorities and police forces, and create anxiety about the control of resources: would it be necessary to 'ring-fence' policing or community safety funds so as to prevent their diversion to other purposes (2008, p 92)? Finally, designing local ('bespoke') systems carries both organisational and political risks:

> The chief drawback is this introduces yet another structure in a complicated landscape and one that may not be skilled to deliver what is required of it. Such localised arrangements may be captured by specific interests and conflict then build with the local police and the police authority. (2008, p 94; emphasis added)

These comments point to a complicated combination of a politics of scale and a politics of policing. Policing needs public input and accountability, not least to overcome problems of legitimacy. But it also needs to be insulated from politics, since politics – in different forms across these quotations – implies a conflict with professional judgement, conflicts over priorities and resources or the risk of capture by 'specific interests' (Newman and Clarke, 2009). The search for a depoliticised public is a common one, but the attempt to hold politics at bay in these ways points to an implicit claim for professional and organisational autonomy in policing priorities. This returns to what we termed the 'knowledge–power knot' in public services (Clarke et al, 2007, pp 114–20) in which professional knowledge claims are intricately intertwined with forms of power and authority. At the core of the knowledge–power knot is the assumption that professionals do, indeed, 'know best'.

In all services, these encounters between publics (individually or collectively) and service providers are fraught (eg in healthcare: see McDonald et al, 2007 on the ethical consumer, and Clarke et al, 2007, pp 130–4 on patient identity). These entanglements are reflected in conflicts and uncertainties about what to call people who use public services (citizens, clients, consumers, customers, users and even survivors, as individual categories). Sustaining these entanglements of knowledge and power has proved increasingly difficult in an era where compliance and deference to authority has been displaced by a variety of democratic and demotic dynamics – insisting on the rights of the people to come to voice; on the importance of transparency; and on the symbolic value of accountability. In our study, we found that one way of reworking the knowledge–power knot was professional and organisational investment in constructing the 'reasonable consumer' (in place of the 'unmanageable consumer') (Gabriel and Lang, 1995; Clarke et al, 2007). Such initiatives involved dialogic or educative encounters between public service organisations and their publics about what might be possible, practicable and productive. The police were no exception, except that the 'reasonable consumer' is replaced by the 'informed community':

'In some ways, we're trying to open up the debate about looking at the public as consumers and having an understanding of what their needs are, and then in return for that being able to move from being what I describe as an ill-informed community to an informed community, then you can actually have some logic to your debate with them.'

(New Town Police senior 02)

We continue to find this one of the most fascinating comments in the whole study. It may be read in several different ways. It can be seen as the calculated recuperation of police power – an informed community is one that understands the world through the eyes of the police. The community comes to be informed by its framing assumptions, calculations and propositions, with the result that the professional judgement of the police is restored as the dominant principle – albeit now buttressed by public support. The comment can be read – politically – as an anxiety about policing being 'captured' or shaped by extreme political forces with 'illogical' demands (targeting specific minority groups or excluding those who do not 'belong' to the neighbourhood, for example). Finally, it might be read as an acknowledgement of the challenges of 'working dialogically': what work needs to be done (and by whom?) to create the grounds for dialogic, deliberative or participatory approaches to policy making? This is the most optimistic reading – and points to a much larger agenda for public service reform in which informed and empowered communities might take an active part in co-producing policy and not just services (Needham, 2007).

References

Atkinson, R. and Flint, J. (2004) *The fortress UK? Gated communities, the spatial revolt of the elites and time-space strategies of segregation*, ESRC Centre for Neighbourhood Research, CNR Paper 17, Bristol: University of Bristol.

Burney, E. (2005) *Making people behave: Anti-social behaviour, politics and policy*, Cullompton: Willan Publishing.

Campbell, D. (1992) 'Police chief admits public faith shaken', *The Guardian*, 18 June.

Clarke, J. (2007) 'It's not like shopping: relational reasoning and public services', in M. Bevir and F. Trentman (eds) *Governance, citizens and consumers: Agency and resistance in contemporary politics*, Basingstoke: Palgrave Macmillan, pp 97–118.

Clarke, J. (2009) 'People and places: the search for community', in G. Mooney and S. Neal (eds) *Community: Welfare, crime and society*, Buckingham: Open University Press.

Clarke, J. and Newman, J. (2004) 'Governing in the modern world?', in D.L. Steinberg and R. Johnson (eds) *Blairism and the war of persuasion: Labour's passive revolution*, London: Lawrence and Wishart, pp 53–65.

Clarke, J., Smith, N. and Vidler, E. (2006) 'The indeterminacy of choice: political, policy and organisational dilemmas', *Social Policy and Society*, vol 5, no 3, pp 1–10.

Clarke, J., Newman, J., Smith, N., Vidler, E. and Westmarland, L. (2007) *Creating citizen-consumers: Changing publics and changing public services*, London: Sage.

Cochrane, A. and Newman, J. (2009) 'Community in policymaking', in G. Mooney and S. Neal (eds) *Community*, Maidenhead: Open University Press/The Open University.

Cooper, D. (1998) *Governing out of order: Space, law and the politics of belonging*, London: Rivers Oram Press.

Crawford, A. (2006) 'Networked governance and the post-regulatory state? Steering, rowing and anchoring the provision of policing and security', *Theoretical Criminology*, vol 10, no 4, pp 449–79.

Crawford, A. and Lister, S. (2004) *The extended policing family: Visible patrols in residential areas*, York: Joseph Rowntree Foundation.

Finlayson, A. (2003) *Making sense of New Labour*, London: Lawrence and Wishart.

Flanagan, R. (2008) *The Final Report of the Independent Review of Policing, conducted by Sir Ronnie Flanagan*, London: Home Office.

Gabriel, Y. and Lang, T. (1995) *The unmanageable consumer: Contemporary consumption and its fragmentations*, London: Sage.

Her Majesty's Chief Inspector of Constabulary (2001) *Annual Report 2000/2001*, London: The Home Office.

Her Majesty's Chief Inspector of Constabulary (2001a) *Open all hours: A thematic inspection report on the role of police visibility and accessibility in public reassurance*, London: The Home Office.

Heward, T. (1994) 'Retailing the police: corporate identity and the Met', in R. Keat, N. Whiteley and N. Abercrombie (eds) *The authority of the consumer*, London: Routledge, pp 240–52.

Home Office (2003) *Policing: Building safer communities together*, London: The Home Office.

Home Office (2004) *Confident communities in a secure Britain: The Home Office Strategic Plan 2004–08*, Cm 6287, London: The Home Office.

Hughes, G. (ed) (1998) *Imagining welfare futures*, London: Routledge/ The Open University.

Hughes, G. (2006) *The politics of crime and community*, Basingstoke: Palgrave.

Hughes, G. and Edwards, A. (eds) (2002) *Crime control and community: The new politics of public safety*, Cullompton: Willan Publishing.

Le Grand, J. (2007) *The other invisible hand*, Princeton, NJ: Princeton University Press.

Leishman, F., Cope, S. and Starie, P. (1995) 'Reforming the police in Britain: new public management, policy networks and a tough "old bill"', *International Journal of Public Sector Management*, vol 8, no 4, pp 26–37.

Loader, I. (1999) 'Consumer culture and the commodification of policing and security', *Sociology*, vol 33, no 2, pp 373–92.

Low, S. (2003) *Behind the gates: Life, security and the pursuit of happiness in fortress America*, New York and London: Routledge.

McDonald, R., Mead, N., Cheragi-Sohi, S., Bower, P., Whalley, D. and Roland, M. (2007) 'Governing the ethical consumer: identity, choice and the primary care medical encounter', *Sociology of Health and Illness*, vol 29, no 3, pp 430–56.

Macleod, G. (2004) *Privatizing the city? The tentative push towards edge urban developments and gated communities in the United Kingdom* (Final report for the Office of the Deputy Prime Minister), London: Department of Communities and Local Government (www.communities.gov.uk/ archived/publications/citiesandregions/privatizingthecity, accessed 17 June 2008).

Mooney, G. and Neal, S. (eds) (2009) *Community: Welfare, crime and society*, Maidenhead: Open University Press/Open University.

Needham, C. (2007) *The reform of public services under New Labour: Narratives of consumerism*, Basingstoke: Palgrave.

Neveu, C. (2007) 'Deux formes de territorialisation de l'engagement dans l'espace urbain', in H. Bertheleu and F. Bourdarias (eds) *Les formes de manifestation du politique*, Tours: Presses Universitaires François Rabelais.

Newman, J. and Clarke, J. (2009) *Publics, politics and power: Remaking the public in public services*, London: Sage.

OPSR (Office of Public Services Reform) (2002) *Reforming our services: Principles into practice*, London: OPSR.

Rose, N. (1999) *Powers of freedom: Reframing political thought*, Cambridge: Cambridge University Press.

Secretary of State for the Home Department (1999) *The Stephen Lawrence Inquiry* (Report of an Inquiry by Sir William Macpherson of Cluny advised by the Right Reverend Dr. John Sentamu and Dr Richard Stone), Cm 4262-I, London: The Stationery Office.

Wakefield, A. (2003) *Selling security: The private policing of public space*, Cullompton: Willan Publishing.

Westmarland, L. (2001) *Gender and policing: Sex, power and police culture*, Cullompton: Willan Publishing.

TEN

The consumer in social care

Caroline Glendinning

Introduction

Consumerism discourses within adult social care, and the corresponding development of mechanisms to facilitate consumer-type choices by service users, have arguably developed further and faster over recent years than in other public service sectors. In addition to the supply-side mechanisms and incentives put in place by successive government regimes, consumer-related developments in social care have also been energetically advocated by articulate users of social care services.

Voluntary and charitable organisations have always played an active role in the provision of social care. However, since the early 1990s successive governments have consistently promoted a market-based 'mixed economy' of social care services, funded by local authorities (and increasingly also by individuals funding their own care entirely from their own private resources) but provided by a range of charitable and for-profit organisations. The promotion of social care markets – with external providers, in contrast to the internal market of the NHS – by the Conservative governments of the 1990s reflected a firm belief in the value of competition in driving down costs and driving up quality within the public sector. There is little to suggest that similar beliefs in the role of markets do not underpin more recent New Labour policies (Glendinning, 2008).

These policy developments have intersected with demands from users of social care services. Since the early 1980s, growing dissatisfaction has been expressed, particularly by disabled people, about the inflexibility and unreliability of local authority-funded social care services. Disabled people have argued for the right to exercise choice and control over their lives by being able to have control over the support they need to live independently. This, they have argued, can be achieved by giving disabled people the cash with which to purchase and organise their own support in place of directly provided services (Glasby and Littlechild, 2006; Morris, 2006).

The current state of consumerism within social care therefore rests upon an uneasy synergy between a highly influential, articulate, 'bottom-up' user movement and the 'top-down' ambitions of successive governments to increase the penetration of market-related mechanisms into the public sector. This synergy also reflects a convergence between a civil rights or social justice discourse and a neoliberal approach (Askheim, 2005; Glasby and Littlechild, 2006; Postle and Beresford, 2006). In contrast, the more recent discourse of consumerism and choice within the NHS may reflect a greater impact of top-down policy pressures (Rankin, 2005).

The particular characteristics of social care itself may also have contributed to the early introduction of consumer-style mechanisms within the sector, ahead of other public services. This chapter will therefore first describe the distinctive nature of social care and argue that there are some very important reasons for paying attention to the exercise of choice in its provision and delivery. It will then outline the introduction and development of consumerist policies and mechanisms within the sector over the past two decades, with a particular focus on policies since 2005. In principle, these mechanisms should go some considerable way to meeting the demands of disabled and older people for greater choice and control over their social care support. However, they also raise important concerns about the nature of collectively funded services; about the balance between individual and collective responsibilities; and about the new roles of citizen-consumers. These issues will be discussed in the final section of the chapter.

Social care – the preconditions for consumerism

Social care has distinctive features that have both facilitated the progress of consumerist approaches and also shaped their impact and outcomes. These features include the fragmentation of provision between multiple charitable, non-profit and commercial organisations; and the marked blurring of boundaries between public and private funding and provision.

Voluntary and charitable organisations have always been significant players in the provision of social care, particularly the provision of more specialist services for people with particular disabilities and problems. Funding traditionally came from a mixture of charitable donations and grants from local and central governments. However, the introduction of quasi-markets within social care in the early 1990s changed this role and the nature of the relationship between the voluntary sector and the state. Quasi-markets reflected a strong suspicion on the part of the (then) Conservative government about the role of local authorities as direct providers of welfare services (Means et al, 2002) and a belief in the value of a 'mixed economy' of social care. This was facilitated by a shift to funding voluntary and charitable provision through contracts that specified tightly the types, levels and quality of services to be delivered; and the encouragement of new private and commercial service providers.

The role of for-profit and non-profit providers has grown exponentially in England since 1993. Most residential and domiciliary services, whether paid for by local authorities or through private purchase, are now provided by independent organisations. For example, by March 2006, almost three quarters of residential and nursing homes were owned by private sector providers and a further 19% by non-profit organisations (all figures from CSCI, 2006a). Independent operators therefore receive most of the estimated £3 billion spent annually by local authorities in England on residential provision (Hirsch, 2005). The residential care market has been subject to significant changes since the early 1990s as large, sometimes multinational, organisations have bought out smaller, family operators and have themselves subsequently been subject to further buyouts and takeovers. 'Residential care is now a commodity and ... is there to be traded and exploited for its surplus value like any other commodity' (Scourfield, 2007a, p 162). This commodity is purchased by local authorities on behalf of poorer clients and by users themselves with assets over a specific limit. The concentration of provision in the hands of a few large providers means that around 20% of older people in residential care live in homes owned by the 10 biggest providers, including BUPA, Southern Cross, Four Seasons and Westminster Healthcare – a trend exacerbated by the large size of many nursing homes.

In contrast, providers of domiciliary services are typically small and local. By March 2006, 4,622 home care agencies in England were registered with the Commission for Social Care Inspection. They include local authority in-house teams, voluntary or non-profit organisations, social enterprises, sole proprietors, partnerships and franchises and limited companies. The average agency provides around 500 hours of care per week, though this masks huge variations. 'Overall most of the industry still has the characteristics of a "cottage industry" dominated by small providers, many of whom are relatively inexperienced in running their own businesses' (CSCI, 2006a, p 27). The market is also unstable, with significant proportions of providers entering and leaving each year.

Public funding for social care falls far short of need. Therefore, unlike the NHS, about half of total spending on social care services comes from private sources: the means- and assets-tested co-payments required by local authorities from users of residential and domiciliary services; or the payments made by people who purchase their care services privately. Private expenditure was estimated to be £5.9 billion in 2005–06 (CSCI, 2008). However, even this significant contribution of private resources is miniscule in comparison to the volume of unpaid social care contributed 'in kind' by family and friends. According to the 2001 Census, there were about 5.2 million carers (1 in 10 of the population) in England and Wales. Of these, two thirds provided up to 20 hours of care per week to a sick, disabled or older person; 11% provided 20–49 hours' care per week; and 21% provided more than 50 hours' care per week. The value of this care across the whole UK in 2007 was estimated to total £87 billion – slightly more than the annual NHS budget for the whole of the UK.

The importance of choice in social care

Choice has been argued to be vitally important in social care. It has been argued that choice, which must be accompanied by control, is fundamental to self-determination, citizenship, social inclusion and human rights. This argument has been advanced most vigorously by disabled people (Morris, 2006), but choice over the delivery and use of services has also emerged as important for older people too (Clark et al, 2004). Wider citizenship debates assume that individuals have the capacity for free choice and that full citizenship involves the exercise of autonomy – the 'ability to determine the conditions of one's life and to pursue one's life projects' (Lister, 1997, p 16). Without choice and control, therefore, neither autonomy nor self-determination – nor, ultimately, citizenship – can be achieved. Although articulated most cogently by younger disabled people, there is nothing to suggest that the same arguments do not also apply to frail older people or to other people who rely on help from others to live an 'ordinary life'.

The capacity to exercise choice and control is also central to concepts of independence (Parry et al, 2004). Exercising choice and control does not necessarily mean performing tasks for oneself. Disabled people have unambiguously associated independence with the capacity to exercise choice and control, rather than with physical self-reliance:

> Independence does not refer to someone who can do everything themselves ... but indicates someone who is able

to take control of their own life and to choose how that life
should be led. It is a thought process not contingent upon
physical abilities. (Barnes, 1991, p 129)

Similarly, Boyle (2005, p 734) points to the distinction between
'decisional' and 'executional' autonomy and suggests that, for frail
older people, poor mental health is more likely to be associated with
constraints on the capacity to make decisions than with restrictions on
the capacity to execute those decisions independently. In this respect
the ability to exercise choice and control over daily activities may be
thought of as a 'good-in-itself' (Giddens, 2003, cited in Lent and Arend,
2004, p 7) because the enhancement of choice will, in and of itself,
increase subjective well-being.

Choice and control is important not just in relation to the timing,
content and delivery of social care and other personal support, but is
also widely acknowledged to be a desirable outcome of social care
services. The capacity to exercise choice and control over daily life is
an outcome commonly desired by older people and younger disabled
adults alike (Vernon and Qureshi, 2000). Thus, good social care and
other support services should enable their users to exercise choice and
control over a wide range of everyday activities and to fulfil the broader
roles, obligations and lifestyle choices they have made and/or aspire
to. These routines may involve considerable levels of responsibility for
others; engagement in paid employment and wider social participation;
and specific personal and domestic tasks. Arguably it is the choice and
control that is facilitated by appropriate social care that has the most
significant impact on experiences of independence, well-being and
social inclusion:

> Self-determination, which is key to disabled people's status
> as full and equal citizens, cannot be achieved without …
> the provision of necessary support; and choice and control
> over that support. (Morris, 2006, p 245)

Choice is also important in the context of the considerable power
inequalities that often pertain between the givers and receivers of social
care, particularly when this includes intimate personal help and/or
psychological support. As Morris (2006) points out, depending on
others for assistance with intimate tasks is not the same as depending
on a mechanic to service a car. While both types of dependency
demand assistance that is reliable, competent and delivered with respect,
additional vulnerabilities derive from the experience of impairment:

> It is hard to maintain adulthood or dignity in the face of being fed with a spoon, having your pads changed or your face and body washed.... To be naked is to divest oneself of protection and disguise.... Nakedness thus creates vulnerability. (Twigg, 2000, pp 45–6)

Having choice over how, when and by whom such assistance is provided is therefore crucially important in helping to redress this unequal power relationship.

Finally, Baldock points out that social care is produced and consumed simultaneously, with the distinction between producer and consumer blurred:

> in particular, the activities and response of the 'user' become part of the quality and success of the production ... the success ... of social care is therefore a collaborative project between helper and user. (Baldock, 1997, pp 82–3)

The distinctive contribution made in the production of social care by those receiving help suggests that their choices and preferences are likely to constitute an important dimension in its overall effectiveness. This latter feature of social care has proved particularly receptive to recent discourses that have advocated the active involvement of users in the co-production of services and has created new links between discourses of consumerism and citizenship. Needham, quoting Alford, defines co-production as 'the involvement of citizens, clients, consumers, volunteers and/or community organisations in *producing* public services as well as consuming or otherwise benefiting from them' (Needham, 2007, p 221; original emphasis). Moreover, the concept of co-production has been linked to the remaking of citizenship. Neither passive consumerism nor citizenship as represented by formal democratic representation any longer provides adequate 'scripts' for the public sector, it is argued. Rather, both consumerism and citizenship can be promoted by the active participation of users in the production of welfare goods and services:

> By putting users at the heart of services, enabling them to become participants in the design and delivery, services will be more effective by mobilising millions of people as the co-producers of the public goods they value. (Leadbeater, 2004, pp 19–20)

In relation to social care, more participative co-production approaches are argued to have the potential to transform relationships between professionals and service users, as they introduce new knowledge – particularly lay and user-derived knowledge – to the procurement and delivery of services (McLaughlin, 2006). Co-production is argued to introduce new incentives for providers to respond to individual demands; and new incentives for service users to optimise how the resources under their control are used in order to increase cost-effectiveness. Co-production approaches:

> create a new way to link the individual and the collective good: people who participate in creating solutions that meet their needs make public money work harder and help deliver public policy goals. Self-directed services work because they mobilise a democratic intelligence; the ideas, know-how and energy of thousands of people to devise solutions rather than relying on a few policy makers. (Leadbeater et al, 2008, p 81)

These issues will be discussed further in the final section of this chapter; the next section summarises the policy measures since the mid-1990s that have promoted consumerism in social care.

The development of consumerism in social care

As noted above, in the early 1990s the demands of disability activists and the Independent Living Movement for control over the cash resources to buy their own support coincided with the ambitions of a Conservative government committed to neoliberal social and economic policies of rolling back the welfare state. By the mid-1990s, many local authorities were circumventing the legal restrictions on giving cash payments to individuals by making indirect payments to a trust fund or third-party organisation which then passed them on to disabled individuals. The 1996 Community Care (Direct Payments) Act (implemented from April 1997) gave local authorities power to make cash payments, in lieu of services in kind, to adults aged 18 to 65 who were deemed 'willing and able' to make the necessary decisions. These direct payments could not be used to purchase healthcare or local authority services or to employ a close, co-resident relative.

Subsequently three developments have taken place in direct payments policy and practice. First, the groups of people able to receive a direct payment instead of services have been extended. From 2000, people in England aged 65-plus have been able to receive direct payments, as have carers, people with parental responsibility for disabled children and disabled 16- and 17-year-olds. Second, to encourage people to take up the direct payment option, a £9 million Direct Payment Development Fund was launched in England in 2003. The fund aimed to stimulate the development of organisations providing information and support to people wishing to use direct payments. Third, section 57 of the 2001 Health and Social Care Act made it mandatory (not just optional) for local authorities to offer direct payments to eligible individuals (that is, those eligible for social care services who consent to and are able to manage payments).

There has been extensive research on the take-up of direct payments, the very uneven patterns of take-up and the factors that appear to facilitate or hinder take-up. Despite the measures listed above, take-up of direct payments has remained low overall and also highly variable – between the different countries within the UK; between local authorities within those countries; and between different groups of social care service users. Take-up rates are highest in England and lowest in Northern Ireland. People with physical and sensory impairments have consistently had higher rates of take-up, while older people, people with learning disabilities and, particularly, people with mental health problems have much lower average take-up rates (Riddell et al, 2005; Priestley et al, 2006). There appears to be a concentration of direct payments among more severely disabled service users and among younger age groups, although no differences in levels of income or wealth are apparent, once benefit levels and age are controlled for (Leece and Leece, 2006). Local political and policy factors also appear to play a significant role (Fernández et al, 2007).

In 2005 the potential for consumerist approaches in social care took a major step forward with the publication of three policy documents. The Prime Minister's Strategy Unit (2005) report *Improving the life chances of disabled people* included a wide range of policy proposals designed to remove the barriers experienced by younger and older disabled people. Proposals included the piloting of individual budgets (IBs); these would bring together the resources from different funding streams (including local authority social care, housing-based support services, adaptations and equipment budgets) for which any individual is eligible into a single sum that could be spent flexibly according to the priorities and preferences of the individual. The IB proposal was repeated in the UK strategy for an ageing population (HMG, 2005) and in a Green Paper on adult social care (DH, 2005) which called for more opportunities for older and disabled people to exercise choice and control over how their support needs are met:

> People could have individual support to identify the services they wish to use, which might be outside the range of services traditionally offered by social care ... For those who choose not to take a direct payment as cash, the budgets would give many of the benefits of choice to the person using services, without them having the worry of actually managing the money for themselves. (DH, 2005, p 34)

The principles underpinning IBs include greater roles for self-assessment, for self-definition of needs and desired outcomes, and for self-determination of the preferred ways of meeting those outcomes. Crucially, IB users should know how much money they are entitled to, how much relevant services cost, and how they can best use the resources available to them to meet their needs – all key characteristics of an informed consumer. The proposals built on the experience of In Control, an initiative originally developed to introduce an individualised approach to funding for people with learning disabilities. In Control connects closely with the principles underpinning direct payments but has a broader aim of redesigning social care systems towards 'self-directed support' (Duffy, 2004). IBs also offer new opportunities for exercising choice and control to people who do not wish to manage a cash budget themselves but prefer instead to receive local authority-commissioned services. The principles of knowing what resources are available for an individual and how much services cost should, theoretically, apply to the choice of local authority service options as well – potentially providing an incentive for councils to match standards of personalised and individualised services that may be offered in the private sector or through cash-based mechanisms (Glasby et al, 2006).

Thirteen local authorities were selected to pilot IBs between 2006 and 2007. A rigorous evaluation of the pilots (Glendinning et al, 2008) revealed that IBs were typically used to fund personal care, help with domestic tasks and social, recreational and leisure activities. People receiving an IB were more likely to report feeling in control of their daily lives, compared with those receiving conventional social care support, although there were variations between different groups of service users – positive outcomes were greater among working-age people with physical or sensory impairments than among older people. Attempts to integrate multiple funding streams in order to increase the flexibility and choice available to an IB holder were largely unsuccessful. Moreover, within the timescale of the evaluation there was little evidence of changes in the responsiveness of local social care markets as a result of their increased exposure to individual consumer demand. Indeed, many providers were protected by their existing block contracts with local authority purchasers, suggesting that developments in consumer responsiveness may take some while to develop. Meanwhile, in December 2007 the Department of Health announced the intention of extending personalised budgets in social care across all English local authorities (DH, 2007).

Consumerism in social care – new opportunities and risks

The role of user-led and advocacy movements in transforming the nature of social care cannot be overstated (Newman et al, 2008). This section discusses the potential opportunities and risks of these new measures to promote consumer choice in social care. The actual extensiveness, depth and consequences of these opportunities and risks are as yet difficult to ascertain; discussion and empirical research have tended to focus on the positive experiences of a minority of users (Scourfield, 2007b).

New opportunities

For many people needing social care support, the opportunities for greater flexibility and the construction of personalised support arrangements are likely to be substantial. Research has already demonstrated how direct payments can significantly improve the quality of life of those using them. Research on people using personal budgets through In Control similarly reveals reports of better health and well-being; improved quality of life; greater social engagement with friends and the wider community; improvements in personal dignity and personal safety; and greater choice and control (reported in Leadbeater et al, 2008). Similar benefits have been reported by some early users of individual budgets (Rabiee et al, forthcoming).

However, requiring that active consumers of social care know the level of resources available to them also has the potential to reveal differences – between localities, between different groups of service users and between users with similar levels of impairment or need for support – in the processes by which individual resource allocations are determined and in the amounts that are available to individual disabled and older people. This is in contrast to current processes, which tend to be shaped by factors such as professional judgements; the extent to which individuals are articulate, able and willing to draw attention to their needs; the availability of family support to reduce immediate levels of risk; and the costs of the services that are actually consumed. Transparency over the amount of money in each personal budget may create new pressures from users, professionals and the public alike for greater clarity and consistency over the criteria used to allocate resources and for greater equity in the resulting allocations (Glendinning, 2007). While this transparency has not so far characterised the allocation of resources for direct payments, it is a fundamental requirement of the individual or personal budget approach.

A third potential gain is for users of social care to be able to purchase ordinary community services – lunch in the local pub rather than meals-on-wheels, a cinema trip rather than attending a special day centre – and for this to lead to greater social inclusion. Again, this is reported by users of direct payments and personalised budgets (Glendinning et al, 2000; Clark et al, 2004; Leece and Bornat, 2006; Glendinning et al, 2008; Leadbeater et al, 2008; Rabiee et al, 2008). However, these gains do not come automatically. Research in England has shown the vital importance of help with planning personalised support arrangements and with managing direct payments or personal budgets. Moreover, a review of research on self-directed support schemes in North America and Australia shows how their success also requires investment in building community capacity and mutually supportive local networks, rather than focusing solely on public service reform (Lord and Hutchinson, 2003).

Concerns and risks

The widespread extension of consumerist approaches within social care also presents risks, at least in principle. Extensive and rigorous research is needed to establish both the extent to which these risks are realised in practice and how far they can be mitigated.

First, high eligibility thresholds currently restrict eligibility for publicly funded social care to those people whose independence is at least at moderate risk. Many will have relatively low levels of economic resources and/or social capital, leading to their being relatively disadvantaged in the role of informed consumer. Some will have poor and fluctuating health; others may have profound cognitive impairments. Many may find it hard to obtain information, weigh up options or make and express choices. For example, people with learning disabilities or dementia may have difficulty in comprehending information, reduced insight into their own circumstances and reduced capacities to appraise the potential benefits and drawbacks of different options. These factors may restrict both their capacity and their willingness to behave as informed, knowledgeable and active consumers. Easy access to information for otherwise disadvantaged service users is key; however, there is little evidence that the information required by active social care consumers is provided in a consistent or meaningful way (Baxter et al, 2008a; Newman et al, 2008). Yet without comprehensive, easily accessible information, and perhaps also help with managing and editing this information, there is a risk that the potential benefits of choice will be inequitably distributed (Lent and Arend, 2004).

More generally, consumerism involves a shift of responsibility, both for managing a fixed level of resource in the form of direct payments or personalised budgets and for ensuring that this leads to agreed outcomes. Scourfield has described this process as the 'managerialisation of the self', whereby the service user takes on more of the functions, risks and responsibilities that were formerly the remit of the state. 'One wonders, though, where this leaves the sections of society that have neither the desire nor the ability to be entrepreneurial and who cannot be self-sufficient' (Scourfield, 2007b, p 119). More evidence is needed on the types of initial and ongoing information and support services that can enable the more disadvantaged consumers of social care to carry out these responsibilities, while at the same time avoiding the reintroduction of paternalistic or controlling professional power.

A second risk, also under-researched, is that consumerist pressures fail to have the expected and desired impact on the behaviours of service providers who, to a greater or lesser extent, may fail to provide the types of services that the individual purchasers of social care desire. Although a large, independent social care market now exists, with potentially far greater flexibility than that which governs the behaviours of large organisational providers in the NHS, the structures and behaviours of social care providers have nevertheless largely been shaped by the purchasing power of large local authority contractors. Consumer choice is only possible if there is an accessible and affordable supply of appropriate service options. Yet some services, for example for people with very high-level or specialised needs, may be in short supply. It is also not clear how far the shift from collective to individual purchasing may encourage providers to behave in ways that maximise their own interests. For example, some providers may provide less-than-impartial information in order to influence consumer choices; others may go further and restrict consumer choice in ways that work to their advantage (for example, through 'cream-skimming' desirable clients).There is no evidence yet of how effective individual consumers might be in creating the kinds of pressures and informational signals that are believed to characterise competitive markets (Richter and Cornford, 2007), nor of the roles that local authorities might play in aggregating and communicating individual choices to potentially responsive providers in order to provide mechanisms 'in which users and providers can discuss service provision away from the point of delivery' (Needham, 2007, p 225).Without such mechanisms, there is a risk that 'individuals will end up in competition with each other over limited resources, an obvious example being personal assistants [employed by direct payment users], who are in scarce supply' (Scourfield, 2007b, p 120). Such problems are already reported by independent domiciliary care agencies, who report tensions between themselves and individual direct payment- or IB-using employers of home care staff over the recruitment and retention of workers (Baxter et al, 2008b).

It is also not clear how far market mechanisms will adequately safeguard the quality of services. Recent policies, in social care as elsewhere, have emphasised the importance of consistency, accountability and protection against risk. It has been argued that the extension of consumerism in social care could signify a retreat from top-down, hierarchical regulatory regimes and a new investment in the power of consumers in the new social care marketplace to lever change through the ways in which they exercise choice (Newman et al, 2008).Yet there is no evidence that consumer-driven regulatory regimes in social care might be effective; and considerable evidence of the profound vulnerability of at least some groups of social care users (McCreadie, 2006).

A third risk concerns the future role of social care professionals, which may be characterised by increasing uncertainty and ambiguity. In demanding choice and control over their support arrangements, disabled people have long challenged professional attitudes and practices, arguing for the right to be viewed as the experts in their own conditions. Proponents of greater consumer choice in public services have argued that this should involve a rebalancing of relationships between producers and consumers of services. More recent advocates of co-production have similarly asserted the potential to transform power relationships between professionals and citizens. Nevertheless, at the same time social care professionals retain major gatekeeping roles in determining the allocation of resources and in approving individual plans for using a direct payment or personalised budget.These roles may involve the exercise of implicit normative judgements or the application of codified formal guidelines on what constitutes an appropriate use of publicly funded social care resources. Is the use of a direct payment or personal budget to fund aromatherapy, a football club season ticket or an internet broadband connection appropriate? In extreme instances, social care professionals retain the capacity to curtail individual choice if it is believed that harm to a vulnerable individual may result.

Co-production models are also argued to involve the valorisation of front-line staff expertise that has developed through repeated interaction with service users (Needham, 2007). Yet the behaviours of front-line staff are at the same time shaped by wider organisational constraints and pressures and these can encourage the development of 'street-level bureaucracies' that reflect a profound lack of sympathy with the interests of service users (Ellis, 2007). By failing to acknowledge the continuing power inequalities between the state, its employees and the users of social care, consumerism masks the 'double dynamics of power ... who identifies legitimate demands/needs; who allocates resources and priorities and who gets to exercise what sorts of choice?' (Clarke et al, 2007, p 251).

Consumerism also risks commodifying and privatising social and collective responsibilities for care. In some respects, these particular risks are no different in respect of social care than in respect of other public welfare goods; they involve threats to the 'publicness' of public services (Clarke et al, 2007) – the commitment to recognising and acting in the wider public interest. However, largely relocating social care from a collective, social domain to the realm of private consumption also fails to acknowledge the common, shared circumstances – particularly illness and advanced age – in which needs for social care most often arise. It also undermines arguments for an 'ethics of care' – the body of theory built upon the positive valuation of women's role in caring that characterised early feminist writing, that has argued for an extension to the public sphere of the virtues and activities involved in care. Tronto (1993), for example, argues that the values associated with care need to be recognised as providing a set of principles about responsibility for the well-being of others that should shape both public and private life. Further, if public policies fail to recognise and support these responsibilities, those involved in providing care to people who are in some way dependent also, it is argued, risk serious threats to their social citizenship (Kittay, 1999).

Conclusions

Driven by the demands of disabled people and other users of social care for greater choice and control over their support arrangements, consumerist mechanisms have existed within social care for some time. Table 10.1 summarises the evolution of these mechanisms, using Le Grand's (2007) dimensions.

The diverse, fragmented, 'mixed economy' that characterises social care quasi-markets should, in theory, provide fertile ground for competition and the exercise of choice between different providers. However, judging from the limited demand for direct payments to date, structural and cultural features of local authority social care services, combined with apparent resistance on the part of potential consumers, appear to have limited the actual practice of consumerism.

However, new policy initiatives – the piloting of individual budgets and the commitment to extend personalised approaches across all English adult social care services – herald a concerted effort to extend the scope of consumerism. Significant changes are now envisaged in who exercises that choice, as the balance of responsibilities for purchasing shifts from block contracting by local authorities to individual budget holders. Like direct payments, these new policies also adopt market exchanges as the method for exercising choice and control – an apparent confusion between the desire for self-direction and '"market populism" .... Choice is good – choice is exercised in the market through exchange – choice in public services needs market-mimicking mechanisms' (Clarke et al, 2007, p 248). It remains to be seen whether the market will in fact respond to these newly empowered consumers; whether the risks associated with the individualised purchase and consumption of services are outweighed by the benefits; and how far the distinctive features of social care, as a normatively infused set of relationships and exchanges that are prompted by difficult personal circumstances, are ultimately compatible with private market transactions.

Table 10.1: Le Grand's dimensions of choice applied to social care

Dimension	Classic welfare state	Conservatives (1979–97)	New Labour (1997–)
Choice of provider (where?)	Local authority in-house services for most people; voluntary/charitable providers for minority (especially with specialist needs)	Until 1993, free choice of residential care funded by individual purchase or social security payments; home care services still largely in-house	Choice of home care services restricted to agencies with local authority contracts; choice made by care managers
		1993 choice of residential care providers with local authority contracts, free choice for self-funders; home care services still largely in-house	Direct payments and individual budgets devolve choice of provider to individual user
Choice of professional (who?)	No choice – local authority staff only	No choice – local authority or private sector care workers	Direct payments take-up promoted and individual budgets introduced, both allow users to recruit and employ their own care workers
		1997 direct payments allow users to recruit and employ their own care workers	
Choice of service (what?)	No choice – type and content of services determined by professional assessment/judgement	No choice – type and content of services determined by professional assessment/judgement	Direct payments allow limited choice over content of service
		1997 direct payments allow (limited) choice over content of service	Individual/personal budgets offer greater choice over type/ content of service
Choice of appointment time (when?)	Limited choice	Limited choice over timing of in-house or independent-sector home care services	Limited choice over timing of in-house or independent-sector home care services
		1997 direct payments allow choice over timing of service	Direct payments/ individual budgets allow choice over timing of service
Choice of access channel (how?)	Local authority professional 'gatekeeping'	1993 local authority professional 'gatekeeping' role increased	Local authority professional 'gatekeeping' role maintained with direct payments/individual budgets
Choice of additional services	Only available for private purchasers	Only available for private purchasers/top-up of local authority-funded provision	Only available for private purchasers/top-up of local authority-funded provision

References

Askheim, O.P. (2005) 'Personal assistance – direct payments or alternative public service: does it matter for the promotion of user control?', *Disability and Society*, vol 20, no 3, pp 247–60.

Baldock, J. (1997) 'Social care in old age: more than just a funding problem', *Social Policy and Administration*, vol 37, no 1, pp 73–89.

Barnes, C. (1991) *Disabled people in Britain: A case for anti-discrimination legislation for disabled people*, London: British Council of Organisations of Disabled People.

Baxter, K., Glendinning, C. and Clarke, S. (2008a) 'Making informed choices in social care', *Health and Social Care in the Community*, vol 16, no 2, pp 197–207.

Baxter, K., Glendinning, C., Clarke, S. and Greener, I. (2008b) *Domiciliary care agency responses to increased user choice: Perceived threats, barriers and opportunities from a changing market*, Social Policy Research Unit, York: University of York.

Boyle, G. (2005) 'The role of autonomy in explaining mental ill-health and depression among older people in long-term care settings', *Ageing and Society*, vol 25, no 5, pp 731–48.

Clark, H., Gough, H. and Macfarlane, A. (2004) *'It pays dividends': Direct payments and older people*, Bristol: The Policy Press.

Clarke, J., Newman, J. and Westmarland, L. (2007) 'The antagonisms of choice; New Labour and the reform of public services', *Social Policy and Society*, vol 7, no 2, pp 245–54.

CSCI (Commission for Social Care Inspection) (2006a) *Time to care? An overview of home care services for older people in England*, London: CSCI.

CSCI (2006b) *The state of social care in England, 2005–06*, London: CSCI.

CSCI (2008) *The state of social care 2007*, London: CSCI.

DH (Department of Health) (2005) *Independence, well-being and choice. our vision for the future of social care for adults in England*, Cm 6499, London: DH.

DH (2007) *Putting people first: A shared vision and commitment to the transformation of adult social care*, London: DH.

Duffy, S. (2004) 'In control', *Journal of Integrated Care*, vol 12, no 6, pp 7–13.

Ellis, K. (2007) 'Direct payments and social work practice: the significance of "street-level bureaucracy" in determining eligibility', *British Journal of Social Work*, vol 37, pp 405–22.

Fernández, J.L., Kendall, J., Davey, V. and Knapp, M. (2007) 'Direct payments in England: factors linked to variations in local provision', *Journal of Social Policy*, vol 36, no 1, pp 97–121.

Giddens, A. (2003) 'Introduction: Neoprogressivism; a new agenda for social democracy', in A. Giddens (ed) *The progressive manifesto*, Cambridge: Polity, pp 1–34.

Glasby, J. and Littlechild, R. (2006) 'An overview of the implementation and development of direct payments', in J. Leece and J. Bornat (eds) *Developments in direct payments*, Bristol: The Policy Press, pp 19–32.

Glasby, J., Glendinning, C. and Littlechild, R. (2006) 'The future of direct payments', in J. Leece and J. Bornat (eds) *Developments in direct payments*, Bristol: The Policy Press, pp 269–84.

Glendinning, C. (2007) 'Improving equity and sustainability in UK funding for long-term care: lessons from Germany', *Social Policy and Society*, vol 6, no 3, pp 411–22.

Glendinning, C. (2008) 'Increasing choice and control for older and disabled people: a critical review of new developments in England', *Social Policy and Administration*, vol 42, no 5, pp 451–69.

Glendinning, C., Halliwell, S., Jacobs, S., Rummery, K. and Tyrer, J. (2000) *Buying independence: Using direct payments to integrate health and social services*, Bristol: The Policy Press.

Glendinning, C., Challis, D., Fernández, J.-L., Jacobs, S., Jones, K., Knapp, M., Manthorpe, J., Netten, A., Stevens, M. and Wilberforce, M. (2008) *Evaluation of the Individual Budgets Pilot Programme: Final Report*, Social Policy Research Unit, York: University of York.

Hirsch, D. (2005) *Facing the cost of long-term care*, York: Joseph Rowntree Foundation.

HM Government (2005) *Opportunity age: Meeting the challenges of ageing in the 21st century*, London: Department for Work and Pensions.

Kittay, E.F. (1999) *Love's labour: Essays on women, equality and dependency*, New York, NY: Routledge.

Leadbeater, C. (2004) *Personalisation through participation: A new script for public services*, London: Demos.

Leadbeater, C., Bartlett, J. and Gallagher, N. (2008) *Making it personal*, London: Demos.

Leece, J. and Bornat, J. (eds) (2006) *Developments in direct payments*, Bristol: The Policy Press.

Leece, D. and Leece, J. (2006) 'Direct payments; creating a two-tiered system in social care', *British Journal of Social Work*, vol 36, pp 1379–93.

Le Grand, J. (2007) *The other invisible hand*, Princeton, NJ: Princeton University Press.

Lent, A. and Arend, N. (2004) *Making choices: How can choice improve local public services?*, London: New Local Government Network.

Lister, R. (1997) *Citizenship: Feminist perspectives*, Basingstoke: Macmillan.

Lord, J. and Hutchinson, P. (2003) 'Individualised support and funding; building blocks for capacity building and inclusion', *Disability and Society*, vol 18, no 1, pp 71–86.

McCreadie, C. (2006) 'The mistreatment and abuse of older people and the new UK national prevalence study', *Journal of Care Services Management*, vol 1, no 2, pp 173–9.

McLaughlin, E. (2006) '"Pseudo-democracy and spurious precision": knowledge dilemmas in the new welfare state', in C. Glendinning and P.A. Kemp (eds), *Cash and care: Policy challenges in the welfare state*, Bristol: The Policy Press, pp 235–48.

Means, R., Morbey, H. and Smith, R. (2002) *From community care to market care?*, Bristol: The Policy Press.

Morris, J. (2006) 'Independent living: the role of the disability movement in the development of government policy', in C. Glendinning and P.A. Kemp (eds) *Cash and care: Policy challenges in the welfare state*, Bristol: The Policy Press, pp 235–48.

Needham, C. (2007) 'Realising the potential of co-production; negotiating improvements in public services', *Social Policy and Society*, vol 7, no 2, pp 221–31.

Newman, J., Glendinning, C. and Hughes, M. (2008) 'Beyond modernisation? Social care and the transformation of welfare governance', *Journal of Social Policy*, vol 37, no 4, pp 531–57.

Parry, J., Vegeris, S., Hudson, M., Barnes, H. and Taylor, R. (2004) *Independent living in later life: Research review carried out on behalf of the Department for Work and Pensions*, Research Report 216, London: Department for Work and Pensions.

Postle, K. and Beresford, P. (2006) 'Making connections; supporting new forms of engagement by marginalised groups', in C. Glendinning and P.A. Kemp (eds) *Cash and care: Policy challenges in the welfare state*, Bristol: The Policy Press, pp 235–48.

Priestley, M., Jolly, D., Pearson, C., Riddell, S., Barnes, C. and Mercer, G. (2006) 'Direct payments and disabled people in the UK: supply, demand and devolution', *British Journal of Social Work*, Advance Access, published 19 July 2006.

Prime Minister's Strategy Unit (2005) *Improving the life chances of disabled people*, London: Cabinet Office.

Rabiee, P., Moran, N. and Glendinning, C. (forthcoming) 'Individual budgets: lessons from early users' experiences', *British Journal of Social Work*.

Rankin, J. (2005) *A mature policy on choice*, London: Institute for Public Policy Research.

Richter, P. and Cornford, J. (2007) 'Consumer relationship management and citizenship: technologies and identities in public services', *Social Policy and Society*, vol 7, no 2, pp 211–20.

Riddell, S., Pearson, C., Jolly, D., Barnes, C., Priestley, M. and Mercer, G. (2005) 'The development of direct payments in the UK: implications for social justice', *Social Policy and Society*, vol 4, no 1, pp 75–85.

Scourfield, P. (2007a) 'Are there reasons to be worried about the 'cartelization' of residential care?', *Critical Social Policy*, vol 27, no 2, pp 155–80.

Scourfield, P. (2007b) 'Social care and the modern citizen: client, consumer, service user, manager and entrepreneur', *British Journal of Social Work*, no 37, pp 107–22.

Tronto, J. (1993) *Moral boundaries: A political argument for an ethic of care*, London: Routledge.

Twigg, J. (2000) *Bathing: The body and community care*, London: Routledge.

Vernon, A. and Qureshi, H. (2000) 'Community care and independence: self-sufficiency or empowerment?', *Critical Social Policy*, vol 20, no 2, pp 255–76.

ELEVEN

Differentiated consumers? A differentiated view from a service user perspective

Peter Beresford

Introduction

Discussion and developments relating to 'the public service consumer' have been constants of growing significance since the late 1970s. This chapter focuses on this issue from the perspectives of people as long-term users of health and social care services. This large group, which includes older and disabled people, mental health service users, people with learning difficulties and others, is one for whom the discourse about the consumer in public services has major ramifications. Yet this discourse is not one in which they can be said to have played a central part, albeit, as we shall see, that they have been enlisted as actors within it.

A key aim of this chapter is to explore both their responses to public service consumerism and the frameworks which they have employed in developing both their own individual and collective identities and actions in relation to public policy and services. I have described this contribution as from a 'service user' perspective because this is a crucial part of my perspective as the author. There is no suggestion that this is the only view that might be offered from a service user's perspective, although the discussion does draw on a wide range of service users' views and discussions.

The role of social policy

A key concern of recent social policy, both in the UK and more generally, has been to develop a changed, more active relationship with welfare users. Yet, so far, social policy texts have had relatively little to say about welfare users. They have paid little (in some cases, no) attention to their perspectives and discourses. In some cases, though, these discourses are far advanced, for example in the case of the disabled people's movement. There is now a range of movements associated with welfare service users, including those of older people, mental health service users/survivors, people with learning difficulties, people living with HIV/AIDS.

Yet, if we take a range of widely used social policy textbooks, discussion of and references to service users, their movements and their critiques are generally very limited or non-existent. It was not until 2008 that the UK Social Policy Association specifically addressed the issue of welfare service users in its student's companion (Beresford, 2008). Yet at the same time, over the last 20 or so years, there has been a growing recognition of the importance of exploring social divisions and issues of diversity in social policy (Williams, 1989; Lavalette and Pratt, 2006). However, this enquiry has barely developed in relation to welfare service users (Beresford, 1997). On the other hand, the social policy literature has paid considerable attention to shifts in the *supply* of welfare provision. This has been true from the emergence of 'welfare pluralism' in the early 1970s, to the pressure for a shift to market supply under the political New Right and the remix of state and private supply and funding under New Labour (Beresford, 2008).

Marian Barnes is one author who has explored the idea of the public service consumer in relation to a group of long-term health and social care service users – mental health service users. She compared groups and organisations of mental health service users and of disabled people (people with physical and sensory impairments). She distinguished between the strategies and approaches of the two, seeing that of mental health service users as based on 'consumerism' and that of disabled people as based on 'citizenship' (Barnes and Shardlow, 1996). In a later book, she again explored the collective action of these two groups in the context of conceptual issues relating to ideas of consumerism and citizenship. However, this time the same distinction was not drawn (Barnes et al, 1999).

Issues of terminology

For me, as someone actively involved in the mental health service user/ survivor movement (and also the broader disabled people's movement), her discussion raises interesting issues about the employment by mental health service users and their organisations of consumerist rhetoric, terminology and ideas. These have frequently been adopted uncritically, as symbols of a determination to speak and act for themselves, by individuals and groups who are not necessarily familiar with their ideological associations or connotations. People's use of such language, the language of 'choice', consumption, purchase of service, market research and the equivalence of mainstream goods and services, may be the only framework for expression to which they have been exposed and with which they are familiar.

There are broader problems with terminology in the field of service user movements and it may not always be wise to interpret its use at face value. There is little agreement about language in this field (Beresford, 2005a). For example, 'service user' is a term frequently used and it will be used here, but it is disliked by many. The proliferation of descriptions and self-descriptions in current use, for example, of mental health service users – consumer, sufferer, service user, survivor, recipient, mad – is testimony to the uncertainties involved. A term like 'disabled person' is valued by many with physical and sensory impairments, but others, including mental health service users and older people, do not necessarily see themselves as disabled people, even if they may be counted as such for policy purposes. Who uses the language is also important. While some mental health service users may seek to reclaim the term 'mad', they are likely to be critical of its popular pejorative use in the media. Language is thus a minefield, and it would be unwise to place too much reliance on external attempts to impose meanings on it.

Differentiation

The differentiation of groups can be used as a means of highlighting divisions between them. In this way, for instance, universalist policies may be presented as partial and inequitable. Thus, in 2008 the right to free bus travel for over-60s was extended to cover all local bus services in England. But the view of one newspaper letter-writer was that this resulted in:

> The rest of us … picking up the tab. The price is the loss of services and amenities traditionally provided by local authorities … for the benefit of the whole community, not just one particular group. (Salt, 2008)

However, as another correspondent replied: 'who picked up the tab for his childhood immunisation and his education?' (Bigwood, 2008).

For service users, the creation of their own organisations and movements based on their differentiation according to their welfare identity, can be seen as an attempt to *overcome* rather than reinforce such divisions. This issue was highlighted in the context of disability in the 1970s. Campaigning on disability issues had been dominated by traditional disability organisations led by non-disabled people. Newly organising disabled people argued that this had misrepresented their rights and needs, encouraged their exclusion from campaigns and the development of policies and philosophies which did not necessarily reflect their aims and objectives (Campbell and Oliver, 1996). They rejected what they saw as the unhelpful prevailing paternalistic model of outside 'experts' identifying and interpreting issues and offering their own solutions to them, relying on 'public education' to bring about change. A crucial example of this was the heated debate that took place between Peter Townsend, the poverty academic, and members of the Union of Physically Impaired Against Segregation (UPIAS, 1975). This represented a key challenge to the construction of disabled people in terms of their poverty.

Anti-poverty, regeneration and other grassroots and community development policies and practices have also come in for criticism for failing to include, on equal terms or in leadership roles, the groups whose rights and needs they place centre stage (Beresford and Croft, 1995). This has, crucially, been true of welfare service users (Hoban and Beresford, 2001; Beresford and Hoban, 2005). Groups of long-term service users, beginning with disabled people, have thus differentiated themselves and highlighted their particular identities in order to take control of activities undertaken in their name and to play an active and equal role in politics, campaigning and policy.

Differentiated, yes – but consumers?

While members of service user movements have clearly sought to differentiate themselves on the basis of identity, their relationship with consumerism demands much closer examination. If we are to gain a better understanding of the values and ideologies underpinning movements of welfare service users, like the disabled people's and mental health service users'/survivors' movements, we are likely to achieve it by examining their development and histories more closely. From the last quarter of the twentieth century onwards, this can be expected to have much to tell us about a number of key contemporary issues operating in politics and public policy, including:

- the tensions between consumerism and democratisation;
- the theory and practice of participation at a time when it has become the setting for such tensions to be worked through;

- the role of service users and their movements as participants and agents in this process.

The disabled people's movement

The UK disabled people's movement developed in the late 1960s and early 1970s out of the carefully documented efforts of some disabled people to escape from institutionalised residential living (Campbell and Oliver, 1996). While it might not be appropriate to characterise the UK disabled people's movement as 'separatist', it has certainly deliberately developed its own agenda, and for a long time has placed much more emphasis on *independent* development than on partnership approaches. Thus it focused on developing its own alternative approaches to policy and provision, and setting up its own, user-controlled organisations (or 'centres for independent living') rather than on primarily seeking to improve and reform existing services (UPIAS, 1977; Campbell and Oliver, 1996; Oliver, 1996). Early on, it developed a clear theoretical and philosophical base both for how it would work and what its goals would be. These are the 'social model of disability' and the philosophy of 'independent living'.

The social model of disability distinguishes between perceived individual impairment – that is to say, the loss or impaired function of a limb, sense or bodily function – and disability – which is taken to mean the societal barriers, oppressions and discriminations that may then be experienced by people with such impairments. Thus, disability is no longer conceived solely as a matter of individual or personal incapacity requiring a traditional medicalised, individualistic response. The social model of disability should not be oversimplified and needs to be understood as a dynamic and developing approach (Crow, 1996; Thomas, 2007). Following from it, the philosophy of independent living challenges traditional understandings of disabled people as inherently dependent and instead posits that to live on as equal terms as possible to non-disabled people, disabled people should be ensured both the support that they need and access to mainstream services and society. The disabled people's movement has achieved major changes in policy and legislation, including the mainstreaming of 'direct payments' to offer people control over their own support as well as anti-discrimination legislation. The social model of disability has become a basis for public policy and the philosophy of independent living has been adopted formally as an objective of UK government policy (Office for Disability Issues, 2008). While it is not easy to measure its influence, and causal relationships are notoriously difficult to prove, the disabled people's movement has been linked with significant cultural and attitudinal change towards disabled people, even if much more remains to be done.

The mental health service users'/survivors' movement

The modern mental health service users'/survivors' movement in the UK developed later, in the 1980s, although precursors involving supportive allies can be traced back earlier (Campbell, 1996). It cannot be said of it, with any confidence, that it has had a major impact on policy and legislation. Instead, as disability legislation in the UK, for example, has increasingly focused on rights and a social model approach, mental health legislation – and this is an international development – has tended to prioritise new restrictions on service users' rights, as happened with the 2007 Mental Health Act. Fundamental differences can be seen between the survivors' and the disabled people's movement. The strategy pursued by the mental health service users'/survivors' movement has been significantly different from that of the disabled people's movement. It has followed much more from a partnership model. Activity has mainly been concentrated in the mental health/ psychiatric system, within its structures and requirements for 'user involvement'. Most of the effort and energy of those mental health service users who become involved has been focused on reforming traditional mental health services. Much of the involvement of mental health service users has been related to the service, policy and practice system(s) rather than to their own agendas. Much of the funded activity of mental health service users/survivors has been in non–user-controlled voluntary and statutory organisations.

Significantly, the best-known campaigning and most radical of the national service user/survivor organisations established in the 1980s, Survivors Speak Out, was an early casualty, losing funding and external support. While some mental health service users/survivors have taken a more radical and separatist position, developing their own initiatives rather than acting in partnership with professionals (O'Hagan, 1993; Mad Pride, 2000), this has not been the main thrust of activity. The approach advocated by the American survivor and activist Judy Chamberlin, doing things 'On Our Own', has been the exception rather than the rule in the UK (Chamberlin, 1988).

Nor has the survivors' movement developed explicit philosophies or theories comparable to those of the social model of disability or independent living developed by the disabled people's movement, even though there can be no question that its members are generally critical of the dominant medicalised individual model operating in the psychiatric system.

But it would also be a mistake to suggest that there is not a set of shared values and beliefs underpinning the survivor movement. The survivor movement and its associated organisations are very conscious of 'the social' in their thinking and activities. Service user/survivor discourses address both material and spiritual issues; the personal as well as the political. However, this still has not led to the widespread development of any equivalent of the social model of disability. There are signs that there is a wariness about doing this, for fear both of imposing another orthodoxy and of coming in for attack for being seen as denying people's personal difficulties and distress (Beresford, 1999; Beresford and Campbell, 2004).

What the movements have in common

If we also include for consideration organisations and movements of other service user groups, for example, older people, people with learning difficulties, people living with HIV/AIDS, the picture becomes even more complex and heterogeneous, with groups having different histories, cultures and traditions. Yet, while the survivors' and disabled people's movements can be shown to have a number of significant differences, they and these other movements of long-term users of health and social care also seem to have some important things in common. All highlight the importance they attach to:

- service users speaking and acting for themselves;
- working together to achieve change;
- having more say over their lives and the support that they receive;
- challenging stigma and discrimination;
- having access to alternatives to prevailing medicalised interventions and understandings;
- the value of user-controlled organisations, support and services;
- a focus on people's human and civil rights and their citizenship – this has emerged later, but is increasingly evident for the survivors' movement;
- being part of mainstream life and communities, able to take on responsibilities as well as secure entitlements. (Beresford and Harding, 1993; Campbell, 1996)

It would be very difficult to see this as a consumerist agenda. This would be true whether it was understood in general terms of the dominance of the market, conventional exchange relationships and purchase of service, or more specifically in relation to current policy making, in terms of quasi-markets and consumer-centred models of decision making, as compared to those based on notions of citizenship and 'publicness' (Needham, 2007). Instead, it is much more clearly concerned with people's desire to be self-determining and to achieve change, individually and collectively, as both means and ends of their action. One thing that we can say is that all these service user groupings seem to have paid serious attention to their own identity, and have generally sought to challenge existing external definitions of who they are and to reshape and reclaim their identity. Significantly, in seeking to do this, none of them has sought to define themself in what might be seen narrowly or broadly as consumerist terms. Instead, as we will shortly see, they have been more often conceived in terms of being liberatory or new social movements. Service users, particularly activist service users, tend not to see themselves as 'consumers'. This is not to say that they may not fit within some understandings of the concept developed by sociologists of consumption (for example, Gabriel and Lang, 2006). However, such discussions have tended not to be ones that service users and their organisations are either part of or familiar with.

Unpicking two related developments

It is helpful at this stage to remember that, over the period that service user movements were emerging in the UK and beyond – the last quarter of the twentieth century – there were *two* distinct but interrelated developments taking place. This can help us to make better sense of the philosophies of these movements and their relationship with consumerism, as well as some of the reasons why and the ways in which these have been different from consumerism. One of these developments was the emergence of the service user movements, but the other, much more visible and much more often a subject for comment, was a shift to the Right in international politics and economics.

The shift to the political Right

The shift to the political Right of the 1970s was given impetus by temporary economic recession, but its influence on both politics and public policy has remained strong ever since. While it found early expression in the UK and the US, it has had much broader international consequences on public policy, having a global influence through the operation of the US, World Bank and International Monetary Fund. With it came a constellation of ideas that have transformed the role and status of the welfare service user. The new political Right, exemplified by the politics of Margaret Thatcher in the UK, disliked state expenditure and intervention, seeing them as inefficient, burdensome and damaging to wealth creation. The state was regarded as an inefficient provider of services, centralising and bureaucratic in tendency. Now the private market and private finance were seen as more appropriate and efficient ways of making provision. Welfare provision, beyond safety-net provision, was also seen as potentially unhelpful, creating dependency and perpetuating a destructive and disaffiliated 'underclass'. Whereas the 'welfare state' was previously presented as a positive, now being a 'welfare state user' was framed in negative terms.

Community care, the policy most central to long-term health and social care service users, became an advance guard for the political Right's shift to the market in the UK (Means et al, 2003). Now most services were to be provided by the 'independent' rather than the state sector. Instead of access to support being based on need, it now increasingly rested on payment for service, based on an exchange relationship. This, like the shift to the market in public policy more generally, was presented in terms of market rhetoric. Now the individual was not to be treated as a passive recipient of public services but as an active customer or consumer, with an emphasis on 'choice', a new emphasis on formal bureaucratic 'quality standards' and the increasing imposition of new regulatory mechanisms to meet requirements for public accountability. Nor did the consumerism of the political Right end with its decline in power. While presented as 'the third way', the politics of New Labour and its international equivalents has maintained the rhetoric of consumerism, underpinned by a managerialist/consumerist approach to policy and provision which continues to be based on a strong role for the market and private sector (Giddens, 1998). The use of market rhetoric, however, did come in for adverse criticism. Service users argued that being a compulsory patient in the psychiatric system or being taken into state care as a child or young person were not comparable with an individual 'consumer' purchasing goods and services. To frame such situations and experiences in terms of 'choice, voice and exit', as some commentators and policy makers did, had little meaning for potentially 'involuntary consumers'. Nonetheless, the language of choice, consumption and being a 'customer' were the terms in which public service use, including use of health and welfare services, was increasingly framed.

Service user movements

The service user movements, however, were never primarily framed in these terms by those who developed and joined them. As we have seen, their concerns were with challenging their negative identities, speaking and acting for themselves, and living on more equal terms in mainstream society (Beresford, 1999; Beresford and Campbell, 2004). Thus, they are not readily conceived of as consumerist movements. There has, however, been some discussion of the kind of movements they might be. A number of social theorists identified the emergence in the late twentieth century of a wide range of groups which they conceived of as 'new social movements', including those of environmentalists, minority groups and welfare recipients (Touraine, 1981; Oliver, 1996). Characteristics associated by theorists with a new social movement include that:

- they remain on the margin of the political system;
- they offer a critical evaluation of society;
- they imply a society with different forms of valuation and distribution;
- the issues which they raise transcend national boundaries. (Oliver, 1996, p 157)

Some disabled commentators have described the disabled people's movement as such a new social movement (Oliver and Zarb, 1989; Davis, 1993). Others have seen the disabled people's movement as a liberatory movement. Tom Shakespeare, for example, has distinguished between post-materialist and liberation movements and argued that the disability movement belongs to the latter category (Shakespeare, 1993; Oliver, 1996, p 158). Discussion about the nature of other movements, like that of mental health service users and people with learning difficulties, is less developed, but significantly, in day-to-day discussion, those involved in them often identify with other new social movements, like the women's, black people's and lesbian, gay, bisexual and transgender movements.

The emergence of user involvement

The two developments which have so far been discussed, the shift to the political Right and the market, and the emergence of service user movements, have one key characteristic in common. Both have had a concern with user involvement which, over the last 25 to 30 years, has emerged as a key issue in social and public policy. In the UK, for example, there are now increasing requirements for user involvement – whether framed as public, patient or service user involvement or 'engagement' – in planning, policy, practice, research and evaluation. This increasingly operates across policies, at local and national levels.

This can be and sometimes is seen as a factor unifying the two developments under discussion. But it may also actually be seen as confusing them and mistakenly encouraging the association of service user movements with consumerism. Indeed, user involvement, in both practice and theory, can be seen as a battleground for the working through of the conflicts that exist between different, competing values and ideas of consumerist and democratic, rights-based ideologies.

Both service users and their movements and market-driven consumerist politics have had reason to be interested in user involvement. For the former, it is clearly associated with the desire for self-determination. For the latter, it closely relates to the rhetoric of the consumer actively involved in influencing the market and choosing goods and services. But what it is crucial to do is not to conflate the different ideologies underpinning these goals and aspirations.

When we look more closely at user involvement two distinct approaches can be identified (Hickey and Kipping, 1998; Beresford, 2005b). First is the managerialist/consumerist approach to user involvement, with its ideological origins in the political Right and the market. Framed mainly in market terms and developed by state and service systems, it has so far mainly been based on consultative models of involvement, operating as a kind of intelligence-gathering/market research activity. It has primarily been concerned with garnering information and seeking to incorporate the public and service users.

Second is the democratic or empowerment approach to involvement that has been developed by service users, their organisations and allies. This has been concerned with redistributing power, increasing user involvement in decision making and bringing about broader social change, so that service users are able to exert more control over their own lives and can have more say in agencies, organisations and institutions which impact upon them. These are very different approaches which should not be confused with each other.

Service users' organisations and movements primarily value getting involved as a means of effecting change. This is the repeated message when they are asked. It is to achieve such change that service users respond to calls and initiatives to become involved (Turner and Beresford, 2005; Branfield et al, 2006). As we have seen, particularly in relation to the disabled people's movement, there is a major concern with achieving people's citizenship rather than with consumer rights. The emphasis has been on involvement to equalise their civil and human rights (Oliver, 1996). A strong altruistic impulse can be detected here. Yet much of the user involvement on offer is based not on a democratic model, but on a managerialist/consumerist model of involvement operating through consultation and market research. As a result, for many service users it can feel like little more than tokenism or a 'box-ticking' exercise (Beresford, 2005b; Stickley, 2006).

Service users as agents in a consumerist world

Thus the models of involvement of service users and those of the state and service systems tend to be aiming and pushing in different and conflicting (if sometimes temporarily overlapping) directions. This is by no means always explicit, although more radical service users, particularly members of the disabled people's movement, have regularly articulated this view. As we have seen, though, user involvement and opportunities for user involvement have been key to service user movements' efforts to bring about change. What this essentially means is a constant process of these movements seeking to turn the opportunities that involvement offers to their own democratic advantage, rather than accepting them on the consumerist terms on which they may be offered. This, of course, is a complex and frequently difficult task. However, service users and their organisations have to operate in societies and structures where, consistently over time, the dominant pressures at work have been for large-scale political and economic change which prioritises the role of the market and state rather than the rights and needs of groups facing particular barriers and discrimination. Service users have sometimes come in for criticism from, or been misread by, those critical of the consumerist market-driven approach, who see them as either colluding with or at the mercy of it. While this may be true in some cases, of course, their main concern has been significantly different. As Oliver and Barnes have helpfully observed of the disabled people's movement, what it has succeeded in doing has been to develop a discourse that is counter to the dominant discourse in politics and social policy (Oliver and Barnes, 1998).

This highlights the importance of seeing service users and their organisations as agents in this process, rather than as mere ciphers reacting to the politics, policy provisions and participatory arrangements around them. For them, the rhetoric of involvement and choice has served as a window of opportunity to work so as to take forward their own liberatory and democratising goals. It is unlikely to be a coincidence that the large-scale emergence of their movements has coincided with such economic and political changes. The latter have offered some supportive and helpful conditions for their advancement – the emphasis on consumption, the 'rights' of the consumer and the litany of 'choice'. Of course, there have been other pressures operating in a different direction; those which have been concerned with restricting state expenditure, increasingly requiring citizens to make their own individualised and market-based arrangements for their welfare and which require increasing reliance on families and other close individuals to act as their unpaid 'carers'. But it would be wrong, as a superficial inspection might suggest, to assume that, because service users and their organisations are operating in a consumerist situation and sometimes consumerist settings, they are necessarily going along with these. What is more often likely to be the case is that they are working within and yet in opposition to consumerist policies and provisions.

Direct payments: a case study

The development of direct payments for disabled people offers a helpful case study to clarify this. The disabled people's movement pioneered direct payments as a means of supporting independent living by putting people in control of the support they accessed, through receiving a cash payment which they could spend as they wished in order to put together the support package of their own choice (Zarb and Nadash, 1994; Hasler et al, 2000; Hasler, 2004). Such direct payments were long opposed in the UK by trade unions like UNISON, as well as by traditional left-of-centre commentators, as representing an individualising, consumerist approach, commodifying need, which would undermine the provision of collective public services. This ignores the reality critiqued by disabled people, that such public services historically tended to be of inferior quality, stigmatising, segregating and unaccountable to service users. Their model of direct payments was linked with the empowering philosophy of independent living and included a key role for the collective involvement of service users and their organisations in providing an infrastructure of support to enable all disabled people to access such a service with the information, advocacy and advice that they required. This is very different from a consumerist model of service provision, and based clearly on the liberatory philosophy underpinning the social model of disability and the values of independent living.

However, what can also be seen from this case study is the way in which the empowering philosophy of direct payments can be and has in some cases been undermined by the way in which payments have been implemented by local authorities. Concerns about 'over-policing' and over-bureaucratisation within inappropriate cost limits have been highlighted by service users and identified by researchers (Glasby and Littlechild, 2002; Leece and Bornat, 2006).

Towards new forms of involvement and action

Not only have the service user movements not been tied to consumerist thinking, but they have also explored and developed new and different forms of democratic involvement and action. It should be remembered that a key trigger for their setting up of their own organisations and movements was that they had been left out of or subordinated in much traditional collective and grassroots action, campaigning, politics and developmental work. Their exclusion can be explained by two factors. First, there does not seem to have been any recognition that their involvement was necessary or possible. Their devalued status, the low value and expectations placed upon them and the apparent preference of non-disabled groups and constituencies to speak and act on their behalf, all contributed to this. But second, and no less important, was the fact that dominant forms of organising, acting and collectivity were frequently inaccessible to them. 'Counter-politics' and 'grassroots' forms of organising were essentially based first on inclusion in the workforce, and then on dominant meeting, speaking and written forms of activity. Service users have been marginalised groups, significantly, excluded from the workforce and often without such skills, capacities and experience.

For this reason, an early distinction that the disabled people's movement drew was between organisations *for* – that is to say, organisations controlled by non-disabled people who traditionally had spoken for them – and the need to create organisations *of* – that is to say, their own disabled people's organisations, under their own control. While traditional organisations for disabled people had been differentiated on the basis of *individual impairment*, for example, for people with cerebral palsy, visual impairments or muscular dystrophy, disabled people began to organise on the basis of *disability*, that is to say, the discriminatory societal reaction that they collectively experienced (Campbell and Oliver, 1996).

Whereas in traditional collective action and organising a distinction has tended to be drawn between self-help and mutual aid activities, and campaigning and change activities, in the service users' movements these activities have tended to be unified. How else would people who had been institutionalised, segregated, had received inferior education and other opportunities, who have physical, sensory or intellectual impairments, be able or equipped to become involved at all effectively? Thus the disabled people's movement emphasised that its concern was with both empowering the individual and securing broader social change, seeing collective self-organisation as the most effective means to both (Campbell and Oliver, 1996; Oliver, 1996).

The importance of empowerment

It is for this reason, perhaps, that empowerment has been a central concept for service users and their movements, despite frequent criticisms that it is a vague and devalued idea. The concept of empowerment came to prominence in the civil rights struggles of black Americans in the 1960s. Its importance for the service user movements is that it brings together and unifies issues of personal and social change. It recognises that only service users themselves can be the source of their empowerment, even if others, including professionals, can support them to achieve it. Critically, it makes clear that personal and social development and change are closely interrelated and that the chances of achieving the latter are compromised without addressing the former. Similarly, focusing on personal empowerment in isolation from issues of broader change comes to be recognised as limited and inadequate (Beresford and Croft, 1995; Jacks, 1995; Shera and Wells, 1999).

A key means to personal empowerment as a basis for wider collective action is *capacity building*. This has become a key concept for service users and their organisations, not least because of the high levels of isolation and disempowerment that they report experiencing (Branfield et al, 2006). This can be achieved through:

* raising people's expectations;
* providing information to increase their awareness and understanding of what is available and possible;

- skill development to become involved in existing ways of working as well as challenging these by developing their own ways of doing things;
- developing service user trainers and educators to do this, establishing 'training for user trainers' programmes and courses. (Beresford and Croft, 1993; Branfield et al, 2006)

An example of innovation

Shaping Our Lives, the independent, UK-based, national user-controlled organisation and network, offers a helpful case study of the innovative approaches of service user movements to organising (see www.shapingourlives.org.uk). Shaping Our Lives was first established in 1996, with a focus on increasing the say and involvement of service users and improving the quality of their lives and the support they receive. It works at national policy level with government as well as with non-statutory organisations, and has close links with local service user organisations. Unlike many service user organisations, it is made up of and works across a wide range of user groups, including people with physical and sensory impairments: deaf people, people with learning difficulties, mental health service users/survivors, older people, people living with HIV/AIDS, people with drug and alcohol problems, users of palliative care services and young people with experience of living in state care. In this way it seeks to avoid arbitrarily excluding people by conforming to the service system's administrative categorisation of people according to its bureaucratic construction of user groups.

Shaping Our Lives has placed an emphasis on inclusion in both its process and its objectives in two distinct but related ways. First, it seeks to work in ways that enable as full and equal involvement as possible. Shaping Our Lives has learned from its own and other people's work that there is a range of groups who tend to be particularly marginalised where collective action and user involvement are concerned. Sometimes called 'hard to reach' groups, they may better be seen as groups facing particular additional barriers and exclusions. They include, for example:

- members of black and minority ethnic communities
- people who do not communicate verbally or in English as their first language
- people with multiple impairments
- people seen as having profound impairments
- homeless people and travellers

- people in the criminal justice system
- refugees and asylum seekers.

There are other groups too. What Shaping Our Lives has learned is that if you are serious about involving *all* service users, then very determined efforts need to be made to access and include such groups. A wide range of supports needs to be put in place to make this possible. Different ways of working are likely to be needed. Shaping Our Lives has developed an access policy and practice to ensure equal involvement which places an emphasis on the need for:

- physical access
- communication access
- cultural access.

To put this in place needs time, effort, commitment, skills and funding. Without doing this, collective action and involvement are likely only to reflect and perpetuate dominant barriers and exclusions.

There is also another key dimension of diversity to address. As yet, what has been highlighted is the inclusion of different groups of service users. Equally important is the need to work for inclusion so as to challenge exclusions related to age, gender, ethnicity, sexuality, belief, class, culture and so on. Shaping Our Lives has worked hard to do this, both in the composition of its management group and the national user group from which this is elected, and in its activities and focus.

One of the criticisms often made of service users' organisations and movements is that involvement in them tends to be restricted to a narrow and 'unrepresentative' range of activists, often called 'the usual suspects'. A large-scale national research and development project currently being undertaken by Shaping Our Lives and supported by the Department of Health, entitled 'Developing diverse involvement: Getting beyond "the usual suspects"', highlights both the barriers to broad-based involvement and ways of overcoming them. Significantly, service users identify as one of the groups who face particular barriers to becoming involved those regarded as the 'usual suspects', who, because of the skill, confidence and experience they have developed in getting involved, are prepared to challenge local and national state organisations and services.

Ways forward

It may be helpful, by way of conclusion, to highlight two key ways in which service users seem to be moving forward.

Key areas for involvement

In the late 1980s and early 1990s, when user involvement began to be embodied in government legislation and guidance, the emphasis was on user involvement in planning services and in individual 'comment and complaints' procedures. This reflects the dominant consumerist agenda. Since then, service users have developed their own priorities for involvement, consistent with their commitment to increasing their say and control and securing their human and civil rights. These include:

* involvement in professional education and training through developing service user trainers to change the culture of welfare and its organisations (Levin, 2004);
* involvement in developing quality standards and outcome measures, to ensure that prevailing policy emphasis on quality and performance indicators is more strongly based on 'user-defined' measures and measurement (Shaping Our Lives et al, 2003);
* involvement in occupational and professional practice, so that the understanding and construction of occupational practice becomes a joint project between service users and workers (Beresford et al, 2007);
* developing user-controlled services and support, at individual level, through the development of self-directed support schemes (like direct payments), and through the expansion of collective user-controlled services (Barnes and Mercer, 2006);
* involvement in research and the development of user-controlled research, so as to equalise research relationships and prioritise empowerment and the generation of broader change as key goals of research alongside the creation of new knowledge (Turner and Beresford, 2005).

The second key issue beginning to be highlighted by service users is the need to form alliances and develop new relationships and solidarity. At first this has been reflected in the desire to form links between different service user movements, and there has been growing interest in this. Even more recently, there have begun to be pleas to develop links with other groups, notably with service workers, carers and now also with those movements based on difference in terms of gender, sexuality, ethnicity, culture and belief (Beresford and Croft, 2004; Campbell, 2008) with which many service users feel they can identify. The emphasis, again, is on democratisation, but now – out of the original impetus for differentiation – is emerging an interest in exploring ways of increasing strength and solidarity through the recognition of common causes.

References

Barnes, C. and Mercer, G. (2006) *Independent futures: Creating user-led disability services in a disabling society*, Bristol: The Policy Press.

Barnes, M. and Shardlow, P. (1996) 'Effective consumers and active citizens: strategies for users' influence on service and beyond', *Research, Policy and Planning*, vol 14, no 1, pp 3 –38.

Barnes, M., Harrison, S., Mort, M. and Shardlow, P. (1999) *Unequal partners: User groups and community care*, Bristol: The Policy Press.

Beresford, P. (1997) 'The last social division?: Revisiting the relationship between social policy, its producers and consumers', in M. May, E. Brunsdon and G. Craig (eds) *Social Policy Review 9*, London: Social Policy Association, pp 203–226.

Beresford, P. (1999) 'Making participation possible: movements of disabled people and psychiatric system survivors', in T. Jordan and A. Lent (eds) *Storming the Millennium: The new politics of change*, London: Lawrence and Wishart, pp 34–50.

Beresford, P. (2005a) '"Service user": regressive or liberatory terminology?', *Disability & Society*, vol 20, no 4, pp 469–77.

Beresford, P. (2005b) 'Theory and practice of user involvement in research: making the connection with public policy and practice', in L. Lowes and I. Hulatt (eds) *Involving service users in health and social care research*, London: Routledge, pp 6–17.

Beresford, P. (2008) 'Welfare users and social policy', in P. Alcock, M. May and K. Rowlingson (eds) *The student's companion to social policy*, (3rd edn), Oxford: Blackwell Publishing, pp 259–66.

Beresford, P. and Campbell, P. (2004) 'Participation and protest: mental health service users/survivors', in M.J. Todd and G. Taylor (eds) *Democracy and participation: Popular protest and new social movements*, London: Merlin Press, pp 326–42.

Beresford, P. and Croft, S. (1993) *Citizen involvement: A practical guide for change*, Basingstoke: Macmillan.

Beresford, P. and Croft, S. (1995) 'It's our problem too! Challenging the exclusion of poor people from poverty discourse', *Critical Social Policy*, Issue 44/45, Autumn, pp 75–95.

Beresford, P. and Croft, S. (1995) 'Whose empowerment? Equalising the competing discourses in community care', in R. Jacks (ed) *Empowerment in community care*, London: Chapman and Hall, pp 59–73.

Beresford, P. and Croft, S. (2004) 'Service users and practitioners reunited: the key component for social work reform, the future of social work', Special Issue, *British Journal of Social Work*, vol 34, pp 53–68, January.

Beresford, P. and Harding, T. (eds) (1993) *A challenge to change: Practical experiences of building user led services*, London: National Institute for Social Work.

Beresford, P. and Hoban, M. (2005) *Effective participation in anti-poverty and regeneration work and research*, York: Joseph Rowntree Foundation.

Beresford, P., Adshead, L. and Croft, S. (2007) *Palliative care, social work and service users: Making life possible*, London: Jessica Kingsley.

Bigwood, A. (2008) 'Crack the code, letters and emails', *The Guardian*, 8 April, p 33.

Branfield, F. and Beresford, P. with Andrews, E.J., Chambers, P., Staddon, P., Wise, G. and Williams-Findlay, B. (2006) *Making user involvement work: Supporting service user networking and knowledge*, York: Joseph Rowntree Foundation/York Publishing Services.

Campbell, J. (2008) *Fighting for a slice or for a bigger cake? Moving from identity politics to consensus action*, The Sixth Annual Disability Lecture, Cambridge: University of Cambridge, 29 April.

Campbell, J. and Oliver, M. (1996) *Disability politics: Understanding our past, changing our future*, London: Routledge.

Campbell, P. (1996) 'The history of the user movement in the United Kingdom', in T. Heller, J. Reynolds, R. Gomm, R. Muston and S. Pattison (eds) *Mental health matters: A reader*, Basingstoke: Macmillan in association with the Open University, pp 218–25.

Chamberlin, J. (1988) *On our own: Patient controlled alternatives to the mental health system*, London: Mind.

Crow, L. (1996) 'Renewing the social model of disability', *Coalition*, July, Manchester: Greater Manchester Coalition of Disabled People, pp 5–9.

Davis, K. (1993) 'On the movement', in J. Swain, V. Finkelstein, S. French and M. Oliver (eds) *Disabling barriers: Enabling environments*, London: Sage in association with the Open University, pp 312–20.

Gabriel, Y. and Lang, T. (2006) *The unmanageable consumer* (2nd edn) London: Sage.

Giddens, A. (1998) *The third way: The renewal of social democracy*, Cambridge: Polity Press.

Glasby, J. and Littlechild, R. (2002) *Social work and direct payments*, Bristol: The Policy Press.

Hasler, F. (2004) 'Direct payments', in J. Swain, S. French, C. Barnes and C. Thomas (eds) *Disabling barriers: Enabling environments* (2nd edn) London: Sage, pp 219–25.

Hasler, F., Zarb, G. and Campbell, J. (2000) *Implementing direct payments: Findings and policy issues*, London: Policy Studies Institute.

Hickey, G. and Kipping, C. (1998) 'Exploring the concept of user involvement in mental health through a participation continuum', *Journal of Clinical Nursing*, no 7, pp 83–8.

Hoban, M. and Beresford P. (2001) 'Regenerating regeneration', *Community Development Journal*, vol 36, no 4, pp 312–20, October.

Jacks, R. (ed) (1995) *Empowerment in community care*, London: Chapman and Hall.

Lavalette, M. and Pratt, A. (eds) (2006) *Social policy: Theories, concepts and issues* (3rd edn), London: Sage.

Leece, J. and Bornat, J. (eds) (2006) *Developments in direct payments*, Bristol: The Policy Press.

Levin, E. (2004) *Involving service users and carers in social work education*, Resource Guide no 2, London: Social Care Institute for Excellence.

Mad Pride (2000) 'Direct approach', *Open Mind*, no 106, Nov/Dec, p 18.

Means, R., Richards, S. and Smith, R. (2003) *Community care: Policy and practice* (3rd edn), Basingstoke: Palgrave Macmillan.

Needham, C. (2007) *The reform of public services under New Labour: Narratives of consumerism*, Basingstoke: Palgrave.

Office for Disability Issues (2008) *Independent living: A cross-government strategy about independent living for disabled people*, London: The Stationery Office.

O'Hagan, M. (1993) *Stopovers on my way home from Mars: A Winston Churchill Fellowship report on the psychiatric survivor movement in the USA, Britain and the Netherlands*, London: Survivors Speak Out.

Oliver, M. (1996) *Understanding disability: From theory to practice*, Basingstoke: Macmillan.

Oliver, M. and Barnes, C. (1998) *Disabled people and social policy: From exclusion to inclusion*, Harlow: Longman.

Oliver, M. and Zarb, G. (1989) 'The politics of disability: a new approach', *Disability, handicap and society*, vol 4, no 3, pp 221–40.

Salt, R. (2008) 'Blazing a trail on a free bus pass, letters and emails', *The Guardian*, 7 April, p 31.

Shakespeare,T. (1993) 'Disabled people's self-organisation: a new social movement?', *Disability, Handicap and Society*, vol 8, no 3, pp 249–64.

Shaping Our Lives National User Network, Black User Group (West London) Ethnic Disabled Group Emerged (Manchester) Footprints and Waltham Forest Black Mental Health Service User Group (North London) and Service Users'Action Forum (Wakefield) (2003) *Shaping our lives – From outset to outcome:What people think of the social care services they use*,York: Joseph Rowntree Foundation.

Shera,W. and Wells, L.M. (eds) (1999) *Empowerment practice in social work: Developing richer conceptual foundations*, Toronto: Canadian Scholars' Press Inc.

Stickley, T. (2006) 'Should service user involvement be consigned to history? A critical realist perspective', *Journal of Psychiatric and Mental Health Nursing*, no 13, pp 570–77.

Thomas, C. (2007) *Sociologies of disability and illness: Contested ideas in disability studies and medical sociology*, Basingstoke: Palgrave Macmillan.

Touraine,A. (1981) *The voice and the eye:An analysis of social movements*, Cambridge: Cambridge University Press.

Turner, M. and Beresford, P. (2005) *User controlled research: Its meanings and potential*, Final report, Shaping Our Lives and the Centre for Citizen Participation, Brunel University, Eastleigh: Involve.

UPIAS (1975) *Fundamental principles of disability*, London: Union of the Physically Impaired Against Segregation.

Williams, F. (1989) *Social policy: A critical introduction*, Cambridge: Polity.

Zarb, G. and Nadash, P. (1994) *Cashing in on independence*, Derby:The British Council of Disabled People.

TWELVE

Authoritative consumers or experts by experience? User groups in health and social care

Marian Barnes

Introduction

The neoliberalism of Margaret Thatcher and her successors has had a profound effect on conceptualisations of the relationship between those who provide health and social care services and those who use them. The reinvention of clients and patients as welfare consumers was intended as one way of subjecting public services to the assumed discipline of the market. If people behaved more like active consumers than passive clients, then, it was argued, this would force services to become more responsive. Politically, the Left was found wanting in terms of its capacity to resist the power of this consumerist rhetoric, not least because welfare services were also under critique from very different quarters for their unresponsiveness and paternalism (Deakin and Wright, 1990). It was not possible simply to defend the existing state of affairs, and consumerism came to be linked with the empowerment of public service users. The mantra of choice appeared to unite those who wanted to dismantle public provision and replace it with the private sector, and service users who were angry and frustrated by their inability to receive services of the type they wanted when they wanted.

The embracing of consumerism by New Labour – albeit in hybrid form along with other projects such as the crafting of more responsible citizens (Clarke et al, 2007; Clarke and Newman, 2007) – indicates the strength of the Thatcher legacy and the extent to which, in practice, relationships between producers and consumers of welfare have shifted. But this does not mean that consumerism offers the most appropriate way of understanding the identities of those who use health and social care services, or the solution to paternalistic welfare provision. I argued against this in 1990 (Barnes et al, 1990) and I see little reason to change my mind. In this chapter I revisit and develop my arguments.

Revisiting choice

The equation of consumerism with the 'empowerment' of service users underpins the strength of the consumerist discourse. It is a claim that continues to be made in the context of the 'personalisation' agenda and the introduction of individual budgets as the preferred model for the delivery of social care (and other) services (Leadbeater et al, 2008). But it is a hollow claim and one that disregards the context and nature of service use in many instances. David Prior and I considered and rejected the potential of consumerism as a route to empowerment on this basis (Barnes and Prior, 1995). We suggested that the following conditions of public service use interact to affect the priority attached to choice and the extent to which it is experienced as empowering:

- coercion – the extent to which seeking to use a service represents a positive decision;
- predictability – the extent to which it is possible to anticipate what that service will be like prior to use;
- frequency – whether service use is one-off, ongoing or a regular aspect of people's lives;
- significance – the importance of the service in affecting the quality of the user's life;
- participation – the extent to which receiving a service requires the active engagement of the service user.

We also went on to suggest that:

1. Use is often compelled by circumstances, people often have little real option about *whether* to make use of services, and use is made at times of particular vulnerability. Thus, although coercion only applies in particular circumstances (eg following child protection or vulnerable adult procedures) it often feels as if there is little choice other than to seek help.
2. It is difficult to find out in advance what services will be like – you have to experience them to really know this. Service use therefore scores low in terms of predictability prior to use.
3. Service use is frequent if not continuous. Users can develop considerable expertise in relation to services and what works for them.

4. Services are likely to play a very significant part in people's lives, affecting basic capacities to function on a day-to-day basis. Hence, getting it right is very important.
5. Many services require the active engagement and cooperation of the user, thus participation is high.

The first two conditions suggest that exercising choice at the point of entry is very difficult, while the other conditions suggest that choice or co-decision making will be important during the course of ongoing service use. That distinction is certainly evident in the responses of service users. Campaigning by disabled people and others has been directed towards ensuring greater accountability of public services rather than arguing for an expansion in the market (Barnes, 1999). Service users have sought greater control over and participation in decision making about the services they receive on a regular basis. The inability to choose who provides personal and often intimate care, at what time services are provided (including what time you can get up and go to bed), or how services are provided (for example, going shopping with someone rather than having shopping done for you), have been significant factors influencing campaigns for direct payments and have led to the adoption of 'personalisation' and individual budgets as the way forward for social care provision across the board (Department of Health, 2005).

What people value about such schemes is precisely the sense of being in control, being able to live their lives the way they want to. But this is rather different from a concept of choice as 'shopping around' within a service marketplace and trusting in the market to ensure quality of provision. It could also be argued that those who have campaigned for direct payments have sought to give up their identities as *consumers* and instead to become *employers* of their own personal assistants. Their relationship with personal assistants is not that of a consumer of services provided by someone else, but that of an employer defining and supervising the work to be done by another. The emphasis on being 'in control', in the context of the expansion of individual or personal budgets, is conceived as turning on their head existing relationships between those who provide and those who use services (Leadbeater et al, 2008). The person receiving services is not a consumer but a planner, purchaser and sometimes employer of those providing support.

What people are really concerned about is the quality of the ongoing relationship with those who provide services and the capacity to negotiate and reach joint decisions about this – a process understood as 'co-production' (Needham, 2008). They are looking for a relationship with someone who offers them respect, a relationship that has continuity, which is based in trust and security, enables people to realise their aspirations, or to live their final months with dignity. While those who have had little experience of being able to choose may initially value the act of choosing per se, ultimately it is the value attaching to the quality of the service that is most important rather than the act of choosing (Clarke and Newman, 2007).

There are some situations in which service use is a collective rather than an individual experience. Relationships between service users attending day centres or living in residential accommodation can be as important as the formal service in determining satisfaction. Users receive both support and friendship from others in a similar position to themselves. There is a danger that promoting individual choice and enhancing individualised solutions can undermine the collective experience of building relationships with other service users. Groch (2001) has demonstrated how deaf culture and consciousness developed from the 'spaces of autonomous action' within segregated schools. User-controlled autonomous action has enabled mental health service users and others to propose their own analysis and solutions (Barnes and Bowl, 2001). Rather than seek a greater range of choices between providers, citizens and service users have collectively worked to improve the opportunity for *voice* to influence services and increase accountability of providers to users. They have recognised the increased potential for influence that comes from acting together, as well as the intrinsic value of coming together with people in similar circumstances (Barnes and Bennet, 1998).

Authoritative consumers

Choice is not the only dimension of consumerism, and Keat et al's (1994) work adopts a rather broader perspective on changing social relations between producers and consumers. They note that the notion of a consumer as someone who purchases commodities in a marketplace does not adequately address the 'character of relations between consumers and producers' (p 2) and they introduce the notion of consumer 'authority' as a way of understanding what might be at stake in reconceptualising this relationship. Nicholas Abercrombie (1994) addresses the 'collapse of authority' and situates the debate about the distribution of authority between producers and consumers in this context. This sociological analysis of the relationship between authority and power – for Weber authority is legitimate power – addresses the way in which expertise can be the basis for sustaining the legitimacy of an authority relationship. Thus, for example, psychiatrists claim particular expertise in diagnosing and treating mental illness, and this gives them the authority to exercise power over those they have thus diagnosed, determining not only how they will be treated medically, but also applying a diagnosis that has considerable significance in constructing broader social relationships. A clinical diagnosis can lead to other identities, such as 'nutter' or 'loony', that have considerable impact on all aspects of people's lives.

Abercrombie identifies other ways in which authority is maintained, in addition to through the exercise of expertise:

- *Deference*. The doctor–patient relationship is a prime example of this.
- *Taboo*. Boundaries cannot be crossed without serious consequences – what would happen if the loonies took over the asylum?
- *Meaning*. In the context of doctor–patient relationships the assignment of a diagnosis defines the meaning of a problem, while in social care contexts professional definition of the severity of needs determines the degree of priority in terms of allocating services.

An analysis that considers the collapse of authority recognises the potential for authority to be resisted as well as maintained. One way in which this happens is through challenging expertise by drawing on other bodies of knowledge – which I discuss below in relation to the development of service user groups. But Abercrombie's analysis of the producer–consumer relationship suggests another aspect of this dynamic which focuses on the third mechanism through which authority is maintained:

> I would argue, control of *meaning* is particularly significant in contemporary societies; that is the authority of the producer is sustained by the capacity to define the meaning of the transaction involved and is lost as consumers acquire that power. (1994, p 50)

Abercrombie argues that contemporary consumption is largely about meaning. Struggles between producer and consumer are struggles not only about what is produced at what price, but also about meaning and the commodification of meaning. Consumer organisations play a significant role in this struggle and, Abercrombie argues, there has been a gradual loss of producer authority and legitimacy as a result of their power – not to control processes of production, but to invest commodities with a different meaning from that which producers might wish to supply.

This resonates with the source and nature of much resistance among service users to professional control over, for example, the meaning of treatments provided for mental illness, or the significance of adaptations to the home to enable disabled people to live as they want. In the case of the former, psychiatrists may argue the value and importance of medication in symptom relief, while service users may resist the experience of what feels like a 'chemical cosh'. In debates over home adaptations service providers may argue for less 'intrusive' adaptations – such as moving a bedroom downstairs – while disabled people and their families may prefer the disruption of a lift that enables all family members to sleep on the same floor (see Barnes, 2007, ch 3). In both instances, what is in dispute is the meaning of the service in the context of what is most important in service users' lives. Few of the users of health services in Clarke and Newman's (2007) study were comfortable about claiming the identity of consumer because this did not 'fit' their aspirations in terms of their relationships with health professionals, and it is precisely this issue of 'meaning' that demonstrates the inadequacy of understanding these processes as disputes over production and consumption.

Rights, citizenship and social justice

In some of my early work exploring reactions to a mental health users' council on a psychiatric ward I encountered substantial differences in the meanings assigned to this activity by the users who were involved and a senior psychiatrist working in the hospital (Barnes and Wistow, 1994). The service users thought that they were engaged in an activity through which they could resist what they experienced as oppressive treatment by doctors in the hospital. For the psychiatrist, on the other hand, the users' council was an opportunity for a therapeutic exercise – people could 'get things off their chests', but without any expectation that what they had to say might represent a legitimate challenge to medical authority and thus be taken seriously as a basis for changes in practice.

Neither of these views about the meaning of this activity locate these service users as 'consumers' resisting the authority of producers. For the psychiatrist it was clearly a question of how what was deemed to be an inappropriate challenge from patients to professional authority might be legitimated in the context of 'therapeutic' practice. The service users were not engaged in a process that Abercrombie has described as fantasising and daydreaming about consumption. What they were concerned with was much more fundamental – their rights to be treated humanely and not to be subjected to treatment that they experienced as worse than the problem that it was meant to address.

Many of the claims that are made by disabled people's groups and others are human rights claims: to be free from discrimination and stigmatisation resulting from the negative identifications associated with age, disability or mental illness. They are claims for *recognition* (Fraser, 1997) – of their capacity for self-determination, for defining their own identities and, in the case of carers' groups, claims for the identity of carer to be recognised (Barnes, 1997). They include claims for rights of access to appropriate services – but these should be understood not so much as consumer rights claims but as claims for the support necessary for living an ordinary life and, in some cases, for survival.

They also include rights claims that are constructed not as rights to services, but as rights to share in activities that are taken for granted as rights of citizenship: education, employment, travel between locations and access to public buildings. These are all claims that those engaged in such struggles much more readily identify as claims of citizenship rather than of consumption (Barnes and Shardlow, 1996; Barnes, 1999; Barnes et al, 1999).

Social movements and social change

While some action among service user and carer groups may be considered to support the identity of users as choosers, and while for many the key objective is to secure more responsive and individually accountable service provision, the user movement has a much broader significance and impact. Collectively, action among service users and carers is characterised by:

- *Diversity*. User movements encompass a wide range of forms of action. This includes: service provision, advocacy, protest action, research and 'partnerships' with service providers. This suggests that we cannot define 'the user movement' in terms of any one particular type of action.
- *Challenge*. At a fundamental level user movements challenge assumptions of expertise associated with professional training and qualification. They also challenge lay assumptions about competence and capacity (or the lack of it) associated with particular conditions or related to age.

- *Networks.* There is an unknown number of individual user and carer groups, based around localities, issues, services or other aspects of people's identities. But both formal and informal networks connect individuals and groups so that the whole is more than the sum of its parts.
- *Values.* User and carer movements pose questions about the way in which we live together and how we regard fellow citizens. Thus their objectives cannot be understood solely in terms of the production of more sensitive or appropriate services, but concern much broader issues of personal and social life.

Melucci (1996) argues that the term 'social movement' is best understood as an analytical concept rather than as one that should be used to define a specific category of collective action. This constructivist approach is one that I am using here to address the meaning and significance of user and carer movements. Such a perspective avoids the dilemmas posed by the diversity and sometimes contradictory nature of actions and objectives which can be identified within user movements. For example, Mad Pride activists have a very different take on what the user/survivor movement is about than do those who work with policy makers to develop new forms of support and service provision. Empirically, we are talking about very different types of action. Yet both can be embraced within the notion of 'social movement'. My aim in the following section is to address the significance of collective action among users and carers in order to understand the nature of the challenge that autonomous action in these contexts has, not only for professionalised welfare services, but for social relations more broadly.

Knowledge/expertise

Another important aspect of the claims made by service user groups is that they are knowledge claims. This is of particular significance in the context of an understanding of the way in which user and carer movements can challenge welfare systems and resist professional authority, and reflects a broader characteristic of identity-based social movements:

> These new social movements created new subjects of knowledge (African Americans, women, lesbians and gay men) and new knowledges.... Black nationalists, feminists, gay liberationists and lesbian feminists produced social

perspectives that were said to express their distinctive social reality: Afrocentrism, feminism, lesbian and gay or Queer theory. (Seidman, 1998, p 254)

Thus, mental health service users, disabled people and carers can also be seen to have produced new 'subjects of knowledge', evidenced, for example, in the burgeoning of research into carers and caring following on from the articulation of the identity of carer. There could be no research agenda about carers without the naming of carer as a distinct social identity. But perhaps more significantly, user movements have produced their own perspectives, frameworks and theories within which their experiences can be understood. The social model of disability can be considered to be a theorisation of the experience of disablement, on a par with feminism as a theorisation of women's experiences of gender relations.

Some have taken this further. Control over the process of knowledge production has itself become a site of struggle in some sections of the user movement. Within the disabled people's movement in particular, there is resistance to able-bodied researchers researching and interpreting disabled people's lives and experiences and, if such research does take place, research relationships are often negotiated such that disabled people control how the research is carried out (Oliver, 1992). Among other sections of the user movement there are more examples of participatory research being undertaken with allies from outside the movement, and both the theory and practice of emancipatory and participatory research are increasingly the subject of advocacy and analysis (eg Barnes et al, 2000; Beresford, 2005).

There are a number of ways in which such developments are significant. When disabled people and other service users carry out research (on their own or with colleagues and allies), the role they play is not that of 'service user', but that of expert and/or colleague. When they also become actively involved in educating and training welfare professionals this can unsettle the usual 'professional–user' relationship, as it is the service user who occupies the position of 'expert' vis-à-vis a trainee social worker, community psychiatric nurse (CPN) or other service provider. The unsettling of social relations in these contexts provides both tangible and symbolic challenges to expected relations, and models alternative possibilities for our understanding not only of the nature of disability or mental illness, but also of what constitutes knowledge and expertise. At an individual and personal level involvement in this type of activity has provided some service users with a long-term source of employment which has further limited their status as 'service users'.

Thus, at both a discursive and a practical level the knowledge claims of service users and their organisations have constituted a significant source of resistance to the power of welfare professionals (Barnes and Bowl, 2001). The connection between knowledge and social action is significant. The goal of creating new meanings and new understandings from the experiences of marginalised and oppressed groups is intimately tied in with broad social change goals. If knowledge is both socially produced and socially constructed, then opening up the production of knowledge to be used in professional education holds far-reaching implications for transformations in the way in which professionals approach their relationships with service users.

Identity

An initial awareness of shared experiences and of their problematic nature has been significant as a basis for action in all aspects of user and carer movements.

The origins of the carers' movement were in the early 1960s, when Mary Webster, an unmarried woman who had given up work to look after her parents, realised that her experiences must be shared by many women of her generation. It was this awareness that enabled her to invite others to join with her to seek recognition for a role that had not previously been identified as of any particular significance. The substantial response to her invitation indicated that there was a considerable number of women who recognised the experience she described and who welcomed an opportunity to articulate that experience collectively. This led to the establishment of an organisation called the National Council for the Single Woman and her Dependants. However, it was some time before that experience and role was articulated as that of 'carers'. That required, first, recognition that the role was one undertaken by people other than single women, and, second, it required the articulation of a collective identity which was distinct from any particular familial or other personal relationship (Barnes, 1997, ch 5). The emergence of the carers' movement can be considered to have created the identity of 'carer' as a social group. That identity is now formally enshrined within official policy (DH, 2008) and from 1995, with the passage of the Carers (Recognition and Services) Act, carers have their own rights to assessment and to have their needs and circumstances considered.

In the case of users of mental health services the shared experience that prompted the first organisations was that of using particular services. Such services were often experienced as unsympathetic if not oppressive – hence the adoption of the identifier 'survivor' among some sections of the movement. This referred not only to surviving mental health problems, but also to surviving the interventions of mental health professionals. One of the fundamental objectives of the mental health service users'/survivors' movement has been to reclaim the right to define their own experiences and their own identity. The stigmatised identity of 'mental patient' creates particular difficulties because of the association between madness and violence in lay discourse, but a professional medicalised discourse of mental illness is also often experienced as inadequate and unhelpful in enabling people to deal with their mental health problems in the context of their lives as a whole. The user/survivor movement has offered a challenge to both lay and professional constructions of the identity of 'mental patient' as incompetent, irrational, dangerous or to be feared (Rogers and Pilgrim, 1991; Barnes and Bowl, 2001).

In the case of people with physical and sensory impairments, the movement has challenged the identities of both 'tragic hero' and 'pitied victim', while also resisting the normalising discourse of rehabilitative medicine and much community care policy which encourages disabled people to aspire to approximations of 'normality' and to develop ways of being 'as if' their bodies were not impaired (Oliver, 1990, 1993). This challenge to a deficit model of disability is particularly marked in the case of deaf people, who have promoted deaf culture as an alternative and equally valuable way of living (Davis, 1995).

Melucci (1985) has suggested that a key characteristic of what he termed new social movements is the way in which shared identities are constructed through frequent interactions focused on action involving movement actors. Thus, while some initial recognition of shared experience is necessary for the first phase of organisation, the process of identity construction is an ongoing aspect of social movement organisation and action. This does not imply uniformity of identity, nor that an end-point can be reached at which a collective identity becomes 'fixed'. In the early years of the disability movement, mobilisation emphasised the similarities of experiences, regardless of the nature of impairment, and located shared experiences within the disabling impact of physical and social organisation that was based in assumptions of the normalcy of able-bodiedness (Swain et al, 1993). However, more recently this position has been critiqued from within the movement for failing to recognise the heterogeneity of disabled people's experiences (Shakespeare, 2006). As the movement has developed, it has become more possible to acknowledge differences among disabled people and the particular oppressions associated with such differences – for example, the importance of beautiful bodies among gay men can make life particularly hard for disabled gay men.

However, the general point is that users' and carers' movements have provided spaces within which identities can be articulated separately from the professionalised construction of such identities by welfare professionals. Separate organisation has made that possible, and continued action enables the process to develop – not only for existing members of the movement but for those who join at a later stage of its development. And this is not just an issue of how individuals might break free from demeaning or stigmatising identities deriving from stereotypical assumptions of incompetence or irrationality, or from medicalised constructions of pathologically malfunctioning bodies or minds. What the social models of disability and ageing, and the less well-formulated but emergent thinking around social models of mental illness, offer are understandings of the ways in which notions of madness and sanity, disabled and 'normal' bodies, youth and age, construct social relations within society.

In his later work Melucci reinforced his emphasis on the cultural significance of new social movements. He wrote: 'Contemporary "movements" assume the form of solidarity networks entrusted with potent cultural meanings, and it is precisely these meanings that distinguish them so sharply from political actors and formal organizations next to them' (Melucci, 1996, p 4). Such movements are concerned less with the distribution of resources within society, and more with a transformation of meanings and values – in this context, with a transformation in the way in which we think about what it is to be old, to be disabled, to provide and receive care, to experience the confusing and sometimes frightening impact of psychological distress, and not only how we organise and provide welfare services to support those in need of support, but also how such experiences define and construct social relations in everyday life.

Hence the diversity of action in which user movements are engaged. Symbolic and cultural objectives concerned with social relations, as well as the design of welfare services, require action within diverse locations – in the interactions of daily life; in the production of media and artistic representations; as well as in interactions between individual service users and welfare professionals and in deliberation about the design of policy and service delivery among politicians and service providers. Such action implies multiple identities, of which that of consumer may be of very limited relevance.

Having a say

Consumers express their views about services via complaints and feedback systems, by taking part in satisfaction surveys or by invoking consumer rights. As the previous discussion has implied, such modes of expression cannot encompass the depth and diversity of means through which people who use health and social care services seek to influence the social relations of welfare. Even within formal welfare systems, having a say about services requires more than customer feedback.

User involvement (variously defined and enacted) is now official policy and forums in which service users deliberate with service providers are widespread. But official willingness to open up processes of decision making to service users and to carers has not always been accompanied by an understanding of the implications for the form which dialogue on issues of policy and service delivery might take. Personal accounts of experiences have been dismissed as 'anecdotes', not worthy of equal consideration alongside the 'evidence' deriving from scientific research or the 'expertise' of professionals. The emotional expression of anger or hurt has caused embarrassed silence or led to accusations of 'bad manners' in settings where conflict tends to be suppressed (Church, 1996). Service providers have expressed discomfort when the agenda has been set by service users and they are asked to respond, rather than to inform. Officials are sometimes reluctant to accept that user groups will themselves determine who will speak on their behalf in deliberative forums, and have sought to exercise control over which service users they are prepared to engage in dialogue with (Barnes, 2002, 2004, 2008).

One aspect of the cultural challenge presented by user movements thus concerns the way in which dialogue about issues of social policy and service delivery takes place. The articulation of different identities and knowledges is accompanied by different ways in which those identities and knowledges can be expressed, which may conflict with the rational instrumental approaches typical in welfare bureaucracies. The insertion of service users into forums previously controlled by officials can challenge the rules of the game in ways that officials may feel very uncomfortable with. Participation within policy forums can also be a process through which identities are constructed rather than represented, and in some instances such processes challenge the binary separation between producer and consumer identities and interests (Barnes et al, 2007).

Conclusion

In this chapter I have examined a number of reasons for disputing the adequacy of a consumerist frame of reference for understanding the challenge presented to health and social care services by user and carer movements. Not only is the consumer as chooser an inadequate conceptualisation of the relationship between users and producers of welfare services, it is also a flawed strategy for empowerment and does not express the broad significance of the collective action that has developed over the last 40 years among users of welfare services. The notion of the 'authoritative consumer' offers some insight into the way in which professionalised meanings have been challenged by the lay knowledge of service users, but even this tends to confine the focus of analysis to the producer–consumer relationship. Collectively, service users have developed alternative ways of understanding disability, mental illness and caregiving, have claimed the right to construct their own identities, and have unsettled taken-for-granted assumptions about social relations not only between providers and users of welfare services at the point of delivery, but also in the process of deliberation about social policies. They have also prompted a more fundamental challenge to the various exclusions experienced by disabled and older people, and by those who live with mental illness. The right to choose who they think they are does reflect a key purpose of user movements and few have voluntarily embraced the identity of consumer in this respect.

References

Abercrombie, N. (1994) 'Authority and consumer society', in R. Keat, N. Whiteley and N. Abercrombie (eds) *The authority of the consumer*, London: Routledge, pp 43–57.

Barnes, M. (1997) *Care, communities and citizens*, Harlow: Addison Wesley Longman.

Barnes, M. (1999) 'Users as citizens: collective action and the local governance of welfare', *Social Policy and Administration*, vol 33, no 1, pp 73–90.

Barnes, M. (2002) 'Bringing difference into deliberation: disabled people, survivors and local governance', *Policy & Politics*, vol 30, no 3, pp 355–68.

Barnes, M. (2004) 'Affect, anecdote and diverse debates: user challenges to scientific rationality', in A. Gray and S. Harrison (eds) *Governing medicine: Theory and practice*, Maidenhead: McGraw Hill/Open University Press, pp 122–32.

Barnes, M. (2007) *Caring and social justice*, Basingstoke: Palgrave.

Barnes, M. (2008) 'Passionate participation: emotional experiences and expressions in deliberative forums', *Critical Social Policy*, vol 28, no 4, pp 461–81.

Barnes, M. and Bennet, G. (1998) 'Frail bodies, courageous voices: older people influencing community care', *Health and Social Care in the Community*, vol 6, no 2, pp 102–11.

Barnes, M. and Bowl, R. (2001) *Taking over the asylum: Empowerment and mental health*, Basingstoke: Palgrave.

Barnes, M. and Prior, D. (1995) 'Spoilt for choice? How consumerism can disempower public service users', *Public Money and Management*, vol 15, no 3, pp 53–8.

Barnes, M. and Shardlow, P. (1996) 'Effective consumers and active citizens: strategies for users' influence on services and beyond', *Research, Policy and Planning*, vol 14, no 1, pp 33–8.

Barnes, M. and Wistow, G. (1994) 'Learning to hear voices: listening to users of mental health services', *Journal of Mental Health*, no 3, pp 525–40.

Barnes, M., Davis, A. and Tew, J. (2000) 'Valuing experience: users' experiences of compulsion under the Mental Health Act 1983', *The Mental Health Review*, vol 5, no 3, pp 11–14.

Barnes, M., Newman, J. and Sullivan, H. (2007) *Power, participation and political renewal: Case studies in public participation*, Bristol: The Policy Press.

Barnes, M., Prior, D. and Thomas, N. (1990) 'Social services', in N. Deakin and A. Wright (eds), *Consuming public services*, London: Routledge, pp 105–53.

Barnes, M., Harrison, S., Mort, M. and Shardlow, P. (1999) *Unequal partners: User groups and community care*, Bristol: The Policy Press.

Beresford, P. (2005) 'Theory and practice of user involvement in research: making the connection with policy and practice', in L. Lowes and I. Hullatt (eds) *Involving service users in health and social care research*, London: Routledge, pp 6–17.

Church, K. (1996) 'Beyond "bad manners": the power relations of "consumer participation" in Ontario's community mental health system', *Canadian Journal of Community Mental Health*, vol 15, no 2, pp 27–44.

Clarke, J. and Newman, J. (2007) 'What's in a name? New Labour's citizen-consumers and the remaking of public services', *Cultural Studies*, vol 21, nos 4–5, pp 738–57.

Clarke, J., Newman, J., Smith, N., Vidler, E. and Westmarland, L. (2007) *Creating citizen-consumers: Changing publics and changing services*, London: Sage.

Davis, L.J. (1995) *Enforcing normalcy: Disability, deafness and the body*, London: Verso.

Deakin, N. and Wright, A. (eds) (1990) *Consuming public services*, London: Routledge.

DH (Department of Health) (2005) *Independence, well-being and choice: Our vision for the future of social care for adults in England*, Cm 6499, London: DH.

DH (2008) *Carers at the heart of 21st century families and communities: A caring system on your side, a life of your own* (www.dh.gov.uk/en/Publicationsandstatistics/Publications/PublicationsPolicyAndGuidance/DH_085345).

Fraser, N. (1997) *Justice interruptus: Critical reflections on the 'postsocialist' condition*, New York, NY: Routledge.

Groch, S. (2001) 'Free spaces: creating oppositional consciousness in the disability rights movement', in J. Mansbridge and A. Morris (eds) *Oppositional consciousness: The subjective roots of social protest*, Chicago, IL: University of Chicago Press, pp 65–98.

Keat, R., Whiteley, N. and Abercrombie, N. (eds) (1994) *The authority of the consumer*, London: Routledge.

Leadbeater, C., Bartlett, J. and Gallagher, N. (2008) *Making it personal*, London: Demos.

Melucci, A. (1985) 'The symbolic challenge of contemporary movements', *Social Research*, vol 52, no 4, pp 789–816.

Melucci, A. (1996) *Challenging codes: Collective action in the information age*, Cambridge: Cambridge University Press.

Needham, C. (2008) 'Realising the potential of co-production: negotiating improvements in public services', *Social Policy and Society*, no 7, pp 221–31.

Oliver, M. (1990) *The politics of disablement*, London: Macmillan.

Oliver, M. (1992) 'Changing the social relations of research production?', *Disability, Handicap and Society*, vol 7, no 2, pp 20–8.

Oliver, M. (1993) *Disability, citizenship and empowerment*, Milton Keynes: Open University Press.

Rogers, A. and Pilgrim, D. (1991) '"Pulling down churches": accounting for the British mental health services users' movement', *Sociology of Health and Illness*, vol 13, no 2, pp 129–48.

Seidman, S. (1998) *Contested knowledge: Social theory in the postmodern era*, Malden, MA: and Oxford: Blackwell.

Shakespeare, T. (2006) *Disability rights and wrongs*, London: Routledge.

Swain, J., Finkelstein, F., French, S. and Oliver, M. (eds) (1993) *Disabling barriers: Enabling environments*, London: Sage.

THIRTEEN

The public service consumer as member

Richard Simmons and Johnston Birchall

Introduction

In a recent study as part of the ESRC/AHRC 'Cultures of Consumption' programme, we asked public service users in social rented housing, social care and public leisure services to describe how they saw themselves and how they were seen by the providers of the services (Simmons et al, 2007a). We were trying to find out what labels they felt comfortable with and how they viewed the labels that were 'stuck on them' by the professionals. The variety of answers was startling, and it was often difficult to generalise from the findings.

One word that our respondents used often was 'member': they saw themselves as a 'member of the public', 'member of the local community' or 'member' of a group of people in need, such as 'mental health service users' or 'people with disabilities'. Where a user group was available, they would also say 'I am a member of the user group', and in one estate that was run by a management co-operative, they would say 'I am a member of the housing co-op'. There is a clear progression here, from a broad identification as a citizen, through a geographical community or community of need, to a formal group that offers membership to service users. What does membership mean? What kinds of membership are on offer in public services and to whom? What are the advantages and disadvantages of being a member? How compatible are the values associated with membership of a formal group with those of communities, or with the broader values of citizenship? Does 'member' participation in governance of a service delivery organisation improve the quality of decision making or confer special benefits on a minority? What are the limits of membership in a public service? Does membership enhance or detract from the 'publicness' of the service? It is these kinds of questions that this chapter seeks to address.

The nature of membership

When asked to choose up to two terms that they felt best described them as users of a particular public service, we found considerable variety among people's responses. Table 13.1 shows the distribution of these identifications.

Table 13.1: Some identifications of people who use public services

	Day care (n=116) %	Leisure (n=318) %	Housing (n=109) %
Member of the public	29.3	34.3	33.0
Customer	17.2	55.7	34.9
Taxpayer	11.2	12.3	11.9
Client	37.9	10.7	13.8
Member of the local community	21.6	23.3	32.1
Citizen	6.9	4.1	13.8
Consumer	8.6	16.0	7.3
Service user	41.4	39.0	22.9

Many of these were a combination of both 'individual' and 'collective' identifications (for example, 'customer' and 'member of the community', or 'client' and 'member of the public'). As Simmons (this volume, Chapter Four) has argued, this distinction between the individual and the collective shows something of the complexity of the identifications of people who use public services. In this chapter we seek to take this distinction in a slightly different direction, arguing that we might also differentiate between different types of collective identification among public service users.

Collective identifications were important to a significant number of people. In day care 50% of people chose at least one or other of the collective identifications offered to them ('member of the public' or 'member of the local community'). The corresponding figure in housing was 58.8%, and in leisure services 63.9%. These findings are supported in the 80 in-depth interviews that we conducted with service users across these three services where, as we have outlined above, ideas of 'membership' often came to the fore.

In their own research in the 'Cultures of Consumption' programme, John Clarke and his colleagues also asked questions about 'Who are you when you use public services?'. Their findings concur, showing that:

> Popular terms among people who use services were ones
> that invoked a sense of 'membership' – relationships of
> belonging in which people are part of something, and feel
> that being a member is a condition of entitlement or access
> to services. Larger collective imaginaries – the public and
> the local community – carry this sense of belonging and
> attachment. Ideas of belonging carry double meanings.
> Belonging can both locate an identity and express a relation
> of ownership: I belong here; this belongs to me. (Clarke et
> al, 2007, p 128)

The idea of the 'collective imaginary' is a useful one to invoke in
relation to larger-scale memberships, such as a 'member of the public'
or 'member of the local community'. According to Bouchard (2003),
the concept of a collective imaginary involves the establishment of
four relationships:

- a relationship to the past, which is expressed in a collective
  memory;
- a relationship to the future, which is expressed in utopias;
- a relationship to space, resulting in a territoriality;
- a relationship to self and to other, giving shape to an identity.

In this way the concept helps to capture some of the important
dimensions that help to describe membership. In our previous work
here, we have identified three important variables: the duration,
extensiveness and intensity of membership (Birchall and Simmons,
2001). These overlap with Bouchard's four relationships. First, the
importance of 'duration' is captured in the longitudinal relationships
Bouchard draws from the past, through the present, to the future. It also
encapsulates members' attitudes to change, especially the pace of change.
For example, as Birchall (1988, p 194) emphasises, 'a too-fast pace of
change destroys customary habits of thinking and acting, and does not
allow for the growth of new ones', while a 'too-slow' pace of change can
also lead to problems such as complacency and disconnection. Second,
as we highlight above, membership varies in 'extensiveness', reflecting
different levels of scale in notions of 'members of the public', 'members
of the local community' or 'members of a formal group'. Scale defines
the boundaries of collective interests and identities; boundaries that
contain spaces where issues such as the jointness of supply of goods,
group homogeneity and positive interdependence all impact on the
possibilities of collective action (eg Marwell and Oliver, 1993; Gavious

and Mizrahi, 1999). As Cornwall (2004, p 75) points out, thinking spatially allows us to consider 'the ways in which particular sites come to be populated, appropriated or designated by particular actors for particular kinds of purposes'.

Third, membership also varies in 'intensity'. Intensity can be characterised as the strength of 'feeling of belonging or of sharing a sense of personal relatedness' (McMillan and Chavis, 1986, p 9). This strength of feeling may be based on place (eg a strong attachment of local populations to their immediate locality; eg Young et al, 1996; Brint, 2001), or on a categorical interest and/or identity – 'which may be as diverse as ethnic origin, religion, politics, occupation, leisure pursuits or sexual propensity' (Mayo, 1994, p 51, after Wilmott, 1984). However, following McMillan and Chavis (1986, pp 9–14), we suggest that the 'belonging' component of membership (ie the sense 'I belong here') is supported by the co-presence of three further variables:

- *Shared connection*: the belief that members share common resources – history, assets, symbols, experiences and so on. It is not always necessary that group members have participated in the history in order to share these common resources, but they must identify with it.
- *Reinforcement, or the integration and fulfilment of needs*: the feeling that members' needs will be met by the resources received through their membership in the group. For any collectivity to maintain a positive sense of togetherness, the association must be rewarding for its members. The receipt of these rewards is often reciprocal, standing in relation to the material and/or non-material contributions of group members.
- *Influence*: a sense of mattering, of making a difference to the group and of the group mattering to its members. It is a bidirectional concept. For a member to be attracted to a group, he or she must have some influence over what the group does. On the other hand, cohesiveness is contingent on a group's ability to influence its members.

When we draw on these kinds of ideas, the nature of membership becomes more apparent. Descriptively, it is built on a sense of belonging ('intensity') within a particular tangible or imaginary space ('extensiveness') over time ('duration'). However, the other dimensions identified by McMillan and Chavis also matter. In another way of understanding membership, derived from an American intellectual tradition relating to farmer co-operatives, Torgerson (1983) identifies the basic dimensions of membership as member ownership, member control and member benefit. These dimensions approximate to McMillan and Chavis's connection, influence and reinforcement, but emphasise a more solid set of connections between individuals and organisations that are explicitly designed to meet their needs. Perhaps for this reason, we find that Torgerson's terms travel better within the public service environment.

To sum up, then, we identify six dimensions of membership:

1. Duration
2. Extensiveness
3. Intensity/Belonging
4. Ownership
5. Control
6. Benefits

The first two of these, duration and extensiveness, are not really independent variables, but are important as background conditions. Also, the meaning of intensity is not as immediately obvious as belonging, and so we prefer the latter term. We end up with four active dimensions of membership – 'belonging', 'ownership', 'control' and 'benefits' – that together should allow us to establish a firmer grasp on different collectivities that we might seek to study. In a moment, we will apply these dimensions at different levels of extensity. We want to move from the larger forms of collective imaginary to make links to smaller-scale and more tangible collectivities in the public service environment, such as user groups and other member-based organisations.

Before we do so, however, perhaps we should ask: why is collective representation important? Why should we have it? Clarke et al (2007, p 141) found that 'collective attachments to local or national bodies expressed through "membership" seemed a more desirable or meaningful form of attachment than the formal status of citizen'. This indicates something of the value and relevance of the idea of membership in public services. Similarly, in our own research we found evidence of demand for relationships that respond both to people's individual and their collective identities – and corresponding evidence that this was not always the relationship on offer (Simmons et al, 2007b). Hence, while one important reform movement within the public sector currently champions the needs and rights of individuals rather than of collectivities (through such mechanisms as personalisation and choice), our findings suggest that there is also scope to develop mechanisms by which people's collective identities and interests might be more effectively recognised (see also Birchall and Simmons, 2004; Simmons et al, 2007a).

How are membership identifications constructed?

Membership implies some sort of collectivity. The dimensions of belonging, ownership, control and benefits help us to examine what membership means at different levels of extensity. First, consider what it means to be a member of the public. Jacqui Ewart (2000, p 2) suggests that the public is brought into existence when it comes to recognise itself in common discourse and symbols, and 'consequently members seek to possess the values and characteristics portrayed therein as a mark of their belonging'. This perspective of the public emphasises the dimensions of 'belonging' and 'ownership'. However, from a different perspective, Stewart Ranson and John Stewart speak of the 'duality' of publicness. This involves 'the need to enable citizens in their plurality to express their contribution to the life of the community and, out of that plurality, to enable a process of collective choice and the government of action in the public interest to take place' (Ranson and Stewart, 1989, p 5). This perspective emphasises collective 'benefits' and 'control'. We believe that each of these perspectives has something important to say about what it means to be a 'member of the public'.

In relation to public services, we might characterise an 'ideal type' member of the public as one who has access to services with the status of citizen, and on the basis of need. There is indirect participation in the governance of public services through voting at national and local elections, and through the use of political voice. What does this member of the public want? Standardised services that do not vary from place to place, with equal access for those in equal need. In terms of our four elements, the sense of belonging may be quite high (although also quite abstract), as may be the sense of ownership (although also quite diffuse). There is a very indirect form of control, but a keen sense of who is entitled and who benefits.

The ideal type 'member of the local community' has a broadly similar profile and set of concerns, even though these are focused at a different level of extensity. This member of the local community wants services that are locally accessible and that reflect local needs and priorities, even if this is within a national framework of public service provision. In terms of our four dimensions, the intensity of belonging is commonly held to be stronger (as well as less abstract), in turn engendering a stronger set of solidaristic values. There is also a greater sense of ownership and loyalty to particular providers (eg local general hospital), a greater sense of control through the relative proximity of local government and greater ability to organise local collective action, and a desire to ensure that those members of the community who should benefit do benefit.

In each of these cases a balance emerges between notions of collective 'identity' ('belonging' and 'ownership') and notions of collective 'interest' ('benefits' and 'control'). This balance is also evident when one considers membership in relation to user groups in the public service environment. Membership of a user group is more sharply focused, being concerned about the collective interests of the group but also about the rights of the individual. In terms of our four dimensions, the sense of belonging may be quite intense, particularly if it is based around an important social category (eg ethnicity, gender, disability). A high sense of ownership is also likely, since the group *is* the members. Within the group there is generally a strong sense of control through direct democracy, and of collective group benefits: a sense of efficacy, confidence in being listened to, etc. However, in public service settings where claims are made by the group over such matters as procedural fairness and resource allocation, members' perception of collective control and benefits is often much weaker.

In her work examining user groups within the governance of welfare, Marian Barnes (1999, p 78) discusses the distinction between identity-based and interest groups. She cites Phillips (1993, pp 146–7), who argues that 'the new pluralism homes in on identity rather than interest groups: not those gathered together around some temporary unifying concern'. Barnes supports this argument, suggesting that:

> Action around a particular 'interest' can be engaged in by anyone, regardless of their personal or social identity. However, white people cannot join some black people's organisations, nor, in many cases, can men participate in action within women's movements.... For groups for whom oppression, difference and exclusion provide a focus for action the issue of identity based on a common experience is a key motivating factor. (Barnes, 1999, p 78)

This recognition of the importance of identity is a welcome step forward from a simplistic view of interest groups 'gathered around some temporary unifying concern'. A considerable part of the value of membership may be contained in members' sense of 'belongingness' within a social category (Turner et al, 1987). This is often supported by a sense of ownership. For example, Peter Beresford (2000) identifies a clear instance where 'ownership' is important in this context, in the reclamation by some mental health user groups of terms such as 'mad'.

However, we believe that to separate out the identity-based and interest-based components of membership would be a mistake; both have their place. This is something that Barnes seems to recognise (but does not make explicit), noting that user groups developed from 'A growing movement among those who were dissatisfied not only with the nature of the services they were receiving, but also with their lack of control over them' (Barnes, 1999, p 75).

In this way, we are able to make important links to both 'benefits' (ie the nature of services) and 'control'. The sense of belonging to a collectivity, and the accompanying sense of ownership this imbues, focuses on identity. The pursuit of member benefits and control focuses on interests. From this perspective, interests and identities are two sides of the same coin, and cannot easily be separated.

Our discussion thus far suggests that the dimensions of membership that we have identified hold firm across a range of settings. In what follows, we seek to examine a fourth level of extensity for membership in relation to public services – where people become formal members of a provider organisation. Member-based provider organisations offer, potentially, the strongest form of membership in relation to public services. Here, membership entails direct involvement in the governance of the provider, sometimes in a single stakeholder form, such as a housing co-operative, sometimes a multi-stakeholder form, as in foundation hospitals. There is a real legal ownership (though generally with a lock on the assets), direct participation in governance, and individual as well as collective benefits (though they still have to be produced collectively).

Member-based organisations in public services

At first, discussion of member-based organisations may seem rather peripheral in relation to public services, as it tends to focus on lesser-known forms of organisation such as tenant management co-operatives (which account for a relatively small proportion of the socially rented housing sector). However, with the emergence in England of Foundation Trust hospitals as member-based organisations and the support of both major political parties for co-operative schools, member-based forms of organisation seem to be taking a more important place in the future landscape of public services.

In a sense, we are going back to the future; historical analysis shows that there have always been membership-based organisations, involved to a greater or lesser extent in delivering public services. Prior to the founding of the welfare state in the 1940s, one of the key institutional forms that welfare delivery took was the friendly society, a membership organisation offering sickness benefits and health insurance. The 'architect' of the British welfare state, William Beveridge, had hoped that a role could be found for these societies, questioning whether the state would be able to combine 'soundness with sympathy', as they did (1948, p 84). Yet the model that came to dominate focused more on a national 'public' via direct delivery of services by the state. Then, in the early 1970s, community organisations that had formed to fight against slum clearance began to develop new forms, such as housing co-operatives and community housing associations that, as a matter of course, offered membership to tenants and the local community (Birchall and Simmons, 2004). A 'pure' form of membership-based service delivery agency was rediscovered.

During the Conservative governments of the 1980s and 1990s some new forms of tenant management organisations emerged, allowing more council tenants to take control of their estates and exercise self-management (Birchall, 1992). In schools, the role of parents was also strengthened in governing bodies, until they became the dominant stakeholder group. However, membership was never seen as a priority in itself (Pollitt et al, 1998). New Labour governments from 1997 onwards continued the trend towards devolution of services, but with a stronger commitment to the idea of membership. An explicit argument for the value of member-based organisations was made by some influential policy analysts who called their approach the 'new mutualism' (Leadbeater and Christie, 1999; Mayo and Moore, 2001; and see Birchall, 2001). This resulted in the new foundation trusts (FTs) being designed around a multi-stakeholder membership of patients, staff and local community (Lea and Mayo, 2002). Leisure trusts have also been developed by local authorities, as an alternative to privatisation, as a way of running leisure services (Simmons, 2004, 2008). As noted earlier, both Labour and Conservative politicians have recently backed the idea of co-operative schools that will be more explicitly owned and controlled by parents. As a result, a range of organisations can now be found in the public service environment that offer formal membership rights to service users.

Evaluations of these forms of organisation are emerging. For example, *The Guardian* surveyed the initial tranche of 20 FTs on their early experiences of operation (Carvel, 2004). This survey found that the inclusion of a wider range of interests in governance, through the idea of membership, has been widely welcomed. FTs like the legitimacy of having a governing council elected by local people, and this is perceived to have led to a greater sense of ownership by the community. This positive assessment finds support in a Healthcare Commission evaluation (Healthcare Commission, 2005). However, some doubts appear here about the confusion between the roles of patients and the public in governance and in wider participatory processes such as Public and Patient Involvement Forums (Healthcare Commission, 2005, p 36). Simmons' (2004, 2008) detailed assessment of the experiences of the new leisure trusts (NLTs) in local government found many similar factors. The inclusion of a wider range of stakeholders, including user members, on the boards of NLTs was acknowledged to have enhanced the level and quality of debate and decision making – even by councillors who had previously exercised direct authoritative control. However, participatory processes to connect these member representatives with their wider constituencies were often weak. Further evidence is provided by recent studies of the longest-standing member-based organisations in the public service environment: tenant management organisations (TMOs) (Rodgers, 2001; ODPM, 2002). In these studies, housing co-operatives are consistently shown to be more satisfying, as well as being more efficient and effective, than the traditional landlord–tenant relationship. As an evaluation by the Office of the Deputy Prime Minister observes:

> TMOs provide a model of what can be achieved by local people in socially excluded communities where training and support is available. They are generally well-run, and more than half are engaged in social and community development activities which contribute to the strengthening of their communities and social networks. (ODPM, 2002, p 5)

Member-based organisations, old and new, have faced a number of similar issues. Prior to the development of the universalist post-war welfare state, mutuals provided a decentralised (localised) source of social support that enabled a degree of flexibility in provisions to fulfil the needs of diverse social groups, as well as mechanisms for members' voices to be heard. Yet the powerful confluence of forces that created the post-war welfare state overrode concerns to retain these important features. Now, as the state is increasingly criticised for its lack of flexibility in meeting the needs of plural populations and for being too distant to enable service users to participate in meeting their welfare needs, member-based organisations are again being invoked, in the belief that they can remedy the defects of universal state provision. The attraction of the idea is clear. However, if these new organisations are not to find themselves rejected and superseded, as the old ones eventually were, a number of lessons need to be learned. These include issues of 'connection with the community as a whole' (Chanan, 2003, p 28) and the ability of member-based organisations to generate and employ 'solidarity inputs' (Lloyd, 2002) in the governance and delivery of the service (Simmons, 2008). We believe that this learning might be underpinned by greater understanding of the dimensions of membership that we have identified.

Let us look now at some relevant member-based organisations – FTs, TMOs, NLTs and co-operative schools – in relation to the four dimensions of membership. Table 13.2 shows the extent to which a sense of belonging, ownership, benefits and control are vested in these forms of organisation.

FTs offer membership to staff, patients and the public that gives them voting rights over a board of governors which then appoints a board of management. While their powers are hedged about with qualifiers, members are clearly able to exercise some control. This compares (Table 13.3) with non-foundation trusts, whose boards are mainly appointed by the Secretary of State for Health, aided by an appointments commission; and with health boards in Scotland, which are also mainly appointed but include some local authority representatives. The individual benefits of member involvement are not obvious, since membership brings no extra rights to patient care. However, members can gain personal satisfaction from involvement and those who are also members of self-help groups and patient groups can gain better collective access to decision making. The sense of ownership and belonging might be expected to be higher in trusts based on a local general hospital than in those that are specialised and are not based on a particular geographical community, although there is no evidence for this at the moment.

TMOs offer membership to tenants (and sometimes to owner-occupier residents), usually on clearly defined estates. They can be expected to score highly on all four dimensions, except that sometimes there is an underlying sense of alienation among residents that testifies to wider issues such as social exclusion, a history of neglect by the 'authorities', the stigma of belonging to an area with a bad reputation, and so on. The alternative, of traditional local authority housing, is generally lower on all counts, although sometimes it delivers effective estate-based services.

Table 13.2: Sense of belonging, sense of ownership, benefits and control in member-based forms of organisation

	Foundation trusts	Tenant management organisations	New leisure trusts	Co-operative schools
Sense of belonging	LOW Belonging is normally associated with community rather than organisational membership	HIGH Strong attachment/ relatedness, tends to grow over time	LOW Belonging is normally associated with community rather than formal membership	MEDIUM/HIGH Relatively strong attachment to organisation for duration of membership
Sense of ownership	LOW/MEDIUM Diffused across large-scale memberships (but encouraging sign-up/election turnout figures)	HIGH TMO are 'of the people and for the people'	LOW Often need to make membership meaningful in a more collective sense	HIGH Membership brings collective rights and responsibilities
Benefits (access to services)	LOW Access via health professionals	HIGH Services available equally to all members as of right (although initial access to membership in part via bureaucratic allocation system)	MEDIUM Membership benefits available on market-based model (depend on purchasing power)	HIGH Services available equally to all members as of right (although initial access to membership in part via bureaucratic allocation system)
Control (representation in governance structure)	MEDIUM/HIGH Patient and public members represented on board of governors	HIGH Management board comprises only tenants	MEDIUM/HIGH Public members generally represented on board	MEDIUM/HIGH Parent and pupil members represented on board

Membership in NLTs may be offered to staff and/or user/community representatives, depending on the legal model used (Simmons, 2004). As far as users are concerned, membership has often been based on 'leisurecard' schemes that had previously operated under local authority control. However, many of these have been expanded, and in some cases voting rights have been added for community board representatives. Comparing Tables 13.2 and 13.3, this has had a more positive effect on the two 'interest' dimensions than on the two 'identity' dimensions, as identity seems to be located more firmly in notions of local community than in organisational membership per se.

Co-operative schools are a new form that has not yet been tried in Britain, and so any view taken has to be speculative. They can be expected to reinforce control by parents (and, hopefully, by children, who have been shamefully left out of the picture in recent reforms) and to strengthen a sense of ownership and belonging. However, our summary in Table 13.3 attests to the fact that parents already have a great deal of formal control over school governing bodies. On the other hand, evidence shows that, in practice, head teachers still have a controlling influence (Ranson et al, 2005a, 2005b; see also Farrell, this volume, Chapter Seven), and that formal control may not lead to control in practice.

This short discussion has shown that building membership into an organisation ought to enhance people's sense of ownership and control and confer tangible member benefits, as compared to non-membership organisations. However, it has also shown that things are not always

Table 13.3: Sense of belonging, sense of ownership, benefits and control in traditional public sector forms of organisation

	Traditional health trusts	Local authority housing	Local authority leisure	Traditional schools
Sense of belonging	LOW Belonging is normally associated with community rather than organisation	LOW/HIGH Attachment/ relatedness varies according to perceptions of estate/locality	LOW Belonging is normally associated with community rather than organisation	MEDIUM/HIGH Attachment to organisation for duration of use
Sense of ownership	LOW Passive recipient or individualised consumer as 'chooser'	LOW Passive recipient or paying customer	LOW Passive recipient or paying customer	LOW/MEDIUM Largely passive recipient
Benefits (access to services)	LOW/MEDIUM Services available but access via health professionals	LOW/MEDIUM Services available but at managers'/ professionals' discretion	MEDIUM Services available on market-based model (depend on purchasing power)	HIGH Services available equally to all parents/pupils
Control (representation in governance)	LOW Patient and public involvement but formal decisions made by managers/ professionals	LOW Tenant participation but formal decisions made by managers/ professionals	LOW Irregular focus groups, customer surveys, but formal decisions made by managers/ professionals	MEDIUM/HIGH Parents represented on governing body, student councils

what they seem, and that the predicted effects of membership models do not always emerge. In terms of 'solidarity inputs', there is a question, which we have explored at length elsewhere, of whether members will be willing to participate (Simmons and Birchall, 2005, 2007). There are also potential questions over the power of members vis-à-vis other stakeholders, such as professionals and managers, to make these inputs count. Without a planned and proactive approach to membership, this may lead to outcomes similar to those noted above for traditional schools, where head teachers often remain 'first among equals'.

However, Table 13.2 suggests another potentially important question in relation to people's sense of belonging. In member-based organisations where a new level of community 'extensity' is formed by organisational boundaries (for example TMOs, co-operative schools), this sense of belonging can become quite highly developed as the 'duration' of membership increases. Yet where a new level of community extensity is not formed by the organisation itself (for example FTs, NLTs), there is a need to invoke a sense of belonging at other levels of extensity if the relationship between notions of interest (benefits and control) and identity (belonging and ownership) is not to become unbalanced. It would seem that the importance of this question therefore depends not only upon the level of congruence between interests and identity *within organisational boundaries*, but also on the level of congruence between these dimensions *at different levels of extensity* over time. Taking this perspective, the importance of the question may also be extended beyond the discussion of member-based organisations alone.

Overlapping memberships: incompatibilities or complementarities between different types of membership?

It is, of course, the case that people often hold multiple memberships – service users can be members of the public, the local community, one or more user groups and a provider organisation all at the same time. In this sense, Clarke et al (2007, pp 141–2) report that:

> Discourses of membership are typically structured around dynamics of inclusion and exclusion in which the different principles of connection may conflict, merge and overlap.... Our respondents draw on all of these larger discourses about community, publicness and nation.... They put them to work in complex reasoning about experiences and expectations of public services. They also use them to

provide a standpoint for critical reasoning about government programmes and proposals.

This idea of people finding a standpoint for critical reasoning is supported by studies that examine different levels of extensity. For example, Dwyer (2002) and Lister et al (2003) indicate how people acquire for themselves common-sense notions of citizenship. Similarly, Bertram (1997, p 565) describes how 'community' stands as a 'social order ... capable of explaining itself at the tribunal of each person's understanding'. In short, for all the inherent complexity involved, users seem to be well aware of (and capable of handling) the tensions between advocating one's own immediate interest and that of one's community or the wider public.

The 'complex reasoning' in which they engage is also, by definition, relational. One example of this follows the eloquent arguments that Barnes (1999) and others (eg Lister, 2001; Newman, 2005) have made about the acceptance of diversity and difference and the importance of recognition and respect in the construction of public services. These authors seem to suggest that 'service use' is insufficient in itself to be seen as the basis for membership of 'user groups', arguing that this does violence to the meaning given to membership by the sense of belonging that members draw from other levels of identification. We have already seen, in the example given by Barnes (1999), how users may invoke here their membership of social categories. By contrast, in her own discussion of user groups, Lister (2001, p 100) argues for the need to compare the particular set of provisions for a specific group with a more 'universal' standard located in citizenship: 'the recognition debate raises wider issues of equality and difference and of universal and particular claims'. In Lister's analysis, the particular and the universal therefore represent two sides of the same coin.

Such matters stand at the heart of debates that connect the different levels of membership we have so far considered: the various claims and concerns of members of the public, members of the local community and members of user groups that emerge from their collective identities. Hence, it is worth noting that such 'relational reasoning' encapsulates much more than simple 'competition' between people's membership of groups at different levels of extensity. While there may well be incompatibilities here that must rely on zero-sum processes for their resolution, there are often also complementarities, where different 'levels' of membership are, in effect, locked together. Here, positive-sum outcomes can be derived from their interaction.

While such tensions may be resolved at the level of the individual, it is often harder to resolve them at the level of the public service organisation. In another important example of the overlap between different 'levels' of understanding, Streeck and Schmitter (1985, p 129) point to the way in which the self-interested collective action commonly associated with member-based organisations may 'strive for a "categoric good" which is partially compatible or identical with a "collective good" for the society as a whole'. This becomes a question of the extent to which the assumed 'collective self-interest' of organisational members (where the sense of belonging is assumed to be atrophied) overlaps with the assumed 'collective interest' of members of the public, or of the community, or of social categories (where the sense of belonging is assumed to be higher). Perhaps in some ways this is becoming an important test – how to structure public service relationships to cater for people's individual self-interest (rational maximisation via autonomous action), collective self-interest (rational maximisation via collective action) and collective interest (the maximisation of collective interests even if this means that individuals must accept less than the personal maximum). Our argument suggests that, where there is sufficient overlap between 'identities' (belonging/ownership) and 'interests' (benefits/control), effective arrangements can be designed to accommodate public service objectives.

At this point we might ask: how do we construct models that build on people's sense of membership? How do we make membership meaningful and more concrete in how we structure public service organisations? Can structured opportunities be made available for people to be members who act back positively on their membership identifications? This may point to a future for more member-based organisations in public service delivery, either where interests and identities may overlap within the organisation (eg TMOs or co-operative schools), or where the organisation is able to invoke the sense of belonging and ownership from other 'levels' to rebalance this relationship. However, this depends, as Streeck and Schmitter (1985) make clear, on the extent of the overlap. It is possible that the use of member-based organisations as a structural form either interacts creatively with people's own sense(s) of membership (making them more energised, loyal, more collectively focused), or that it interacts destructively (making them more cynical and/or withdrawn). In the public services, where user expectations are based on a wide range of values, this overlap may only be achievable in particular contexts (Simmons, 2008).

Yet, of course, this is not to say that a change in structural form is the only way in which collective interests and identities can be recognised. Some of the values, systems and practices commonly associated with member-based organisations can continue to be strengthened within other structural forms (Birchall and Simmons, 2004). Here we argue that a key task of institutional design in the public sector (and the institutional effort expended in support of that design) is to find a way to ensure that all user voices are included (Simmons et al, 2006). Hence, while membership-based organisations and self-governance make sense in some contexts, ongoing discourses of co-production and empowerment continue to make sense in others. Even better that, in all such contexts, these strategies are combined intelligently with individualised approaches such as personalisation and choice – again, these approaches should not be seen as automatically in competition with more collective ways of organising. A more planned and proactive approach to the design and management of public services might enable the many compatibilities between such individual and collective approaches to be developed.

To conclude, the idea of membership has an important place in discussions of the consumer in public services. However, we believe that there is currently insufficient clarity about the term and its various meanings. A partial membership is potentially against the public service ethos, but a more inclusive approach that takes account of the values, systems and practices of membership is not. The challenge to service providers is to recognise both (a) the different levels of membership and (b) the interaction of the four dimensions of belonging, ownership, benefits and control. The former helps us to understand the nature of people's identifications and interests and, importantly, the connections that they make between these different levels. This can help to avoid the peril of *oversimplification* – for example, that which accompanies the perceived 'universalism' of members of the public, or the perceived 'particularism' of user groups. The latter helps us to break down the categories of interest and identity into a relatively manageable set of operationalisable dimensions. This can help to avoid the opposite peril of *overcomplication*, putting levers into the hands of policy makers and providers so that when they make the offer of membership they can have confidence in making it work.

References

Barnes, M. (1999) 'Users as citizens: collective action and the local governance of welfare', *Social Policy and Administration*, vol 33, no 1, pp 73–90.

Beresford, P. (2000) *Mental health issues: Our voice in our future*, London: Shaping Our Lives/National Institute for Social Work.

Bertram, C. (1997) 'Political justification, theoretical complexity, and democratic community', *Ethics*, vol 107, no 4, pp 563–83.

Beveridge, W. (1948) *Voluntary action*, London: Allen and Unwin.

Birchall, J. (1988) 'Time, habit and the fraternal impulse', in M. Young and T. Schuller (eds) *The rhythms of society*, London: Routledge, pp 71–90.

Birchall, J. (1992) (ed) *Housing policy in the 1990s*, London: Routledge.

Birchall, J. (2001) *The new mutualism in public policy*, London: Routledge.

Birchall, J. and Simmons, R. (2001) 'Member participation in mutuals: a theoretical model', in J. Birchall (ed) *The new mutualism in public policy*, London: Routledge, pp 202–25.

Birchall, J. and Simmons, R. (2004) *User power*, London: National Consumer Council.

Bouchard, G. (2003) *Raison et contradiction: Le mythe au secours de la pensée*, Québec: Nota bene/Céfan.

Brint, S. (2001) '*Gemeinschaft* revisited: a critique and reconstruction of the community concept', *Sociological Theory*, vol 19, no 1, pp 1–23.

Carvel, J. (2004) 'NHS ties are cut – but the red tape remains', *The Guardian*, 13 December.

Chanan, G. (2003) *Searching for solid foundations: Community involvement and urban policy*, London: Office of the Deputy Prime Minister.

Clarke, J., Newman, J., Smith, N., Vidler, E. and Westmarland, L. (2007) *Creating citizen-consumers*, London: Sage.

Cornwall, A. (2004) 'Spaces for transformation?', in S. Hickey and G. Mohan (eds) *Participation: From tyranny to transformation?*, London, Zed Books, pp 75–91.

Dwyer, P. (2002) 'Making sense of social citizenship: some user views on welfare rights and responsibilities', *Critical Social Policy*, vol 22, no 2, pp 273–99.

Ewart, J. (2000) 'Capturing the heart of the region: how regional media define a community', *Transformations*, vol 1, no 1, pp 1–13 (www.cqu.edu.au/transformations).

Gavious, A. and Mizrahi, S. (1999) 'Two-level collective action and group identity', *Journal of Theoretical Politics*, vol 11, no 4, pp 497–517.

Healthcare Commission (2005) *The Healthcare Commission's review of NHS foundation trusts*, London: Healthcare Commission.

Lea, R. and Mayo, E. (2002) *The mutual health service*, London: Institute of Directors and New Economics Foundation.

Leadbeater, C. and Christie, I. (1999) *To our mutual advantage*, London: Demos.

Lister, R. (2001) 'Towards a citizens' welfare state: the 3+2 "R"'s of welfare reform', *Theory, Culture and Society*, vol 8, nos 2–3, pp 91–111.

Lister, R., Smith, N., Middleton, S. and Cox, L. (2003) 'Young people talk about citizenship: empirical perspectives on theoretical and political debates', *Citizenship Studies*, vol 7, no 2, pp 235–53.

Lloyd, P. (2002) 'Tackling social exclusion with social enterprise organisations', Paper to SME Seminar Series, Small Business Research Centre, Kingston University, May.

McMillan, D. and Chavis, D. (1986) 'Sense of community: a definition and theory', *Journal of Community Psychology*, vol 14, no 1, pp 6–23.

Marwell, G. and Oliver, P. (1993) *The critical mass in collective action*, New York, NY: Cambridge University Press.

Mayo, E. and Moore, H. (2001) *The mutual state*, London: New Economics Foundation.

Mayo, M. (1994) *Communities and caring: The mixed economy of welfare*, London: Macmillan.

Newman, J. (2005) 'Regendering governance', in J. Newman (ed) *Remaking governance: Peoples, politics and the public sphere*, Bristol: The Policy Press, pp 81–99.

ODPM (Office of the Deputy Prime Minister) (2002) *Tenants managing: Evaluation of tenant management organisations in England*, London: ODPM.

Phillips, A. (1993) *Democracy and difference*, Cambridge: Polity.

Pollitt, C., Birchall, J. and Putman, K. (1998) *Decentralising public management*, London: Macmillan.

Ranson, S. and Stewart, J. (1989) 'Citizenship and government: the challenge for management in the public domain', *Political Studies*, vol 37, no 1, pp 5–24.

Ranson, S., Arnott, M., McKeown, P., Martin, J. and Smith P. (2005a) 'The participation of volunteer citizens in school governance', *Educational Review*, vol 57, no 3, pp 357–71.

Ranson, S., Farrell, C., Peim, N. and Smith, P. (2005b) 'Does governance matter for school improvement?', *School Effectiveness and School Improvement*, vol 16, no 3, pp 305–25.

Rodgers, D. (2001) 'Housing cooperatives and social exclusion', in J. Birchall (ed) *The new mutualism in public policy*, London: Routledge, pp 60–71.

Simmons, R. (2004) 'A trend to trust? The rise of new leisure trusts in the UK', *Managing Leisure: An International Journal*, vol 9, no 3, pp 159–77.

Simmons, R. (2008) 'Harnessing social enterprise for local public services: new leisure trusts in the UK', *Public Policy and Administration*, vol 23, no 3, pp 278–301.

Simmons, R. and Birchall, J. (2005) 'A joined-up approach to user participation in public services: strengthening the participation chain', *Social Policy and Administration*, vol 39, no 3, pp 260–83.

Simmons, R. and Birchall, J. (2007) 'Tenant participation and social housing in the UK: applying a theoretical model', *Housing Studies*, vol 22, no 4, pp 573–95.

Simmons, R., Birchall, J. and Prout, A. (2006) 'User involvement in public services: "choice about voice"', Social Policy Association Conference, University of Birmingham, July.

Simmons, R., Birchall, J. and Prout, A. (2007a) *Our say: User voice and public service culture*, London: National Consumer Council.

Simmons, R., Birchall, J. and Prout, A. (2007b) 'Hearing voices? User involvement and public service cultures', *Consumer Policy Review*, vol 17, no 5, pp 234–240

Streeck, W. and Schmitter, P. (1985) 'Community, market, state – and associations?', *European Sociological Review*, vol 1, no 2, pp 119–38.

Torgerson, R. (1983) 'Alternative ownership and control mechanisms', in P. Farris (ed) *Future frontiers in agricultural marketing research*, Ames: Iowa State University Press, pp 316–34.

Turner, J., Hogg, M., Oakes, P., Reicher, S. and Wetherell, M. (1987) *Rediscovering the social group: A self-categorization theory*, Oxford: Blackwell.

Wilmott, P. (1984) *Community in social policy*, London: Policy Studies Institute.

Young, K., Gosschalk, B. and Hatter, W. (1996) *In search of community identity*, York: Joseph Rowntree Foundation.

FOURTEEN

Conclusion: the consumer in public services

Richard Simmons and Martin Powell

Introduction: choice is 'not the only fruit'?

A key focus for the contributors to this book was to think about the 'differentiated consumer' in public services and what it meant from their perspectives in relation to public services and consumption. Their contributions show that people are working with a wide range of understandings in this regard. In this chapter we will attempt to make sense of this by returning to some of the themes set out in the Introduction. First, we recognise that many different faces and mechanisms of consumerism exist. This helps us to identify who it is that presents themself when they use public services and what their expectations might be, as well as what responses they might face from public service providers. Second, we acknowledge the role of different public service contexts, and that what works in terms of consumerism and choice for some people in some settings may not be universal. Third, we acknowledge the role of values – not only in underpinning difference in consumer faces and mechanisms, but also in how these differences are recognised and applied in different public service contexts.

One of the key aims of the book is to go beyond the 'consumer as chooser'. In doing so, we have adopted the subtitle 'Choice, values and difference', as we believe that each has an important part of the story to tell. Current debates in the public services have often turned on relatively simplistic notions of the consumer as chooser. *Choice* within public services is variously presented here as a public service 'good' or a public service 'bad'. In relation to this form of consumerism, certain competing *values* are either brought to the forefront or pushed to the background of debate. For example, Jones (Jones and Needham, 2008) suggests a range of consumer values such as competition, representation, access, choice, information, safety, equity and redress (see also Potter,

1988; Policy Commission on Public Services, 2004). More than 20 years ago Clode et al (1987, p 5) also pointed to the enduring conflict between the fundamental values of liberty and equality (to which we might add the often-forgotten member of that famous trilogy, 'fraternity'). Unsurprisingly, this conflict has not yet been resolved and continues to underpin a good proportion of the debates about choice (and the consumer as chooser) in public services. In this sense, such debates are inherently political and it seems entirely appropriate for this book to open with an assessment of the 'new politics of consumerism' (see Shaw [Chapter Two], and Needham [Chapter Three]). Our need to understand these politics comes in spite of the attempts of some of those concerned with the delivery of public services to present choice as a straightforward and 'technical' matter. As Keat et al (1994, p 15) suggest, the difficulties encountered here are of a 'normative and not merely practical' nature:

> In particular, one cannot simply assume that the preferences of individual users are sacrosanct here (that is, consumer authority): questions of value, and of policy, inevitably arise, that should be debated and decided by people acting collectively as citizens in the democratic, political domain, rather than as individual consumers in a quasi-economic one.

Potter (1988, p 156) continues in similar vein:

> the apolitical nature of consumerism, and the fact that it is grounded in economic theory, means that it is not equipped itself to develop this kind of swapping of roles between the governors and the governed, the administrators and the administered. Consumerism's primary role is to place consumers' preferences on the agenda, rather than to encourage consumers to take account of the preferences of others.

Again, such arguments are enduring. As Clarke (Chapter Nine) points out, there may be conflict between choice and equity (ie principle), but also between choice (responsiveness) and evidence-based policy ('what works is what counts') (ie pragmatism). For example, the public may want 'bobbies on the beat', but 'experts' consider that it does not work. Hence, in one very public recent debate with a colleague about consumerism in public services, Needham (Jones and Needham, 2008, p 76) argues that consumer preferences should be seen as important, but neither subordinate nor superordinate in discussions to those of other key constituencies – such as workers, civil society groups and citizens.

Within this debate, Needham (Jones and Needham, 2008, p 74) also argues that Jones works with a very broad conception of the consumer in public services (see Powell et al's narrow vs broad view of consumerism in Chapter One). This conception sees the term 'consumer' as 'the overall term for all individuals. All of us consume goods and services, from various providers, public and private. Within that broad category individuals can have many relationships with producers/providers' (Jones and Needham, 2008, p 70). The first key message of this book follows from this – if the broad category is to be of use, then perhaps we need to understand more about the 'many relationships' involved. It is in this sense that we use the word '*difference*'. Such understanding leads us on to consider the ways in which this difference has effects on the relationships between public service users and providers – for example, through choice and voice. In a moment we will consider two important dimensions of how these relationships are constructed in our consideration of the different 'subjects' of consumerism, and of different consumer 'mechanisms'.

However, taking this perspective leads us on a return journey, back through values to choice. Not only do consumers have different types of relationships at different times in different public service 'spaces', they can also have different values that they hold dear in relation to public services. Such value pluralism can apply both within and between individuals and groups. This means that attempts to establish consensual discourse around one particular value are unlikely to succeed. This returns us to choice. There may be times when consumers themselves wish for a 'narrow' conception of their role, in which they are at liberty to make self-regarding choices from a menu, based on the best information available to them. However, as Gabriel and Lang (2006) powerfully argue, while this may be the case for some people some of the time, it will rarely be the case for all people all of the time. We therefore need to look 'beyond the consumer as chooser'. Broader conceptions of consumers' role in public services might see them attempt to engage with tensions between different values – for example, equality or fraternity – that lead them towards other modes of discourse – for example 'standardisation' or 'co-production' (see Needham, Chapter Three). In this sense, as we attempt to look beyond the consumer as chooser, we can perhaps observe that choice-based consumerism is 'not the only fruit'.

The parameters of consumerism

In Chapter One we set forward some of the key issues that would inform our discussions. These issues bring us to another of the book's key messages: that the parameters of consumerism are unclear. One of these issues regards the 'subjects' of consumerism, or who it is that presents themself when they come to use public services. Another concerns what we have termed 'consumer mechanisms', or the ways of working through which public services relate to these people. These issues have been taken forward in interesting ways by our authors which lead us towards the above message, that in today's public services we must learn to cope with 'difference'.

The 'subjects' of consumerism

A first cut at the question of 'who' it is that presents themself when they come to use public services relates to the ongoing debate started in Chapter One, over the nature of 'consumers' vs 'citizens' vs 'clients'. We can ask here whether policy makers and academic commentators regard the people who use public services as 'consumers' (or citizens, or clients) – and whether the public regard themselves in these (or other) ways (see Clarke et al, 2007). In Chapter One we drew attention to current narratives suggesting a move from 'citizens' (or in some service contexts, 'clients') to 'consumers', or perhaps hybrid 'citizen-consumers'. The evidence from the book on this question points in some interesting directions. For example, Laing et al (Chapter Five) point to the ways in which some 'clients' in professionalised services have become more active and agential 'consumers as choosers'. Overall, they plot a trajectory away from the traditional trusting and 'compliant' client in public services, towards a range of other behaviours that are more overtly consumerist ('triangulating' information from the internet, discussing service options, making choices). However, while the overall trajectory may show a movement in this direction, this is not to say that everybody makes this journey – nor that those who do, do so at the same pace. Laing et al suggest that the picture is much more differentiated and 'messy' than this. In another context, Beresford (Chapter Eleven) directly challenges the label of 'consumer' in relation to social care service users, preferring to examine developments more in terms of social rights and social justice that square little with 'consumerist' narratives. As he puts it, service users are: 'differentiated – yes, but consumers?'. Clearly not all are convinced by the notion of the consumer in relation to public services. This is supported when we look at how the people who use public services see themselves. Clarke (Chapter Nine) and Simmons and Birchall (Chapter Thirteen) each show that few of the people who use public services saw themselves as consumers (or citizens), but more as patients (healthcare), service users, members of the local community, members of the public – or, if there was a cash nexus (housing, leisure), customers. As a result, we find ourselves agreeing with Keat et al (1994, p 15), that the 'distinction between citizen and consumer is increasingly difficult to articulate in an unambiguous fashion' – only perhaps now, 15 years later, even more so.

This observation leads us to a 'second cut' at our question of who it is that presents themself when they come to use public services. In other words, should we attempt to distinguish users of public services through terms such as 'clients', 'citizens' or 'consumers', or through other schemes that attempt to determine different faces of the consumer? In some subject areas (in particular, marketing and social psychology) the idea of using 'segmentation' or 'clustering' techniques to differentiate between people with similar characteristics has become widespread and common. In Chapter One we introduced the idea, following Gabriel and Lang (1995), of the *'unmanageable'* consumer. Gabriel and Lang use this concept to describe nine types or 'faces' of the consumer, so encouraging the rejection of one-dimensional views. We find healthy support in this book for taking a similar stance in relation to public services. Hence, in Chapter One, Powell et al talk of the *'X consumer'* – in other words, there are different types that defy easy pigeonholing. Laing et al (Chapter Five) introduce the idea of the *'post-modern'*, or *'fragmented'* consumer. Here, the people who use public services fall into different quadrants, only one of which resembles the stereotypical 'consumer as chooser'. In Chapter Four, Simmons uses another original framework to analyse difference, pointing to consumers who can be *'differentiated'* according to how they see themselves and the depth of their relationships with the services they use. Simmons' framework provides eight categories, in which again only one can be thought of conventionally as the consumer as chooser. Indeed, throughout the book, this notion is challenged again and again.

In his chapter Shaw (Chapter Two) talks of how the narrative of consumerism sees the consumer as *'king'*, and how political discourse anticipates the development of more *'assertive'* consumers. This picks up on the classic ideas of the consumer as chooser that have often been used in argumentation and rhetoric – either approvingly by policy makers, or perhaps as a straw man by those less favourable. Other chapters certainly see things as less clear-cut. For example, Powell and

Greener (Chapter Six) talk of *responsible* or *ethical* consumers; Laing et al (Chapter Five) of the *reflexive* consumer; and Clarke (Chapter Nine) of *reasonable* consumers. It is hard to see how these characterisations fit easily with purer notions of the 'utility maximiser'.

Other characterisations are equally problematic for notions of the consumer as chooser. In Chapter One we put forward ideas of the *Young* consumer (after Michael Young, who saw consumers as a third force in civil society alongside capital and labour). This consumer is aware of his/her status and prepared to use this as a platform to negotiate, rather than necessarily as a way to 'win' in a zero-sum game. Similarly, Powell and Greener (Chapter Six) speak of the *activist* consumer. Taking their identity from their consumption and using it as a basis for collective action, such consumers also appear to go beyond the supermarket model. Mills provides us with specific examples in what he has termed *rebel* consumers: squatters, rent strikers, collectivists. Indeed, it has been convincingly argued that tenant groups are formed not of local citizens, but of service consumers (Birchall, 1992). This leads us to Simmons and Birchall's conceptions of the *consumer as member* in Chapter Thirteen and possibilities that arise for collective action that can entail taking on responsibility for the actual control of services – for example, in tenant management co-operatives. These collective conceptions of consumers (see also Farrell, Chapter Seven) clearly come from a different place than the stereotypically individual consumer as chooser, but we find good arguments for the need to accommodate them.

At this point, some would argue that the entire notion of the consumer starts to unravel: Barnes (Chapter Twelve), for example, questions whether we are speaking of *authoritative* consumers. Instead she rejects this notion, suggesting that people who use public services need to be recognised as having more to offer in the relationship – for example, strong collective identifications, essential expertise and direct experience. Beresford (Chapter Eleven) picks up this theme, suggesting that the use of consumerist discourses conceals the ways in which social care services have been the site of important struggles between service users and producers, and diminishes the ongoing importance of these actors' roles. Neither author denies that we are looking at diverse populations, but each considers discourses of social movements, collective action and empowerment to be more appropriate than those occurring within explicitly 'consumerist' frames. We therefore need to ask whether consumers are necessarily individuals, or whether collective conceptions can apply (see Hilton, 2003).

Table 14.1 is a tentative attempt to map some of the different types or 'faces' of the consumer that have been introduced in the course of this volume onto the earlier table featured in Chapter One. It comes with a clear and serious 'health warning' – it is difficult to find exact equivalences between concepts derived from a public service perspective and those derived in the different environments described by these other authors on consumerism. As a result, some of our consumer types occur in more than one place. However, we offer it as a potentially useful tool in beginning to build bridges between these two literatures.

While it remains unclear how elastic the concept of consumerism can be, and how far it can be stretched in the collective and voice directions, it does appear that collective aspects of consumerism such as buycotts (eg Fairtrade) and boycotts (eg rent strikes) have been neglected (see Malpass et al, 2007). In another, similar, edited volume, Deakin and Wright (1990, p 14) eschew any neat demarcation between a 'consumerist' and a 'collectivist' approach (see Hoggett and Hambleton, 1987) in favour of an approach which acknowledges that the empowerment of public service users will come through a package of provisions that draw upon a variety of perspectives. However, as we can now go on to consider, some commentators, such as Hood et al (1996), have asserted that different types of consumerism may be incompatible with each other, and so a 'pick 'n' mix' may not be possible.

Consumer 'mechanisms'

The second way in which the parameters of consumption are unclear concerns what we have termed consumer 'mechanisms'. It should be noted here that consumer *discourse* does not necessarily translate into consumer *mechanisms* – in other words, calling someone a consumer does not necessarily make them so unless appropriate mechanisms of choice and voice are present. In Chapter One we revisited some older themes/frameworks of consumerism (eg Winkler, 1987; Potter, 1988; Hood et al, 1996), which we will use to inform our discussion. However, we start here with another of these frameworks: Hirschman's (1970) classic trilogy of 'exit, voice and loyalty'. We see in the above characterisations of the consumer in public services at least two of these mechanisms at work. Hence, notions of the 'consumer as chooser' emphasise exit as the most important mechanism, while for 'assertive consumers', 'activist consumers' and the 'consumer as member' the emphasis appears to fall more squarely on voice. At this point, however, we might ask what happened to loyalty. Does this relate more closely to notions of the client, placing trust in others to make choices on

Table 14.1: Different consumer 'faces'

Gabriel and Lang (2006)	Edwards (2000)	Aldridge (2003)	This volume
CHOOSER: rational consumer, requiring genuine options, finance, information	KING: 'an unconstrained rational actor seeking to maximise positive personal outcomes' (p 12)	RATIONAL ACTOR: 'calculative and selfish' (p 18)	KING (Shaw, Ch Two) RATIONAL ACTOR (Simmons, Ch Four) ACTIVE CONVINCED (Laing et al, Ch Five) EMPOWERED (Mills, Ch Eight; Glendinning, Ch Ten) AUTHORITATIVE (Barnes, Ch Twelve)
COMMUNICATOR: using goods to communicate, leading to conceptions of the consumer as VICTIM, ARTIST or EXPLORER	See VOYEUR		
REBEL: using products in new ways as a conscious rebellion. Also refers to active rebellion (joyriding, looting, etc)	CRIMINAL: the professional shoplifter, causing costs to be passed on to other consumers		ALIENATED (Simmons, Ch Four) ACTIVE SCEPTIC (Laing et al, Ch Five) REBEL (Mills, Ch Eight)
IDENTITY SEEKER: as in social identity, gained from a group. Citing Bauman on the decline of the work ethic	See VOYEUR	COMMUNICATOR: maintains that these faces are the same	REPRESSED CONSUMERS (Simmons, Ch Four) COLLECTIVE (Farrell, Ch Seven; Beresford, Ch Eleven; Barnes, Ch Twelve) MEMBER (Simmons and Birchall, Ch Thirteen)
HEDONIST OR ARTIST? consumption as pleasure, noting that pleasure may be socially constructed	See VOYEUR		

Table 14.1: continued

Gabriel and Lang (2006)	Edwards (2000)	Aldridge (2003)	This volume
VICTIM: referring to both created wants and consumer protection, although focusing on the latter, as in Aldridge	VICTIM: either seduced into buying unnecessarily or buying the wrong product	VICTIM: the rational actor making a mistake, or being incorrectly informed/ advised	SUBJECTED (Simmons, Ch Four) MARGINALISED CONSUMERS (Simmons, Ch Four) COMPLIANT SCEPTIC (Laing et al, Ch Five)
ACTIVIST: generally a potted history of consumer activism, from the Co-op to modern ethical/ environmental groups	ANTI-CONSUMER: participating in boycotts, demonstrations, etc, consuming specific products	See COMMUNICATOR	'YOUNG' (Powell et al, Ch One) REPRESSED CONSUMERS (Simmons, Ch Four) ACTIVE SCEPTIC (Laing et al, Ch Five) ACTIVIST (Powell and Greener, Ch Six) COLLECTIVE (Farrell, Ch Seven; Beresford, Ch Eleven; Barnes, Ch Twelve) EMPOWERED (Mills, Ch Eight; Glendinning, Ch Ten) MEMBER (Simmons and Birchall, Ch Thirteen)
CONSUMER OR CITIZEN? Tracing the tension between two concepts	N/A	Maintains that this is not a face of the consumer	CO-PRODUCERS (Simmons, Ch Four) RESPONSIBLE (Powell and Greener, Ch Six) COLLECTIVE (Farrell, Ch Seven; Beresford, Ch Eleven; Barnes, Ch Twelve) REASONABLE (Clarke, Ch Nine)
EXPLORER: consumers buying without a clear idea, bargain hunting	VOYEUR: window-shopper; strongly tied to the role of consumption in identity formation. Could also apply to ARTIST, COMMUNICATOR or IDENTITY SEEKER	DUPE: characterisation of the critique of rationality, dominated expressive. Could also apply to several other categories in certain contexts.	SELF–EXCLUDER (Simmons, Ch Four) DELEGATORS (Simmons, Ch Four) COMPLIANT CONVINCED (Laing et al, Ch Five)

their behalf? While 'responsible' or 'reasonable' consumers might be expected to use voice when appropriate, they might also be thought of as relatively loyal. Further, in their framework Laing et al (Chapter Five) suggest that, of the people who use professionalised services, 30% fall into a 'compliant convinced' category of users who implicitly trust service professionals (see Le Grand, 2003). This provides evidence of the continued existence in public services of what Baldock and Ungerson (1994) have termed 'clientism' (see Chapter One), which is also bound up with more 'passive' forms of relationships. Hence, although today's consumer is often constructed in current discourse as being more active in either 'choosing' or 'voicing' opinions (see the 'choice vs voice' debate discussed by Powell et al [Chapter One] and Simmons [Chapter Four]), it seems there is a significant number of people who retain these more passive relationships with public services – particularly in professionalised contexts. This has implications for different models of provision, for example suggesting that some consumers will benefit less than others from greater 'choice', at least without appropriate support (Clarke, Chapter Nine; Glendinning, Chapter Ten; but see Le Grand, 2007).

Recently, Le Grand (2007) has proposed a framework that distinguishes between different elements of choice for the 'consumer as chooser'. He argues that, although voice and representation have their merits, 'in most situations policies that rely on extending choice and competition among providers have the most potential for delivering high-quality, efficient, responsive, and equitable services'. Unsurprisingly, having recently worked as an adviser within the British government at the highest levels, his ideas have been influential (see Shaw, Chapter Two). Le Grand sets out five dimensions of choice – asking where, who, what, when and how. The service-related chapters of this book pick up on this framework and show how the different elements have applied in different service contexts at different times. While consumerism in public services has been important for both recent Conservative and New Labour governments, the history of consumerism is of longer standing (ie it was not introduced in 1979, or in 1997). Our chapter authors plot the trajectories of change here, asking whether there has been increasing emphasis on consumption and choice.

Table 14.2 brings together some of their findings. It shows that there has been a movement in the general direction of greater choice, from the classic welfare state, through the conservative governments of 1979–97, to the New Labour governments since 1997. The pace of this change has also quickened to some extent over the last 10 years, both through the extension of schemes and ideas first promoted by the Conservatives and through new developments. The table shows that some of these changes have been more significant than others. In terms of choice of provider, the Right to Buy, choice of school and direct payments are the main examples. In terms of access channels, 'choice-based lettings', 'choose and book' and NHS Direct may also be considered important developments.

We should stress here that most of the cells in this table could be said to show relatively limited movements in the direction of 'consumerism'. Some may say that there is not much 'choice' (even in the latest period), others that consumers have only been offered choices in some areas – mainly 'where' and 'how'. In this way, often the introduction of greater choice has been piecemeal and only at the peripheries of service provision. Further, even where choice has been successfully introduced through such mechanisms as Right to Buy, choice of school and direct payments, this has not been uncontroversial (for example, accusations have followed these policies of 'residualisation', 'cream-skimming' and the 'privatisation of risk' respectively). Choice can therefore increase the conflict between key values such as liberty, equality and fraternity. These things suggest that there may be limits to the extent to which choice can be applied in the public sector. Once again, we seem to find ourselves looking beyond the 'consumer as chooser'.

In response, this book shows how a greater diversity of consumer 'mechanisms' needs to be considered in the public services. In another useful framework, Hood et al (1996) hint at this diversity, describing 'sixteen ways to consumerise public services'. According to Hood et al (1996, p 43), despite – or maybe because of – all the talk about 'consumerisation' in public management, there is no standard scale of consumerisation. They discuss two possible ways: the hierarchical and the dimensional themes. The first, following Arnstein (1969), is a unidimensional 'ladder' of consumerisation. The second is a multi-dimensional approach, such as access, choice, information, redress and representation (Potter, 1988). They combine both approaches, with two dimensions of active and passive; and direct and indirect power. This produces four archetypical forms of co-production (direct/active- ie full 'DIY public services); representation (indirect/active, eg plebiscitary-type direct decisions); product choice (direct/passive, eg electricity supplier); and regulation (indirect/passive, eg adjudication of consumer complaints). Within each type, there are Arnstein-type ladders, making 12 cells, and some 'in-between types making 16 cells in total'. They conclude that public services can be brought under user control in very different ways: the key questions concern 'putting which consumers in what driving seat' (p 49; see Greener, 2003).

Table 14.2: Applying Le Grand's dimensions of choice

Dimension	Classic welfare state	Conservatives (1979–97)	New Labour (1997–)
Choice of provider (where?)	Typically limited – choices largely made on behalf of users, eg GP referral to hospital; use of catchment areas dominant in education. What choice existed was localised: eg choice of GP in health. Exit to private sector possible in health and education for those able and willing to pay	Choices still largely made on behalf of users, although some decentralised, eg GP fundholding. Some elements of choice introduced: eg nursery education voucher (1996); direct payments in social care (1997). Localised choice extended: eg to choice of GP, added choice of school. Some new categories of provider added: eg schools (CTCs, GM schools); Large-Scale Voluntary Transfer (LSVT) housing associations and choice of landlords under 'tenants' choice'; expansion of private security services. Exit to private sector extended with Right to Buy in housing	Nursery voucher removed (1997). However, in health: free choice of NHS or private (2008); in social care: expansion of direct payments (DPs), individual budgets (IBs) (2005). Localised choice maintained/extended: in health: 'choose and book' (2003); in education: catchment areas put back in place alongside choice of school. Further new categories of provider added. In health: foundation hospitals; in education: foundation, community, voluntary aided and aided schools (1998), city academies; in policing: continued growth of private security services. Exit to private sector extended through shared equity schemes in housing

Table 14.2: continued

Dimension	Classic welfare state	Conservatives (1979–97)	New Labour (1997–)
Choice of professional (who?)	Limited in all services except health, where choice of GP	Still limited. To choice of GP in health added choice of landlords in housing (formation of tenant management organisations, LSVT and 'tenants' choice')	Some limited changes. In health: choice of GP, NHS Walk-in Centres, NHS Direct; in housing: extension of tenant representation on TMO and HA boards, choice of landlord through tenant ballots; in policing: 'personalisation' of local beat officers; in social care, DPs/IBs allow users to recruit and employ their own care workers
Choice of service (what?)	Limited in all service areas	Still limited. In health: possibility of private room for those willing to pay; in education: some new choices over types of schools and their specialisms; in housing: incentives for tenants to vote for Housing Action Trusts; in policing: contracted policing and public order services – sports events, retail malls etc	Still limited in health and education, although new developments around the Baccalaureate and continuation of choices around types of schools and their specialisms. In housing: choice of houses through choice-based lettings; choice of decorative schemes (individual); choice of estate services (collective). In policing: new emphasis on neighbourhood, community and local partnerships discussing services. In social care: DPs/IBs allow greater choice over type/content of service
Choice of appointment time (when?)	Limited: usually dictated by professionals, eg health: appointment time and 'wait'; housing: allocation governed by waiting list	Still limited	Still limited, although new developments in health: choose and book; in housing: choice of access times for tradesmen in some cases, choice of payment methods in some cases; in policing: managerial pressure on response times and 'reassurance policing'; in social care, DPs/IBs allow choice over timing of service

Table 14.2: continued

Dimension	Classic welfare state	Conservatives (1979–97)	New Labour (1997–)
Choice of access channel (how?)	Limited	Limited	Some important new developments. In health: NHS Direct (telephone and www), text messages for results, choose and book to set appointment times; in housing: 'choice-based letting' – advertised online and in local newspapers; in policing: addition of non-emergency telephone numbers to supplement – and divert from – 999
Choice of additional services	Limited	In health: possibility of private room for those willing to pay	In health: private rooms, telephones and TVs, food choice; in housing: some landlords offering priced additional services, mainly or only available for private purchasers/ top-up of LA-funded provision

Some might regard the Hood et al (1996) dimension of 'representation' as voice – an alternative to rather than a part of (choice-based varieties of) consumerism. However, it is clear that it is possible to see beyond such narrow 'charm school' (Potter, 1988) or 'supermarket model' (Winkler, 1987) varieties of consumerism. Do different consumption/ choice mechanisms exist? Barnes and Prior (1995, p 53) write that the celebration and expansion of individual choice has been a core objective of government policy over the last 15 years. For example, according to the Citizen's Charter (1991, p 4), where choice and competition are limited, consumers cannot as easily make their views count. In many public services, therefore, we need to increase both choice and competition. They continue that there are four means of increasing choice in the Citizen's Charter: privatisation of public services; contracting within the public sector; developing choices within the public sector; consultation (p 53). The conditions of public service use include coercion, predictability, frequency, significance and participation. It is possible to identify the circumstances in which these different dimensions of service use can combine to create situations where choice, even if it exists, is unlikely to be experienced as empowering, or may generate confusion and uncertainty which could be experienced as disempowering. They examine factors such as lack of information, influence, confidence in what is available, experience/skill in making choices; crisis situations; where choice creates a dilemma; when choice is not an option (p 55). They conclude – in contradiction to the Cabinet Office (2005) and Leadbeater (2004) – that user empowerment is more likely to be achieved through voice rather than choice (p 58).

Barnes picks up these themes again in Chapter Twelve, reiterating that consumerism can disempower service users (see Glendinning, Chapter Ten). Instead she supports empowerment through social movements and collective action (see also Beresford, Chapter Eleven) and advocates an approach based on citizenship rather than consumption. This, of course, stands in direct contrast to Le Grand's (2007) advocacy of choice over voice. At this point we might ask: is Barnes too optimistic regarding citizenship while Le Grand is too optimistic regarding consumerism? Certainly there is evidence that, on its own, voice has traditionally proved insufficient to empower service users in their structurally less powerful roles relative to producers (eg Marquand, 2004). As Simmons (Chapter Four) points out, questions therefore arise as to how, where, when and for whom voice allows service users to 'have a say and make a difference' (see also Simmons et al, 2006, 2007). From Hirschman's (1970) framework of exit, voice and loyalty to the present day, it has been recognised that choice should not be considered in isolation. This book suggests a more balanced position: that both choice and voice are necessary. In one form of this argument the then Schools Minister, David Miliband, put it like this:

> Choice and voice are strengthened by the presence of each other: the threat of exit makes [service providers] listen; the ability to make your voice heard provides a tool to the consumer who does not want to change [provider] every time they are unhappy. (David Miliband, speech, 18 May 2004)

In this view, voice needs to be linked to choice (or the 'threat of exit') to be effective: 'choice gives power to voice' (Le Grand, 2006, p 4). However, Simmons (Chapter Four) argues that while choice indeed gives power to voice at the level of the *individual*, at the level of the *collective* this is a less tenable proposition. Instead, he argues, giving power to collective voice requires greater attention to the strengthening of possibilities for co-production that stand outside the narrow confines of consumer choice. Again, this involves taking a wider view of the consumer in public services (see Clode et al, 1987; Deakin and Wright, 1990). As a result, Needham (Chapter Three) indicates that the relationship between the different narratives of standardisation, differentiation and co-production can lead to tensions in the layers between them. As we suggested earlier, New Labour policy has pursued a path to take the consumer from passive to more active positions (Shaw, Chapter Two). This may involve choice, yes; but arguably also co-production (see Glendinning, Chapter Ten; Barnes, Chapter Twelve).

In sum, in this book we bring together an analysis of difference in both 'consumer types' and 'consumer mechanisms'. We believe this is a novel combination – some commentators such as Gabriel and Lang (1995) simply discuss types, while others such as Hood et al (1996) discuss only mechanisms. By bringing the two together more explicitly, we hope to find ways to develop more productive understandings of how different consumer types might respond to different consumer mechanisms. For example, for the stereotypical 'consumer as chooser', the key mechanism is 'choice' rather than voice. But other 'consumer' types we have identified seem to have associations with other mechanisms. For example, for the 'consumer as activist' the key mechanism may be voice rather than choice. However, in each case, the fact that demand for either choice or voice is dominant does not mean that demand for the other is absent. Hence, in each case, what kinds of choice and voice are required? Further, will different people want different things at the same time? Or will the same people want different things at different times? The coexistence of different consumer types within the public service environment suggests that they will. It may therefore be increasingly hard to satisfy their various demands with an insufficiently multidimensional approach.

These themes are important and likely to be the focus of continued debate, especially, as we have noted, because they remain dynamic over time. As background and contextual issues for different public services, they are also important. This brings us to the next key message of the book: that context is important. In itself, this may seem a relatively banal statement. However, given the pervasiveness of 'universal' discourses around such issues as choice, it seems worth restating. It points to a need to understand what it is about context that makes variation from 'one-size-fits-all' consumerist perspectives desirable. Hence, it pushes beyond simplistic questions of 'what works', to ask what works for whom, where, when and in what ways. It is, perhaps, in answer to these kinds of questions that the understandings of 'difference' that we have discussed can be most usefully applied.

Context is important

Following on from our discussion of difference in the previous section, we can briefly ask questions about 'consumer types' and 'consumer mechanisms' in the range of contexts described in this book. Hence, we might ask: do the different faces/types have any resonance in different policy areas? Are consumers choosers in education but victims in healthcare? Does government assume that consumers are choosers, and what follows if this assumption is not correct? Have consumers changed over time: were they victims but are now rational actors? Similarly, we might ask: does the form or content of consumer choice and/or voice vary in different services? Do the different conditions of public service choice and/or voice (Barnes and Prior, 1995) mean that reforms are differentially empowering or disempowering in different areas?

In Chapter One we suggested that consumption may indeed be contextual, with different versions of consumerism more appropriate for certain people (eg Laing et al, typology, Chapter Five; Simmons, Chapter Four, Figures 4.1a and 4.1b) and different services (Simmons, Chapter Four) at different times. This is consistent with the view that we should talk less of voice versus choice, but instead more of voice plus choice – how best to have a say and make a difference. This view shares some overlaps with the Arnstein-type 'ladders of consumerism' suggested in Hood et al's (1996) framework. As with Arnstein's original ladder of participation, there is no presumption that one rung on the ladder is necessarily better than another. To take such a view would be to neglect consideration of the context.

To some extent, this may be what has happened at the level of central government. As Shaw (Chapter Two) points out, there has been an assumption here that the private sector is more responsive than the public sector. Or, as former prime minister Tony Blair once famously put it: 'You try getting change in the public services – I bear the scars on my back after two years in government' (Blair, 1999). This assumption has been matched with another, that consumers are empowered in the private sector, but not as citizens in public services (see Le Grand, 2003). However, as Needham (Chapter Three) points out, behind this rhetoric of 'differentiation' (D) (found in Blair's speeches, command papers and local authority corporate plans) have been other narratives – 'standardisation' (S) and 'co-production' (C) – that have assumed equal or sometimes greater importance. Particularly noticeable here are differences between services. For example, Needham shows that health and education remain subject to highly 'standardised' narratives at all levels, while in law and order 'co-production' emerges as particularly important. Meanwhile, she points out, welfare is subject to an entirely different prioritisation of narratives by Blair (C–D–S), the command papers (D–S–C) and local government (S–C–D). What must now, perhaps, be unpicked is the appropriateness of these narratives at each level – and what different public services might do to respond.

Powell and Greener (Chapter Six) consider the differences in public services that have led Potter (1988) to ask in relation to consumerism, 'Does the coat fit?'. They cite Titmuss (1968), who identifies 13 characteristics that show healthcare not to be a consumer good. They also note how consumerist discourse does not necessarily lead to greater choice. For example, the 1989 Conservative internal market introduced little in the way of choice, and perhaps reduced choice in some ways – with patients following the money rather than money following the patients. They close, however, by asking whether market mavens have equivalents of public progressives – in other words, whether 'good' consumers can help all (eg through complaints, or buying products with, for example, lower salt, or refusing excessive packaging). However, they leave open this question of whether public service consumers help others in addition to themselves – particularly where there is what the economists call 'excludability'. In a 'zero-sum' game with limited available resources, they warn that competition to secure those resources may mean that 'good' consumers think only of maximising their own utility – and therefore that choice can raise inequalities (see Clarke et al, 2007).

Farrell (Chapter Seven) picks up on this point, showing how, if some parents secure the best school places, there will be fewer left for others. She indicates an important difference between making a choice and expressing a preference. She points out that parental 'choice' of school has largely represented the latter, leading to the perverse effects of parents' well-known attempts to manipulate the process via catchment area rules. This has seen the introduction of a random allocation procedure (or lottery) in some locations to help 'level the playing field'. Farrell's chapter also shows how the frequency of choice varies between different public services. For example, parents may choose schools at (say) ages 4 and 11, but some people make healthcare and social care (or even housing) choices more frequently. The potential for disruption to their child's development means that exit is rarely considered, leaving voice (and/or loyalty) as the main mechanism for parents' ongoing relationship with the school. This is consolidated by the lack of choice over their child's teacher (allocated by head teachers) or over content (largely defined by the national curriculum). Taking these factors together, parents' ongoing relationships with the school are therefore certainly not founded on ideals of the 'consumer as chooser'.

Mills (Chapter Eight) considers the development of consumerism in housing. Here, a dramatic form of choice has been given through the 'Right to Buy'. However, for those unwilling or unable to buy their own homes, many have also been given a choice of landlord through such initiatives as large-scale voluntary transfer. As with the choice of school in education, however, this choice is not one that is available to be made frequently, and is one that generally leaves tenants locked in to a relationship with whichever landlord is voted for by the majority in the ballot. Another choice here is self-management: tenant management organisations exist in many parts of the country and have generally proved quite effective (Rodgers, 2001; ODPM, 2002). This form of choice represents collective rather than individual empowerment. Again, this stands in contrast to stereotypes of the 'consumer as chooser', even though tenants here may be seen as being empowered as consumers (the basis for their collective identity being use of the service) rather than as (the more common collective category of) citizens.

Glendinning (Chapter Ten) turns these categorisations around, suggesting that social care service users are required to make claims for inclusion as citizens in order to ensure equal access to the benefits of public service consumption. Examining the provision of 'direct payments', she argues (as does Beresford, Chapter Eleven) that while this policy found fertile ground in a neoliberal environment favouring 'privatisation' in all its forms, its roots were demand led and the result of a civil rights or social justice discourse rather than an explicitly consumerist one. In other words, direct payments were the result of particular social categories (eg disabled people) arguing collectively for greater equality and autonomy, but not the result of pressure from individual consumers for greater choice. Even though direct payments and individualised budgets certainly allow individuals greater choice, these individuals stand simultaneously in a number of other relationships, for example as employers and co-producers. Once again, models of the consumer as chooser seem rather inadequate in this context (see also Barnes, Chapter Twelve).

In his chapter, Clarke (Chapter Nine) reiterates a point he has made previously about public services: that 'it is not like shopping' (Clarke, 2005; Clarke et al, 2007). There are perhaps few better examples of this than the services provided by the police. Of course, the perpetrators of crime generally 'consume' these services against their will and so can hardly be constructed as 'choosers'. However, the victims of crime also face very limited choices. For example, they cannot choose protection from another police force from a different part of the country if they are dissatisfied with the service they receive. Despite the presence of government league tables, neither can citizens easily choose the most lenient force for speeding (see Tiebout (1956) – voting with your feet). Unsurprisingly, therefore, the consumer as chooser is another insubstantial (if not invisible) figure here.

At this point we should point out that none of the above arguments takes an ideological position against choice. As Shaw points out in Chapter Two, the government has considered it a legitimate aim to support greater choice in helping 'pawns' become 'queens' (Le Grand, 2003). Hence, Le Grand (2007) has argued that for those disempowered by producer-dominated public services, including those from marginalised sections of the community, there is generally limited voice. Greater choice may therefore provide new ways to counteract producer power. Further, even if consumers have limited voice *and* choice, there is still the question of which is the least worst. Choice, then, can be seen as an important part of the toolkit of ideas in relation to public services. Nevertheless, all the above contributions seem to be saying that there is a danger in seeing the benefits of choice too narrowly – in that this can:

1. lead to representations of the public service consumer as 'chooser';
2. affect the mechanisms by and through which producer–consumer relationships are constructed.

As we have demonstrated, such constructions and representations are often unrealistic, failing to fully reflect the nature of consumers in the wide range of public service contexts in which they are found. As Shaw (Chapter Two) also points out, this range of contexts is complicated further by the plurality and diversity of service providers increasingly found in the public services. Private and social enterprises have been added to the 'delivery' portfolio, along with 'membership' organisations such as hospital foundation trusts and tenant management organisations (Simmons and Birchall, Chapter Thirteen). Such developments could be expected to have further effects that are worthy of study. Hence, as Warde (1996, p 309) puts it in the conclusion to another similar edited text: 'The restructuring of welfare has significant and varied effects for citizenship as well as for individual customers and clients. Generally however, little attention is paid to the consequences for social relations of substitution of one mode of provision for another.'

Conclusion: going 'beyond the consumer as chooser'

The consumer as 'chooser' has become part of the fabric woven together in the public services by the 'warp' of top-down, supply-side processes (eg neoliberalism, government rhetoric, policy exhortations), and the 'weft' of bottom-up, demand-side processes (eg individualisation, loss of deference for authority). However, as such, it should perhaps be seen as only one important strand. The contributions to this volume show that there are many faces of public service users that both compare and contrast with the consumer as chooser, and many service 'mechanisms' that vary in their compatibility with this (stereo)type.

Leading sociologist Zygmunt Bauman (2003, 2007) portrays consumption as a solitary activity. Even in a more classic sense of consumption, however, this is open to challenge – clearly he has never heard of the Campaign for Real Ale! Our analysis suggests that to individualistic models of the consumer based on choice may be added other 'faces' or 'types' that may be more collective, and which function/are empowered via other mechanisms such as voice. Cabinet secretary Andrew Turnbull (2003) sees choice positively, as 'disruptive governance':

> People have written about disruptive technologies. I would describe choice as disruptive governance. It really forces you to change your view of the world. It is at this point that power really shifts. It is like that inversion of magnetic north to magnetic south that scientists talk of, where accountability for the first time really starts to flow downwards. (cited in Leadbeater, 2004, pp 45–6)

We might suggest that different varieties of choice might be even more disruptive in this sense – especially when linked to different varieties of voice. In support of this perspective, Gabriel and Lang (2006, p 173) write that some see the notion of the consumer as being too individualistic, restrictive, in short irrecoverably hijacked by the political Right, and resurrect an older idea propounded by the founder of the UK's *Which?* (formerly the Consumers' Association) and National Consumer Council, Michael Young, who envisaged organised consumers as a third force for the citizenry, alongside labour and capital. Clode et al's (1987) edited collection featured a foreword by Young, who issued a typical challenge: 'The successors of Beveridge therefore need to come out of the wood and show what the new welfare could be like without the New Right to direct it.'

In response, the different contributions to this book suggest that many of the faces of the consumer in public services cannot be translated directly from the private sector. In other words, consumption in the public services is 'not like shopping', or at least – as Powell and Greener (Chapter Six) would have it – not *simply* shopping (cf Diamond, 2007). In another, similar, edited volume, Deakin and Wright (1990, p 214) point to 'the concept of public services as an indispensable element in the structure and values of our society'. This indicates something of the distinctiveness of public services that is inherent in notions of a 'public service orientation' and 'public value' (see Clarke and Stewart, 1986; Moore, 1995). Meanwhile, as Warde (1996, p 311) observes, 'the field of consumption remains one of partial, competing perspectives … [between] the instrumental imperatives of material life and the normative grounding of all social action'. We might suggest that the increasing complexity of public service contexts, and the differentiated nature of public service consumers (eg Simmons, Chapter Four; Laing et al, Chapter Five), means that these instrumental imperatives and normative groundings are becoming less clear-cut.

Certainly, the 'faces' of the consumer that we have revealed in this book are sufficiently differentiated for no one-size-fits-all approach, whether paternalist or consumerist, to work effectively in different contexts. As a result, as Hood et al (1996) point out, we often find ourselves faced with either 'pick 'n' mix' or 'painful trade-offs'. Their analysis is based on the observation that 'different state traditions emphasize consumerism in different ways, and that different forms of public service consumerism may be incompatible with one another' (Hood et al, 1996, p 43).

Incompatibility is one lens through which to view Hood et al's (1996) consumer mechanisms. However, it is also perhaps a regressive one, anticipating zero-sum outcomes and providing justifications for the promotion of 'narrow' approaches to the relationships between public service users and providers. The notion of *complementarities* provides a second lens that accepts difference and perhaps instead looks for positive-sum outcomes from a 'broader' set of relationships. We believe it is important to consider *both* the incompatibilities *and* complementarities between different approaches. The challenge for public services can be seen as minimising the former while maximising the latter. The first step here is acknowledging difference. The second is learning how to work effectively with it in particular public service contexts.

As a result, we think it is important to recognise the different types/ faces of the consumer – or 'who' it is that uses public services. As we suggested in Chapter One, there is a need to focus on consumers (plural) rather than *the* consumer. This diversity suggests that one-size-fits-all approaches (even where this is a 'consumerist' version ostensibly offering individual 'choices') are therefore unlikely to succeed. What works for one consumer may not be best for all consumers. This means that it is also important to recognise that there are different consumer mechanisms – or 'what' can be done to provide the basis of the relationship between public service users and providers. By bringing together in this book this analysis of difference in both 'consumer types' and 'consumer mechanisms', we believe we are charting new territories that today's 'modern' public services must seek to explore. In some contexts, it may be easier to overcome incompatibilities and find complementarities than in others – because of the diversity of their user populations (or lack of it) and/or because of the diversity of mechanisms that they employ to engage with users (or lack of it). This book has shown how using choice as the main mechanism for building relationships between users and providers is problematic, and that voice is often of at least equal importance. In this way, unlike shopping (Clarke, Chapter Nine), choice is one important value among many which people expect to be taken into consideration within the public service environment. For example, 'liberty' to make differentiated choices must compete with 'equality' in public service standardisation narratives and 'fraternity' in notions of co-production and membership (Needham, Chapter Three; Simmons and Birchall, Chapter Thirteen). Values are influential – not only in underpinning differences in consumer faces and mechanisms, but also in determining how these differences are recognised and applied in different public service contexts. Choice (and voice), values and difference each have an important part of the story to tell. By helping to understand differentiated consumers in public services, and what can be done to respond to them in different contexts, they suggest how more progressive relationships may be built – relationships that move beyond the current emphasis on the 'consumer as chooser'.

References

Aldridge, A. (2003) *Consumption*, Cambridge: Polity.

Arnstein, S. (1969) 'A ladder of citizen participation', *Journal of the American Institute of Planners*, vol 35, no 4, pp 216–24.

Baldock, J. and Ungerson, C. (1994) *Becoming consumers of community care: Households within the mixed economy*, York: Joseph Rowntree Foundation.

Barnes, M. and Prior, D. (1995) 'Spoilt for choice? How consumerism can disempower public service users', *Public Money and Management*, vol 15, no 3, pp 53–8.

Bauman, Z. (2003) *Liquid love: On the frailty of human bonds*, Cambridge: Polity.

Bauman, Z. (2007) *Consuming life*, Cambridge: Polity.

Birchall, J. (1992) 'Council tenants: sovereign consumers or pawns in the game?', in J. Birchall (ed) *Housing policy in the 1990s*, London: Routledge, pp 163–89.

Blair, T. (1999) Speech to the British Venture Capitalists Association, London, July.

Cabinet Office (2005) *Choice and voice in the reform of public services: Government response to the PASC report – choice, voice and public services*, London: Cabinet Office.

Citizen's Charter (1991) Cm 1599, London: HMSO.

Clarke, J. (2005) 'Competitive choice or relational reasoning?', Paper to 'Cultures of Consumption' Seminar, 'Choice and Voice in Public Services', HM Treasury, London, 24 June.

Clarke, J., Newman, J., Smith, N., Vidler, E. and Westmarland, L. (2007) *Creating citizen-consumers*, London: Sage.

Clarke, M. and Stewart, J. (1986) 'Local government and the public service orientation', *Local Government Studies*, vol 12, no 3, pp 1–8.

Clode, D., Parker, C. and Etherington, S. (eds) (1987) *Towards the sensitive bureaucracy: Consumers, welfare and the new pluralism*, Aldershot: Gower.

Deakin, N. and Wright, A. (1990) *Consuming public services*, London: Routledge.

Diamond, P. (ed) (2007) *Public matters: The renewal of the public realm*, London: Politicos.

Edwards, T. (2000) *Contradictions of consumption: Concepts, practices and politics in consumer society*, Milton Keynes: Open University Press.

Gabriel, Y. and Lang, T. (1995) *The unmanageable consumer: Contemporary consumption and its fragmentations*, London, Sage.

Gabriel, Y. and Lang, T. (2006) *The unmanageable consumer* (2nd edn), London, Sage.

Greener, I. (2003) 'Who choosing what?', in C. Bochel, N. Ellison and M. Powell (eds) *Social Policy Review 15*, Bristol: The Policy Press, pp 49–68.

Hilton, M. (2003) *Consumerism in twentieth century Britain*, Cambridge: Cambridge University Press.

Hirschman, A. (1970) *Exit, voice and loyalty*, London: Harvard University Press.

Hoggett, P. and Hambleton, R. (1987) *Decentralization and democracy: Localising public services*, Bristol: SAUS Publications.

Hood, C., Peters, G. and Wollmann, H. (1996) 'Sixteen ways to consumerize public services: pick 'n' mix or painful trade-offs', *Public Money and Management*, vol 16, no 4, pp 43–50.

Jones, G. and Needham, C. (2008) 'Debate: consumerism in public services: for and against', *Public Money and Management*, vol 28, no 2, pp 70–6.

Keat, R., Whiteley, N. and Abercrombie, N. (eds) (1994) *The authority of the consumer*, London: Routledge.

Le Grand, J. (2003) *Motivation, agency, and public policy: Of knights and knaves, pawns and queens*, Oxford: Oxford University Press.

Le Grand, J. (2006) 'Choice and competition in public services', *Research in Public Policy*, Issue 2, Bristol: Centre for Market and Public Organisation.

Le Grand, J. (2007) *The other invisible hand*, Princeton, NJ: Princeton University Press.

Leadbeater, C. (2004) *Personalisation through participation*, London: Demos.

Malpass, A., Barnett, C., Clarke, N. and Cloke, P. (2007) 'Problematizing choice: responsible consumers and sceptical citizens', in M. Bevir and F. Trentmann (eds) *Governance, consumers and citizens*, Basingstoke: Palgrave, pp 231–56.

Marquand, D. (2004) *Decline of the public*, Cambridge: Polity.

Moore, M. (1995) *Creating public value: Strategic management in government*, London: Harvard University Press.

ODPM (Office of the Deputy Prime Minister) (2002) *Tenants managing: Evaluation of tenant management organisations in England*, London: ODPM.

Policy Commission on Public Services (2004) *Making public services personal*, London: National Consumer Council.

Potter, J. (1988) 'Consumerism and the public sector: how well does the coat fit?', *Public Administration*, vol 66, no 2, pp 149–64.

Rodgers, D. (2001) 'Housing co-operatives and social exclusion', in J. Birchall (ed) *The new mutualism in public policy*, London: Routledge.

Simmons, R., Birchall, J. and Prout, A. (2006) 'Choice about voice', Paper presented at Social Policy Association Conference, Birmingham, July.

Simmons, R., Birchall, J. and Prout, A. (2007) 'Hearing voices? User involvement and public service cultures', *Consumer Policy Review*, vol 17, no 5, pp 234–40.

Tiebout, C. (1956) 'A pure theory of local expenditures', *The Journal of Political Economy*, vol 64, no 5, pp 416–24.

Titmuss, R. (1968) *Commitment to welfare*, London: George Allen and Unwin.

Turnbull, A. (2003) Speech at launch of 'The Adaptive State: strategies for personalising the public realm', London: Demos, 12 December.

Warde, A. (1996) 'Afterword: the future of the sociology of consumption', in S. Edgell, K. Hetherington and A. Warde (eds) *Consumption matters*, Oxford: Blackwell, pp 302–12.

Winkler, F. (1987) 'Consumerism in health care: beyond the supermarket model', *Policy & Politics*, vol 15, no 1, pp 1–8.

Index

Page references for notes are followed by n